Early Years Practice

GETTING IT RIGHT FROM THE START

Early Years Practice

GETTING IT RIGHT FROM THE START

Nóirín Hayes

Gill & Macmillan

Gill & Macmillan
Hume Avenue
Park West
Dublin 12
with associated companies throughout the world
www.gillmacmillan.ie

© Nóirín Hayes 2013

978 07171 5720 4

Print origination by O'K Graphic Design, Dublin
Printed by GraphyCems, Spain
Index by Cliff Murphy

This book is dedicated to the memory of Daisy Corrigan, Educator
(1913–1997)

Sapientia et virtute

Acknowledgements

This book has been influenced by the many conversations and discussions I have had with students and colleagues in early education, both in Ireland and further afield. It has been nurtured by the wonderful and trusting team at Gill & Macmillan. It would not have been possible without the support of my family and friends. To one and all, thank you.

Contents

CHAPTER 1

Considering Practice in Early Years Settings

[I]n order to develop . . . a human being, whether child or adult, requires . . . progressively more complex, reciprocal interaction with persons with whom he or she develops a strong, mutual . . . attachment. (Bronfenbrenner & Evans 2000:122)

This book is about early years practice. Practice makes the curriculum visible. It is what we do every day in day-to-day living with young children. It is not a separate activity or a discretely defined part of our behaviour; rather it is a combination of the education and care we provide for young children and through which we exhibit our interest in and understanding of how we educate our youngest children. This book is not a handbook or a manual. It is written on the assumption that the reader – whether student or practitioner[1] – is keen to learn more about practice and the elements that go to make up the rich, nurturing and enhancing worlds of early years settings. The book is intended to be the starting point for a collective conversation about early years practice that is derived from our knowledge and experiences. It is a conversation with many participants; a space where the ideas and arguments of the book form the basis of further conversations and discussions to maintain the flexible, responsive and flowing process that is early years practice. It is intended to be a conversation that can be returned to reflectively, either alone or with colleagues.

As with any conversation, it is important that participants know what values, beliefs and understandings inform different perspectives. It is also important to develop a shared language.

Researchers tell us that the quality of a child's early years experiences is crucial for overall learning and development and can have a profound impact on later life success. The quality of these experiences depends on a number of factors, and one of the central

[1]   A range of titles are used for professionals in the field of early childhood education, but in this book I will use the term 'practitioner' to refer to those working with children from birth to six years of age. This captures childminders, preschool staff, teachers and students in practice.

influencing factors is the style and content of the day-to-day practice of the early years practitioner. We also know that if practice is to be effective in supporting learning and development it must be informed by theory; that is, we must know *what we do* and *why we do it*. The most effective practices are those that are guided by clearly understood principles and informed by a solid understanding of learning and development. It is therefore important that practitioners feel confident in discussing and reflecting on the principles of their practice, their pedagogy. Ireland has seen a rapid growth in early years provision over the last decade and the training necessary to bring all practitioners up to a minimum level of qualification is still under way. However, early years practice can be supported and enhanced from within settings and through quality practice placements in training. We are fortunate in Ireland in having two national practice frameworks for working with children from birth to six years – Síolta, the national framework for quality, and Aistear, the national curriculum framework – which provide a common language and a common frame for developing early years practice. While they are different in their overall focus, they have both emerged from engagement with the early years sector and they share a common set of principles. This provides Irish early years practitioners with a common framework in which to begin the conversations that will articulate and support early years practice.

To that end, this book will discuss what constitutes good practice in early years and exactly why good practice *is* good; it will consider the research evidence on the impact of early experiences on learning and development and it will explore in detail both Síolta (CECDE 2006) and Aistear (NCCA 2009a, 2009b) to illustrate how these two practice frameworks can be used together to enhance the day-to-day practice of early years practitioners and continue to support the learning and development of all children.

From the very beginning of life children are curious and socially competent. They are active in their communication and engagement with the people, places and objects that comprise their learning environments. This view of the child as an engaged, active participant in the world around them reflects the growing scientific understanding we have of the dynamic and interactive process that is child development, and it also reflects a rights-based perspective of children, recognising them as individuals who are learning and developing in the social world. Central to children's learning and development are the many relationships in which they participate in all their learning environments. While the various social relationships children form with adults and other children are important, their interactions and relationships with materials and objects are also important.

The role of the adult in all relationships is most effective when 'present' with and for the child in that moment, in an attentive way, within a carefully prepared environment that allows for exploration and play to encourage children to become more self-controlled and self-disciplined in their learning and their relationships. Such a role can often mean standing back and observing, assessing the situations observed and informing future planning and provision.

Right from the start a child's temperament contributes to the quality of their interactions, which in turn impact on other aspects of development such as attention. The adult has a central role in being attuned to such contributions, and able to read the communications carefully and respond sensitively to children's behaviour. Wolfe and Bell (2007) found a relationship between infant temperament and working memory performance in early childhood. These associated characteristics highlight the importance of early learned regulatory and attentional behaviours and the impact of these early skills on later development.

The early years practitioner works as part of a complex and dynamic context, whether in the home or in a specialised early years setting. To develop and sustain quality early years practice, which is both personally satisfying and positive for young children, it is valuable to recognise that there is a rich theoretical and conceptual backdrop to good-quality, effective practice. Recognising what high-quality early years practice looks and feels like in an early years setting allows the practitioner to reflect on their own day-to-day practice and contributes to the virtuous cycle of learning and developing.

However, quality is a difficult concept to define and some authors suggest that trying to define it is like searching for 'fools' gold' (Penn 2009). Nonetheless in practice we should be questioning the quality of our practice, challenging ourselves and others to consider what quality might mean for a particular setting or child at a particular time. To achieve this, there are advantages in keeping up to date with contemporary research and pooling insights from neuroscience with developmental psychology, education and other disciplines to highlight the connectedness between the social, physical, linguistic, cognitive and emotional experiences of young children and associated implications for practice and for learning and optimal development (Dalli *et al.* 2011).

Practice is about the care and attention we give to the child 'in the now' when we think of the 'whole child in context'. This attention to the 'now' is most effective when it is practised by adults who know what their practice is and why it is as it is. It goes beyond naming the constructs of early education and care into the translation of those constructs into the day-to-day relationship with and between adults and children. Knowing and understanding the science of development and learning and continually updating this knowledge through accessing relevant resources helps to make sense of why certain practices are worthwhile and others less so. It provides a language and a voice in which we can articulate, discuss and explain what we do, because we have evidence to support us. This in turn allows us to consider our own practice in a more rigorous way, giving us confidence that what we do is appropriate, beyond the mere opinion that 'we know it works'. Knowing how children learn and develop helps us explain why what we do is so important and a unique feature of the early years period of education.

CONTEMPORARY CONTEXTS FOR EARLY YEARS PRACTICE

Young children learn and develop in the midst of society and they are influenced not only by their immediate environments but also by the policies that support and assist families in raising children and the attitudes and values that societies have in respect of children and families. A number of international and national developments can be seen as directly influencing the daily work of practitioners in early childhood settings. Internationally one of the defining moments in relation to our approach to children came in 1989 with the publication of the United Nations Convention on the Rights of the Child (UNCRC). Ratified by Ireland in 1992, this document is a profound commitment to children and young people and lays out a blueprint for how we, as adults, can respect and support children and young people. It has shaped the contemporary image of the child as an active participant in his or her own learning and development.

Specifically in relation to early education, which is not a named right in the Convention, the UN Committee on the Rights of the Child has issued a General Comment No. 7 on 'Implementing Child Rights in Early Childhood' (2005). The general comment recognises early childhood as a critical period for realising children's rights and elaborates, in some detail, how early childhood services can provide for young children in a rights-based framework. Hayes and Kernan (2008) noted that globalisation and mobility has also had an impact on how society considers children, with increased attention to the centrality of principles of social inclusion and respect for diversity reflecting the growing heterogeneity of societies. Specifically in relation to early childhood, there has been a growth in the professionalisation and recognition of the early years workforce through expanded training opportunities and expectations. This is evidenced in the vibrant national and international community of early years professionals, academics and policy thinkers. At a policy level, the recognition of the importance of early childhood is evidenced by, among other international initiatives, the Start Strong initiative from the Organisation for Economic Co-operation and Development (OECD), which continues to provide a rich source of information on international themes and practice supports through its early childhood education and care toolbox (OECD 2012). The European Union (EU) has become increasingly interested in the area of quality early childhood in the context of the Europe 2020 strategy (European Commission 2010) and a number of Council of Europe reports have identified quality early education for children as central to the successful implementation of labour market initiatives and the concept of lifelong learning.

For many years Ireland had a limited involvement in the lives of young children and there was minimum attention to or support for the development of an early years sector. In response to the increasing demands for provision arising from changing family structures and work patterns, there has been unprecedented investment in the expansion of places and the infrastructure to manage such developments. The growth of local childcare support networks and improved co-ordination across the national voluntary organisations has given an increased visibility to the sector that was missing in the 1990s. The National Children's Strategy (2000) recognised that children are active agents in their development and that they both affect and are affected by the environments within which they grow. This view of the 'whole child' has informed the wide variety of policies, strategies and regulations impacting on the lives of children that have emerged over the last decade. The establishment in 2011 of the Ministry for Children and Youth Affairs – incorporating the Office of the Minister for Children and Youth Affairs (OMCYA) – has the potential to enhance cohesion and integration across the range of policy issues impacting directly on young children's lives, including early years provision. The ministry's lead on the development of an Early Years Strategy has important implications for the landscape of early childhood education and care over the next decade.

Early years practice must also conform to a number of legal requirements and national standards and guidelines. In the Irish context the key regulations are the Child Care (Pre-School Services) (No. 2) Regulations (2006). Of particular relevance to the topic of early years practice is Regulation 5 on the Health, Welfare and Development of the Child, which notes that 'Each child's learning, development and well being needs should be met within the daily life of a service through the provision of the appropriate opportunities, experiences, activities, interactions and materials' (DoHC 2006:36). Early years services must also comply with employment and health and safety legislation. A number of practice guidelines and standards should inform early years practice, including Síolta, the National Quality Framework (CECDE 2006), Aistear, the Early Childhood Curriculum Framework (NCCA 2009a), the National Standards for Pre-School Services (DoH 2010), Diversity and Equality Guidelines (OMC 2006) and *Children First: National Guidance for the Protection and Welfare of Children* (DCYA 2011). Information and details on all the above can be accessed through the relevant websites. The purpose of these regulations, standards and guidelines is to draw attention to the critical role of all professionals, including early years practitioners, in working with and protecting children and to provide a robust system within which children are protected and allowed to develop in safe, healthy and enhancing environments.

At a local level there has been funding for the county/city childcare committees to develop policies and resources to support and enhance the quality of provision. This has been accompanied by national initiatives involving the early years sector in its widest sense. This approach was particularly evident in the development and publication of Síolta (in 2006) and Aistear (in 2009), which created a rich basis for considering practice within services for young children. There are also a number of financial supports available to settings, including the capitation subsidy for providing the Free Preschool Year. In an effort to support and enhance the quality of practice within this initiative, incentives are also available to settings to employ qualified staff, and this move is also supported by the commitments on training reported in the *Workforce Development Plan* (DES 2010). These initiatives provide Ireland with the structures and the opportunity to follow other countries towards supporting and developing a graduate-led, diverse professional base to enhance the quality of service provision and the experiences of young children.

UNDERSTANDING CONTEMPORARY CHILDHOODS

The active and competent nature of all children, whatever their age, is recognised in our National Children's Strategy, which puts forward the following vision for Irish children:

> An Ireland where children are respected as young citizens with a valued contribution to make and a voice of their own; where all children are cherished and supported by family and the wider society; where they enjoy a fulfilling childhood and realise their potential. (DoHC 2000: 4)

It is clear from the above that Ireland recognises that children are active agents in their development. This point is further strengthened later in the strategy: 'children affect and are in turn affected by the relationships around them' (DoHC 2000:26). As active participants in our society, children have a right to expect that their early childhood settings, wherever they are and of whatever type, will challenge and excite them, provide safety and security and enhance their overall development and learning.

Children are the social group most affected by the quality of early childhood services. While this may appear self-evident, there may also be some complacency about what actually happens to children in their everyday experiences and a general assumption that by just attending an early years setting children will develop and progress positively. This is not the case and research evidence suggests that to achieve positive outcomes in children attending early years settings they must be of high quality, particularly for children who may be identified as coming from more disadvantaged backgrounds. Indeed, there is some evidence to suggest that low-quality early years experiences are of little or no benefit to young children and their families (Sylva *et al.* 2011). In fact the quality of everyday experiences in early years environments – wherever children are – has a profound influence on them. Young children are not merely recipients or consumers of a service but are deeply influenced, individually and collectively, by their early years experiences.

Children learn in context; the ordinary spaces, places and people they encounter make up that context. Adults who are attuned, who are 'watchfully attentive' and who are mindful in their day-to-day practices with children can make an important and positive contribution to their learning and development. There is no need to distance children from society in an effort to enhance their learning and development – indeed, actively linking early years settings to other important environments in the lives of young children and carefully managing the various transitions they make is seen as an important dimension of quality early years practice. Early years practice is a process that is happening in early years settings every day; it is the curriculum made visible – even where the curriculum may not be readily definable.

This book is intended as a contribution to explaining why practice is so critical, what it is about quality practice that has such a huge impact on young children's learning and development, and why. Early years settings – including the home environment – are complex learning environments with many overlapping interactions between children, adults, materials and ideas.

In addition to being influenced by the learning environment and the people therein, children are also influenced by the beliefs others have about how and what they should learn. Children learn in social and physical environments, developmental niches (Super & Harkness 1986), the characteristics of which are, to a large extent, determined by adults but are also influenced by other elements. Based on their beliefs about development and their expectations, adults select and provide experiences they believe are important for children and will prepare children for their future. These socialisation processes occur at different levels and so can be studied at different levels.

We all carry beliefs about children, how they develop, what they need, how best to ensure the best for them, how to encourage good behaviour and so forth. In previous writing I have identified some basic core beliefs I have about early childhood (Hayes 2010). I restate them here because I believe it is important that each reader understands what informs the points I make about early years practice. In presenting them I hope that you can draw on your own beliefs and your experiences of early years practice to reflect on what they might mean to you. If you have different priorities or beliefs, it is useful to name them and to consider why this might be the case.

First, I hold the child as *central*. Each child is an individual born into a particular socio-cultural context. It is within this context that the child develops and, in turn, influences context. In working with children we must take the time and interest to develop our own skills and knowledge to allow for the individuality of each child to flourish. Second, I believe that the child is basically *good*. No child is born bad, although many are born with considerable disadvantages. It is essential that early years practitioners believe this. Underpinning more rigid practices and punitive styles is the belief that children need to be taught to be good. Rather, I believe they need to be rewarded for behaving as we expect them to and assisted in understanding why certain behaviours are considered inappropriate. Third, I consider that in our tendency to segment the child as we try to unravel the influences that shape her life we must not lose sight of the *interaction* between different aspects of development at different stages. The holistic development of the whole child in context is what we must strive to achieve in our planning and practice. Fourth, I believe that the child is an *active agent* in her learning rather than a passive receiver of information. This belief has serious implications for practice and requires that adults allow children the freedom to make mistakes, to solve problems and to find solutions rather than interfering too soon in an activity or rushing to show children how, for instance, to 'draw the cat' or 'cut out the picture'. Fifth, I believe in the *importance* of the early years. I do not hold the extreme view that there is no hope for change after the child has reached the age of, say, seven. However, I do believe that the foundation for much future learning, behaviour and success is laid down in the very early experiences of a child. It is unacceptable to say that a trauma will affect a young child less than an older one simply because they do not appear to understand it – it is this very fact of childhood understanding that makes early experiences so important, and that places an important obligation on early years practitioners to be sensitive to children's experiences and how they might be affecting them. This sensitivity requires that you recognise that what something means to you may not, in fact, reflect what it means to the child. Finally, I believe in the powerful *role of the adult* in the young child's life. The quality of interactions and relationships is emerging from scientific research as a key factor in enhancing the learning and development of young children. Adults are significant in that they can expand the experiences and the horizons of the child during the early years by their attention, interests, listening skills, observations and the provision of opportunity. Adults must, of course, also recognise their limitations. There are environmental influences and the influence of other adults, for example, that will prevail in certain circumstances (Hayes 2010:viii–ix).

THE EARLY YEARS PRACTITIONER

Effective early years practice and pedagogy integrates education and care with learning, development and experiences for children. We need to consider and understand exactly what the integration of education and care means in practice, what challenges it poses and what opportunities it can provide. While initial training is important, all early years practitioners benefit from the opportunity for ongoing professional development – whether through externally provided programmes or through an in-house environment that supports reflective and informed practice at the individual and team level. Such opportunities contribute to creating a community of learning, a critical and questioning environment that is alert to the impact and effect of day-to-day practices.

Mitchell and Cubey (2003) identify eight characteristics of a quality approach to professional development that can inform the development of a critical learning path to practice:

1 'Incorporate participants' own aspirations, skills, knowledge and understanding into the learning context.' To achieve this there needs to be a safe and open environment that encourages practitioners to look at themselves and their strengths and weaknesses to form the basis of ongoing professional development. It recognises that shared learning can enhance not only an individual's learning but also the overall quality of the early years environment.

2 'Provide theoretical and content knowledge and information about alternative practices.' This challenges practitioners to continue to keep up with emerging research and knowledge about early years practice through reading, attending seminars, accessing resource materials and using them as the basis for personal reflection and group discussion.

3 'Investigate pedagogy within their own early childhood settings.' It is always easiest to start from where you are. Using honest examples or vignettes from your own early

years settings and critically considering them in the context of, for instance, Aistear and Síolta can give ideas on how to progress, enhance or provide the language that allows you to describe your practice more clearly.

4 *'Draw on personal experience for data analysis.'* Here the authors identify the practitioner as an active researcher. Carefully documenting observations for later critical analysis enables this type of approach to considering practice and reviewing the effectiveness of certain approaches. It can pose new and unexpected questions and also provide insight into activities or relationships that might be easily overlooked if not recorded and considered.

5 *'Provide opportunities for critical reflection to challenge assumptions and extend thinking.'* While it may be simple to quickly review your practice, it is a great deal more difficult, but ultimately more valuable, to critically evaluate your practice to explore the values and beliefs that influence you. This requires planning and time and so needs local leadership in settings and a commitment from all practitioners.

6 *'Support educational practices that are inclusive of diversity.'* We are all different, all unique, and so we all contribute to the diversity of settings. As a result of greater mobility and increased immigration, the extent of diversity in groups has grown and brought with it both riches and challenges. Explicitly discussing diversity in the context of practice provides us with the time and space to plan and develop inclusive early learning environments.

7 *'Help participants to change educational practices, beliefs, understanding and attitudes.'* Changing hearts and minds is not easy – even where people are willing to question themselves. It is important that due attention is paid in discussion to the needs and rights of others and that space is allowed for constructive argument and differing views. It is through discussion and argument that we can find new and often better ways to practise.

8 *'Help participants to gain awareness of their own thinking, actions and influence.'* In order to grow in awareness we need to have the desire to do so. Where practitioners are collectively committed to achieving the best possible quality of practice there is an aim that can act as the driver for change. Where the context for this element of professional development is a safe one, where participants trust and respect each other, there it is most likely that everyone gains increased awareness of their thinking, their beliefs and how these can impact directly on practice through influencing our responses to behaviour, our expectations of different situations, our tolerance of change. Practitioners who recognise the importance of self-awareness and show a willingness to change and learn are certainly going to be more motivated in their daily work in early years settings than those who have become complacent.

Essentially, the points raised by Mitchell and Cubey highlight the importance to practice of engaged, attuned and reflective practitioners and offer some suggestions on how to access those aspects of ourselves that we may not bring to mind in the day-to-day routine of early years practice but that inform our actions and ultimately influence our interactions with the children in our settings.

Our own history and experiences of learning – even if we are largely unthinking in relation to them – inform and influence our practice in ways that may not always be useful. Fleer (2003) talks about the constraints that can impact on our work if we assume a shared understanding of commonly used references, ideas or constructs. She argues that we need to give more attention to our 'taken for granted' or tacit knowledge and how it can impose on our practice. As in many different professional areas there is a language specific to early education. We talk of 'high-quality early education'; of our practice being 'child-centred'; we recognise the child as an 'active agent' in their learning; we work with the 'whole child' and recommend that we listen to the 'voice of the child'. However, if not used carefully and with thoughtful reflection, these concepts can become meaningless. We need to know exactly what we mean when we say we work with the 'whole child'. We need to know why we believe this to be important. Unless we truly understand what we mean when we use these important concepts to explain our practice, we may in fact strip away the rich and unique features of early education. Fleer warns against the limiting nature of what she calls this 'taken for granted' knowledge that can become part of the language of early education. She argues that it is important for practitioners – if they are to practise in effective and dynamic ways – to interrogate such 'taken for granted' ideas; to unpack what they really mean and to share our understandings with colleagues so that a common understanding of practice emerges.

Just speaking the language of early childhood is not sufficient – the real challenge is to take language and get behind the real meaning. However, understanding the meaning only becomes real in a social context – it is socially constructed – and we adults can experience this through reflecting and challenging our own 'taken for granted' practice with others with the aim of actually reframing our practice in light of new understandings. Johnson (1988) believes that all those working in education come to their practice with informal theories about children's learning and development, informed by their training and their own experiences. As they derive from our own learning experiences, we often own them much more readily than we accept the implications of theory and research from so-called child development experts. Our implicit beliefs about child development and how children learn, termed 'folk pedagogy' by Bruner (1996), do need to be challenged in the context of contemporary understandings. Training for working in early education must include a strong element of child development along with content or subject knowledge and principles of practice.

We carry tacit knowledge and some of the myths from our past with us into our practice. But the knowledge base around child development and learning is expanding all the time and some of our tacit knowledge may be wrong or out of date. It is important to adopt a critical spirit in our approach to language and our grasp of knowledge and take time to consider the assumptions we make. Unless we are willing to challenge and explore our own assumptions, we may never really provide our young children with the rich learning environments they need to experience in order to be able to adapt to the changing world.

Of course, the 'knowledge' we routinely use provides us with a familiar structure and it may be uncomfortable to reflect on or question it. However, without reflection we merely replicate what we have always done and do not afford a space within which to challenge ourselves and develop our professionalism. The taken for granted – tacit – knowledge is rarely articulated, discussed or made visible; it is just 'the way things are'. Fleer (2003) identifies four of these tacit assumptions, which, she argues, influence early years practice. These four examples of 'tacit knowledge', which may be uncritically accepted, are often evident in the language of early years practice. They provide a useful starting point for discussions of beliefs and values we might hold about the way children learn and our role as practitioners in the process.

The first assumption relates to how we position the child. Do we see the child as part of the wider world or as part of the early years setting? This can affect the extent to which we broaden our own and children's experiences. A child-centred focus can distance the child from the reality of the world, from the world of adults and older children. Fleer suggests that we consider a richer concept, one of child-embeddedness, to capture the idea of the child growing and developing as an active participant in the midst of society. Key learning from science and evidence from wider cultural practices illustrate the importance of inclusive, relational, interactional pedagogy. This is a pedagogical approach I describe elsewhere as a nurturing pedagogy (Hayes 2007; Hayes & Kernan 2008). How we consider the child in relation to the world also impacts on how inclusive we intend to be in planning the learning environment. Fleer suggests that practitioners reflect on the environmental organisation in early years settings to allow for more fluid circulation with less emphasis on 'corners', and a broader range of materials with a wider range of objects that represent more of the ordinary and the familiar to children.

The second assumption Fleer considers is how we view children as learners. Do children actively construct knowledge or do they learn from being told? They can be seen as active, participating meaning-makers or as passive recipients of knowledge. The meaning of *active* needs careful consideration. It is not about physical activity alone: it includes being actively engaged in whatever is happening; active listening; and careful, active observation – from careful observation a child may expand what they are doing. There is a key role for the adult here in acting as a model for learning – showing rather than telling. Think about what that might mean to your practice in light of some recent example you can bring to mind. Understanding children's active engagement allows you to see where and how you might provide them with challenge and work with them in their zone of proximal development (ZPD) – the construct developed by Vygotsky to capture the idea of learners striving towards the next stage.

A third assumption evident in the language of early years refers to how we balance the individual with their social orientation. While it is important to understand the child as an individual, it is also important to see the child as a learner within a group as well as in an environment specific to the child. While individual development and learning may be a focus, we know that children are social beings, social learners, that while they are independent they are also interdependent. Children like to be with other children; they share knowledge and so extend their knowledge; they enjoy succeeding in groups and learn how to cope with failure too (Kernan & Singer 2010). As adults, we understand the value of working as a team, working together in discussion and in learning. It is similar for even very young children and so we should plan for both the individual developing child and also for the interdependent child.

Finally, Fleer questions the assumptions underpinning how we consider conversations. Children are embedded in the social world and are active in their communication with it through various verbal and non-verbal processes. In our practice, do we see both child and adult as partners in learning together, or separate from each other with the adult in the powerful position? While there is of course an inequity between the child and the far more experienced adult, this does not negate the value of considering children as partners. The process of distancing children is well bedded into society and so there is a need for explicit consideration of 'conversational opportunities'. Carefully planned child-friendly environments facilitate social and collaborative learning. Real, meaningful communication between adults and children (and children and children) is not simply about reading stories or asking questions. In fact, limiting conversation and dialogue to a question and answer style of communication or to organisational and management activities is insufficient and also disrespectful to children. It runs counter to an inclusive and respectful early years pedagogy that underlies a democratic approach to practice, which research suggests equips children with important developmental proficiency.

It is useful to review current understandings of how early years practices impact on children. Such a review can act as a stimulus for practitioners to reflect on their practice and the quality of provision for young children so that the experiences in early years settings will be a positive and affirming one for all those involved. The adult, and their style of engagement, has a profound impact on the learning experiences of children. The contemporary view of children as active agents in their learning requires practitioners to recognise and respond to the reality that even the very youngest children contribute to the context and content of their own development. This is not to underestimate the dependence of the child or the very powerful, protective role of the adult. It does, however, challenge adults to reconsider practice and to take account of the rich and diverse nature of each child when planning early care and education, designing learning environments and providing learning opportunities. The adult sets the scene for children's sense of engagement with the world and provides a context within which children can be seen and valued for their own sake and in the here and now.

EARLY YEARS SETTINGS

While the family is recognised as the central space for early education, learning and development, families increasingly share the early care and education of their children with different types of early years setting. These settings are a part of the wider society and have links with other educational, social and cultural settings in the wider community. They provide an important bridge, for children and parents alike, from the seclusion of the home through the early years setting into the local community and wider society. Early years settings therefore provide an important service for all families, but their role is particularly vital for minority or marginalised parents and their children. While the direct role of the practitioner is often characterised in terms of their work with the children attending settings, it is important to recognise that they play an important indirect role in creating these links across various systems, particularly in relation to influencing and supporting the home learning environment.

Research shows that early childhood experiences are important to children in their daily life and into their future. Children are deeply influenced, individually and collectively, by their early years experiences. The quality of everyday experiences in the early years – wherever children are – has a profound influence on them. Indeed, it is the day-to-day interactions and experiences that drive their development. They are active participants in our society and have a right to expect that early childhood settings will challenge and excite them, provide safety and security and enhance their overall development and learning. Viewing children as participants in the early childhood process allows adults to work with children as well as provide for children. In general, children are motivated to learn, to seek meaning in their world, and they expect that the adults they meet will assist them in this endeavour. It is in the immediate, day-to day experiences that children learn about the world around them; the ordinary things in their lives have the potential to be extra-ordinary, to act as the foundation for new knowledge. The adult can help make experiences of the ordinary into rich and meaningful learning experiences by using careful observation and reflection to inform their practice and their engagement with children. Through informed and attuned practice adults can expand children's language, thinking and understandings, they can fire children's curiosity, imagination and creativity, and challenge and extend their skills through encouraging mastery and positive learning dispositions.

Children's curiosity and desire for knowledge is evident in their play, their exploration, their questions and their behaviour. In order to make the most of their early years, children need adults who trust them, adults who are excited, inspired and challenged by them. If the child is seen as the centre of practice the day-to-day curriculum will reflect this. In early years settings with good-quality practices the adults actively include children in the regular experiences of the setting, engage with children and learn from them, and enhance the learning opportunities for them. This approach to practice is informed by a belief in the active nature of child development and includes the child as a partner in development. Such an approach to practice reflects a shift away from a more traditional didactic practice to a more integrated, social and interactive approach.

The design, organisation and resourcing of the early years setting is central to practice and the early learning process. Settings, both indoor and outdoor, should be safe while also providing rich and varied opportunities for exploration, play and risk-taking. However, while planning and organising the setting is important in early years practice, it is insufficient in itself. We know from research that settings that meet the static requirements of quality may not be effective in enhancing children's learning and development because it is the process, what happens on a day-to-day basis, that is at the heart of quality early years practice. Research suggests that the most effective practice is found in settings with well-trained, well-informed staff who are familiar with child development and subject material, who recognise and respond to the dynamic and individual nature of development in the early years, and who can work with an emerging curriculum that is driven by the interests and experiences of the children and the opportunities afforded by the environment (OECD 2006). A curriculum framework, such as Aistear, provides a rich basis for such practice. Cultivating positive learning dispositions and feelings in young children leads to positive outcomes in social, linguistic and cognitive development and the skills necessary for later school success. It is a holistic, adaptive and, ultimately, more effective approach to early education. The process of quality practice is dynamic and interactive, reflecting the dynamic and interactive nature of learning and development, and it requires that practitioners are responsive and reflective throughout both their planning for and their engagement with children.

Implicit in the practice outlined above is a commitment to democratic principles that recognise the need to respect and engage meaningfully with children. This approach is reflective of an understanding of early childhood education and care settings as sites of democratic practice where children and adults can participate collectively in interpreting experiences and shaping decisions affecting themselves (Moss 2007). Changing practice to meet the new vision of early years practice, a vision based on scientific understanding of development and contemporary approaches to children, is not an easy task. It requires ongoing practice, learning and reflection so that we get it right from the start and continue getting it right.

This book is intended as a contribution to:
- widening our common understanding of and language about why practice is so critical
- recognising what it is about quality practice that has such a huge impact on young children's learning and development
- understanding why the quality of practice is so important.

While it includes illustrative examples, this is not a book of examples of 'good' practice; rather, it is intended to prompt discussion and reflection on the quality of practice in the average early years setting, drawing on the experience of the practitioner or student, and to provide opportunities for considering everyday practice in the context of the two pillars of practice, Síolta and Aistear. It provides readers with a research context that will help locate quality early years practice within a shared language, reflecting a shared understanding. It does so by illustrating points of practice, with reference to examples drawn from both Síolta and Aistear, and explores why practice is important and what aspects of practice matter most to positive child development and professional satisfaction. It is not a manual of exercises; it is intended to be the start of an ongoing conversation towards strengthening our understanding of the impact of early years experiences on children and their families, and providing the sector with a shared language with which to raise the awareness of others of the importance of this period of education and the critical role played by early years practitioners.

Rather than approaching the use of Síolta in terms of 'doing this or that standard', or Aistear by way of attending to this particular theme or that principle, this book suggests that you look to your own practice and derive your use of the frameworks directly from it. You are probably already doing much of what is suggested in the illustrations, but you may not be reflecting on it or theorising it sufficiently to fully understand – and evaluate – the potential impact on the learning and development of the young children in your setting. This is as true of the childminder with a small number of children in her own home as it is of students in practice or those working in more formal settings. Maximising the use of Síolta and Aistear in the infant classes of the primary school is a particular challenge because teachers are trained specifically to implement a prescribed curriculum, which is quite different from the curricular framework proposed by Aistear.

This chapter has considered what high-quality early years practice is and has raised a number of opportunities and challenges to achieving such practice. The next chapter considers the research that explains why this quality practice is important and how it impacts on children's development and learning. Chapter 3 reviews the development of Síolta and Aistear and presents the similarities and differences between these two important early years practice documents. In each of Chapters 4–7, we take one of the Aistear themes, discuss the focus of the theme and, drawing on illustrations of practice from Aistear, present an integrated approach to linking Aistear and Síolta in practice by working across the Standards and Components of Síolta and the Learning Goals and Aims of Aistear. Chapter 8, the final chapter, reviews the previous chapters in order to present an integrated reflection on early years practice. This reflection is intended as a contribution to the conversation proposed above, so that we can all work towards achieving, supporting and sustaining high-quality early years practice that gets it right from the start.

CHAPTER 2

Understanding Early Years Practice

Research from a variety of theoretical perspectives suggests that a defining feature of a supportive environment is a responsible and responsive adult. (Bowman, Donovan & Burns 2001)

It is not enough to simply know that what we do is right; we need to be able to explain to ourselves and others *why* what we do is right. In order to be able to talk about early years practice at this deeper level, it is necessary to recognise that practice is not simply a technology – doing what the book says. It is more complex than that; it is informed and guided by adult expertise and understandings of learning and development.

Recognising the importance of linking what we know about child development and learning to the day-to-day practice of early education brings the discussion of practice into the area of pedagogy; the theory of practice. Alexander (2004) highlights this link between practice and knowledge when he describes pedagogy as the 'act and discourse of teaching'. It can be seen as the art of translating agreed principles into responsive and flexible practice to meet the needs of children as individuals or as a group in the particular context of the day. However, it is not easy to describe the art of early years practice.

Most of us involved in working with young children became involved because we value children, we enjoy their company and we feel we can contribute to their overall development and well-being. Early childhood education and care has been slow to gain recognition in Ireland as a key educational provision for young children that is critical to their early learning, health and well-being. However, it has now matured to the point where national curriculum, quality and regulatory frameworks have emerged from within the sector. These frameworks focus on the first stage of education (0–6 years) and have introduced a shared terminology that can break down barriers in the sector and bring together those who work across the different settings, from childminders through various early years settings to primary teachers in infant classes. This emerging common terminology has derived from a common vision and a shared set of principles; it provides practitioners with the opportunity to consider their role, reflect on their practice, assess the needs of the sector and participate in the growth and transformation of the sector. The pedagogy of Irish early education is reflected in the way we talk about our practice and translate the framework principles into everyday practice.

International research suggests that practitioners in the early years are not confident about talking about their practice or about analysing and critically evaluating the impact of their practice on the young children they work with, and there is no reason to expect things to be all that different in Ireland. In a study of pedagogical effectiveness in early learning, Moyles and her colleagues (2002) noted that practitioners were reluctant to engage in pedagogical discussions and found it difficult to articulate or describe in any detail the specifics of their practice that were important to them or the values, beliefs and principles underpinning their practice. They also found that '(W)hilst principles (beliefs and values) underpinning practice were evident in . . . documentation . . . they appear to be the least well-developed area of practitioners' knowledge and understanding. Provision of materials tends to dominate activities' (Moyles, Adams & Musgrove 2002:131). It seems that doing early years practice is often easier than describing or discussing it.

This is short-sighted, for a number of reasons. In the first place it can lead to practice becoming mundane, routine and lacking in challenge. This can impact directly on children and learning opportunities can be lost. This in turn can limit the satisfaction of the adult that derives from quality practice. While the Moyles study found that the ability to articulate and reflect on practice was related to the level of training, it also found that this ability was linked to the 'ethos within settings, which positively promotes self-evaluation and reflection and adopts strategies for developing these' (Moyles, Adams & Musgrove 2002:130). This suggests that leadership and teamwork are important in sustaining and enhancing the quality of practice in early years settings. We know from research that purposeful teaching and learning occurs when practitioners' own understanding and knowledge informs their practice. This is most effective when coupled with the provision of rich and relevant learning experiences that assist young children, even the very youngest, to make sense of their experiences in the world around them.

We recognise that children grow and develop within society and that they are therefore impacted on by many factors – some more directly than others. The direct influences are those located close to children's experiences: the home, and the variety of early years settings they may attend at different times. Older children have a wider set of settings, including schools, youth settings, sports clubs and so on. Recognising this is one thing, but understanding how it actually influences child development and what implications it has for early childhood practice is more difficult. To begin to understand this it may be useful to review the situation with the help of a table.

THE BIO-ECOLOGICAL SYSTEMS PERSPECTIVE

Ecological systems	Definitions	Examples
Microsystems	Part of the environment with which young children are directly in contact	Child's relationships with mother, father, siblings, grandparents, peers and early years professionals
Mesosystems	Links between microsystems	Parents' relationship with early years professionals; early years professionals' links to home, school and community groups
Exosystems	Systems in which young children do not directly participate, but which nevertheless exert an indirect influence on their development	Mother's or father's work conditions; Síolta and Aistear frameworks; regulations and law
Macrosystems	Overarching structures of the particular culture that influence young children's development	Parental belief systems, customs and lifestyles

Source: Bronfenbrenner & Morris (1998).

In considering the complexity of interactions influencing the development of an individual, many people have found Bronfenbrenner's bio-ecological model of development a useful model with which to think about the dynamics of development and the implications for practice (Bronfenbrenner & Morris 1998). The bio-ecological model reflects our current understanding of the integrated and dynamic nature of learning and development. This model recognises that individuals are embedded in, and affected by, different systems or contexts. These influences can be at a distant, or distal, level – referred to as the macrosystem – or at an immediate, or proximal, level – referred to as the microsystem. The model also draws attention to the need for practitioners to pay close attention to the complexity of interacting systems and the interactions between and within those systems. The systems identified in the model are called the microsystem, the mesosystem, the exosystem and the macrosystem.

The child's most familiar *microsystem* is the family, but the microsystem also includes other settings such as early years settings and schools. The *mesosystem* is often the most difficult level to grasp as it refers to the communication and interaction between the various elements of the model; of most immediate relevance to the early years practitioner is the communication between the child's microsystems of the home and the early years setting. The third level in the system is the *exosystem,* which refers to factors that are external to the children and adults but that nonetheless impact on them, such as early education policy and frameworks like Síolta and Aistear. Finally, the *macrosystem* represents the influence of such factors as societal values and the position of the child in general and the early years child in particular. This last system can be seen to include the vision for Irish children in the National Children's Strategy (DoHC 2000) and the government commitment to making children more visible as citizens in the Irish Constitution, Bunreacht na hÉireann. (The Thirty-First Amendment of the Constitution (Children) Bill was passed by referendum on 10 November 2012.)

These systems, or levels, are organised from those closest (*proximal*) to the child to those whose influence is distant and indirect (*distal*). The model, characterised as a set of nested levels with the child at the centre, has been used as a guide in early education, most notably by the New Zealand Ministry of Education in the development and implementation of their early years curriculum (Ministry of Education (New Zealand) 1996). There is also evidence of its influence in both the Síolta (CECDE 2006) and Aistear (NCCA 2009a) frameworks, which, for instance, devote a lot of attention to the importance of links (mesosystems) between early years settings and the home environment (microsystems).

Human development, especially in its early phases, takes place through processes of progressively more complex reciprocal interactions between an active and evolving person and the persons, objects and symbols in their immediate environment. We understand that to be effective, these interactions must be positive and occur on a fairly regular basis over extended periods of time. This in part accounts for why humans have much longer childhoods than other species. Such enduring forms of interaction in the immediate environment are referred to as *proximal processes* and have been called the 'engines of development'. Examples of these important enduring patterns of proximal process are found in feeding or comforting a baby, playing with a young child, child–child activities, group or solitary play, storytelling, active listening, reading, learning new skills, athletic activities, problem solving, caring for others in distress, making plans, performing complex tasks and acquiring new knowledge and know-how (Bronfenbrenner & Morris 1998:996).

To be developmentally effective these activities must occur on a regular basis over time and continue long enough to become increasingly more complex; mere repetition does not work. Second, developmentally effective proximal processes, or interactions, cannot be just one-way; there must be engaged interaction in both directions. In the case of interpersonal interactions, this means that there must be a degree of active engagement between all those involved in the exchange. Finally, proximal processes are not limited to interactions with people, but also can involve interactions with objects and symbols. In these latter circumstances, for reciprocal interactions to occur, the objects and symbols in the immediate environment must be of interest, in a meaningful way, and should invite and reward attention, exploration, manipulation, elaboration and imagination. It is clear that the adult, parent or early years practitioner has a significant role in the quality of child development; and a critical feature of this influence is the quality of the interactions facilitated and encouraged within the setting.

CONSIDERING THE NATURE OF CHILD DEVELOPMENT

When reflecting on early years practice in terms of its effect on children's development it is useful to take some time to consider what is meant by the term 'development'. The concept of development has two dimensions – the normative and the dynamic. The idea of development has come to suggest a progression from one place or state to another along a reasonably predictable path. We learn about children's development in terms of different stages and we come to know what to expect of a child at particular ages. This understanding of a general developmental pattern has proved useful when considering how an individual child is doing in comparison to others of the same age. It is the basis of many standardised tests or assessments that are carried out to establish whether a child has achieved certain milestones such as walking, talking, reading and so on. We call this *normative development* – considering each individual child's development against a standard (or norm) that is normal for most children at the same age in the same cultural context. This normative approach to development has also given rise to the idea that there are activities and behaviours that are appropriate at certain ages, and we can find many materials designed for use with children of specific ages. An example of this approach is the publication of the *Developmentally Appropriate Practice* (DAP) handbook (Bredekamp & Copple 1997), which documents materials and activities that are identified as either 'appropriate' or 'inappropriate' for children at different ages and stages of their lives. The description (or, as some see it, prescription) of 'appropriate' is closely tied to a normative view of development and is based on the notion of development as a continuous progression toward adulthood. However, while the normative approach to development can be useful in certain situations, it has been found to be limiting in respect of early education. This is partly due to the fact that there is such a wide span of what is normal behaviour, particularly in any group of very young children; what may be appropriate for one child of a given age may not be appropriate for another of the same age. The reality of this variation in development has been taken into account in both Síolta and Aistear, where the guidance on age ranges shows overlap: birth–18 months, 12–36 months and 2½–6 years.

It is, however, important, from a practice point of view, to understand that there is a *dynamic* dimension to individual development. This dimension introduces the idea of the interaction of changes in development over time and points to the complexity of development: there can be a developmental link between two dissimilar behaviours. For instance, a child's ability to engage in make-believe play at the age of three years is related to word reading at the age of five years. So we can see how important free pretend play is in any literacy strategy – even though pretend play rarely looks like reading! Dynamic development challenges us to consider what is best for the individual developing child at this moment, in this context. The essence of practising developmentally, then, is rising to the challenge of valuing the moment for its immediate developmental contribution to a child while at the same time acknowledging (but not overemphasising) its potential in respect of later development. It also forces us to recognise that activities and behaviour now can impact on later aspects of development. Different behaviours may serve both present and future development. This reality is one that early years practitioners need to understand and have confidence in as it provides a strong theoretical defence for the focus of quality practice in early years settings.

Viewing development as a dynamic and discontinuous process, or as a 'to and fro' process, allows us to view behaviour and development in early childhood as adaptive to the immediate demands of the child in context. Such an approach to early education is not tied to the age and stage of development of the child but rather is linked to the socio-cultural context of development for the child in the present. It is exemplified by the practices at Reggio Emilia in Italy and in the Te Whariki early years curriculum of New Zealand, where pedagogy is directed by the connections, interactions and relationships between children and the wider world and by social, physical and emotional elements, rather than by any prescribed expectations of developmental outcomes. It is also implicit in Aistear, which in both its design and content reflects this view of development as dynamic.

Contemporary views of children characterise them as active participants in their own learning who, from their earliest days, construct models of their world, and their place in it, from their experiences and the opportunities available to them; a socio-construction model of development. They do this in the midst of a number of social contexts, as illustrated by the bio-ecological model of development. In their behaviour children exhibit and develop dispositions or habits of mind, which have a profound influence on them and direct the way in which they develop their skills and broaden and deepen their knowledge. Indeed, Bronfenbrenner writes that '[I]n order to develop – intellectually, emotionally, socially and morally – a human being, whether child or adult, requires . . . the same thing: active, progressively more complex interaction with persons with whom he or she develops a strong, mutual . . . attachment' (Bronfenbrenner & Evans 2000:122). Research has found that the quality of interactions is closely related to developing and sustaining behavioural dispositions, which can be either positive (generative) or negative (disruptive).

It is all very well to recognise that the quality of the interactions a child experiences, whether with people, objects or materials, is important to development; but what exactly does that mean for practice? Why does the quality of interactions have important implications for development and for the effectiveness of early education? What is the power of interactions and the important role of the adult in planning for and facilitating them? In early education practice adults get the opportunity to guide and assist children in learning more positive, generative dispositions that contribute both to their immediate well-being and their later adjustment to school and society in general. Developmentally generative dispositions are important in positive learning and development and they involve curiosity; the tendency to initiate and engage in activity, alone or with others; a responsiveness to initiatives by others; a readiness to defer immediate gratification in pursuit of long-term goals. In contrast, developmentally disruptive dispositions that can inhibit learning and development include impulsiveness, explosiveness, distractibility, inability to defer gratification and, in a more extreme form, a readiness to resort to aggression or violence; or, at the opposite pole, apathy, inattentiveness, unresponsiveness, lack of interest in one's surroundings, feelings of insecurity, shyness, or a general tendency to withdraw from

activity (Bronfenbrenner & Morris 1998:1009). Through reflective observation of children and their interactions, where records are revisited, reviewed and discussed, adults can come to understand the characteristics of the child and the environment, which will facilitate positive development and learning.

EDUCATING AND CARING FOR THE WHOLE CHILD[1]

Effective early years practice, whether with infants or with children of four and five years of age, demands a great deal from the adult. As we have seen above, research by Moyles found that, in general, early years practitioners resist talking enquiringly about their practice. Stephen (2010) supports this finding when she makes the point that practitioners are often willing to talk about *what they plan* for children and *what they do* with them but are less likely to discuss *why they do things* – what might be called their underlying pedagogical perspective. This inability to articulate a practice philosophy may reflect the absence of a common language of early education; one that captures the sophisticated understandings of child development and learning necessary to allow busy practitioners to plan for and respond effectively to children in the day-to-day messiness that is early years practice. Stephen, referring to a 2000 paper by Stengel, concludes that 'we have not yet developed a language for teaching that combines the "language of technique" (what is effective) with the "language of manner" (what is ethical, moral or caring)' (2010:24).

We do have some elements of a common language of early education in Ireland, and these derive from the Síolta and Aistear frameworks. These frameworks were developed in close consultation with the sector and were informed by national and international research. To contribute to and strengthen the development of a common language and to make visible the underlying principles of effective and caring early years practice I have argued elsewhere that there is a need to explicitly value the care element of early years practice. This is important because care has been seen as something that just happens when adults are with children, but those working in early years practice know that it is so much more. For this reason it is important to find a way of thinking and talking about care practice that recognises the central role of care in quality early education and respects the role of the adult in providing a caring environment. Reconceptualising care as nurture can contribute to highlighting the educative nature of care practice in the early years and contribute to enhancing the status of the care concept in the field (Hayes 2007, 2008, 2012). Despite many endorsements of the value of balancing the care and education elements of early education, there remains a tendency to underestimate the educative role of caring. The idea of considering care as nurture gives it an active connotation and implies that the adult has a responsibility to provide nurturance and to actively foster and encourage learning and development rather than to simply care for, mind or protect the child. To nurture requires an engaged, bidirectional level of interaction and confers on the early years practitioner an enhanced educational role. Such a shift in emphasis should lead

---

1   Parts of this section are derived from Hayes (2007 and 2012).

to a visible change in the language and discourse of early years practice and provide a language in which to describe the day-to-day practices of caring for and educating young children in line with Aistear and Síolta, respectively, while also raising the expectations and status of early years practice.

Nurturing pedagogy in early years practice

Nurturing children's learning as part of a caring educative process requires that adults develop skills of observation and reflection to allow for the non-intrusive planning and the provision of learning environment that support and extend children's own learning and quality interactive opportunities. Skills of observation and reflection are central to a nurturing pedagogy. They enhance practice and planning; are manifest in well-managed and yet reasonably flexible practice; and assist in the provision of a learning environment that includes children, and supports and extends children's learning. This allows for more careful attention to positive interactions between both child and adult and child and child. It also allows for planning by the adult for future opportunities that might extend the child's own learning, giving a key role to the adult which takes the child, rather than prescribed curricular content, as central. It encourages the movement away from the more traditional organisational/management role of the practitioner and strengthens the focus on their educational, pedagogical role.

Linking the term 'nurture' rather than 'care' with pedagogy is intended to focus attention on the implications of this shift in focus for practice. The term 'pedagogy' captures the idea of a dynamic practice, the kind of practice we know is necessary to support children's holistic learning and development. 'Pedagogy' captures the integrated processes of caring, educating and learning alongside the principles, theory, values and approaches that underpin daily work with young children in the range of early childhood settings. 'Pedagogy' is a more powerful, richer word than 'practice' alone as it suggests a theoretically informed practice that encompasses the many processes involved in children learning and adults creating learning opportunities and environments that engage, challenge and interest young children. It acknowledges the sound theoretical base of day-to-day practice and also focuses attention on the everyday learning that adults themselves engage in, as they observe, reflect on and critically analyse the content and approach to their work with young children, alone and with other adults.

Combining the word 'pedagogy' with the term 'nurture' is intended to strengthen the early years professional space. The word 'nurture' has quite a different tone from the word 'care'; 'nurture' is more engaging and active than 'care'. The verb 'to care' is almost custodial in tone and implies a minimum of interaction; the adult merely provides for and looks after the child; and to those outside early education, the complexity involved in such early years practice is not immediately evident. 'To nurture', on the other hand, conveys a more engaged level of interaction and suggests that the adult actively nourishes, rears, fosters, trains and educates the child through his/her practice.

Relationships and interactions are central to a nurturing pedagogy. There is a rich tapestry of relations between children themselves, between adults and young children, between adults and their colleagues and the parents of the children they work with, and between learners and the environments where learning takes place. Interactions are critical spaces for learning not only for the individual but also for groups. To create a significant shift in understanding the role of care in practice it is necessary to explicitly acknowledge the critical contribution of this interpersonal aspect of early education, to make it visible, to realise it in the practice of the everyday interactions, or *proximal processes*, that act as the engines of development (Bronfenbrenner & Morris 1998).

A nurturing pedagogy is a style of practice that may be new and may feel a little uncomfortable to begin with. It suggests a very different practice from the one that many of us experienced in our own education. It involves letting go of some of the older, more traditional ideas about the relationship between the adult and the child, the learner and the teacher, which view the adult as the source of knowledge and the child as the recipient of this knowledge. Quality early years practice relies less on a content-led curriculum and more on a framework of values and principles within which to work. It is explicit in engaging children, respecting them and integrating the learning opportunities provided across the care and education dimensions. It builds on the individual capabilities and dispositions of the child within the social context and derives from the belief that it is the close interactions, the proximal processes, between children and other children, adults and the environment that drive development and learning. Responding to our understanding of early childhood development requires that we prioritise relationships and interactions over direct instruction and teaching as the cornerstone of early educational practice. A nurturing pedagogy fosters these processes of interaction, dialogue and planning, leading to the shared construction of knowledge, between children and adults, within the context of an emerging curriculum that is responsive to the child in the immediate now. Reflecting on practice in this way provides a common language and opens up opportunities for discussing the central features that make early years practice unique and that are evident when observing skilled practitioners at work.

THE IMPORTANCE OF QUALITY PRACTICE

Research tells us that to be effective for young children early years experiences need to be of a high quality. But what is meant by *high quality*? Defining the quality of early childhood experiences is difficult. It is often approached by distinguishing between the more static and measurable aspects of quality, known as structural qualities, and the more fluid or process aspects. Structural quality refers to such visible and measurable elements as the adult:child ratio and the environmental, health and safety aspects of a setting. Process quality, on the other hand, is more difficult to measure. It refers to the unique features of a particular setting and includes such things as the general quality of interactions, the ethos, the responsiveness to individuality within the group and the atmosphere of a setting. The early years practitioner and the quality of their practice is central to process quality.

Identifying quality indicators for structural and process quality in early years settings is a complex undertaking and a task that must evolve with due regard to the context of early education. Quality means different things to different interested parties or stakeholders. Nevertheless, practitioners and policy-makers are faced with the challenge of providing effective early education based on their current understanding of quality and in light of existing standards (French 2003). To recognise and enhance quality, our understandings must be informed by the most up-to-date data in respect to how young children develop and learn and the role of the environment in that development.

While there is debate in the field about the definition and measurement of quality, there is general consensus among early childhood professionals regarding the types of quality indicators that are useful and desirable. The environment should be well organised, stimulating and attractive to the child; it should be uncluttered and pleasing to the eye; it should have responsive and well-trained staff working within a flexible and balanced curricular framework. It should provide opportunities for individual and small group activities and have generous adult:child ratios. A US National Research Council report on quality early education (Bowman, Donovan & Burns 2001), drawing on an extensive review of research, placed the responsibility for quality firmly with the adults. Adults who are attuned, who are 'watchfully attentive' and mindful in their day-to-day practices, really make a difference. The report identified the key features of quality early education as practitioners who: demonstrate a high level of appropriate training; give specific attention to individual children; work with small groups of children; and use strategies that are responsive to the child's interests and normal developmental needs. Adults are the key people in the lives of children and are the most important tools of practice. To be effective they also need to be confident in their knowledge and skills and value the work they do. Rosenow (2012) observes that those working with or for children should nurture themselves as tenderly as they nurture the children in their care and they should delight in the wonders of the world and be eager to share them with children.

We also know from research that quality early years environments should provide opportunities for children to carry out learning activities without undue interference from adults, but with assistance when necessary. Enabling environments, both indoor and out, are those that provide opportunities that are exciting, interesting and challenging for children and that encourage children to engage in activities that challenge them, that build on their existing skills and competencies, encouraging the expansion of these skills to new and more complex tasks and supporting them in a view of themselves as competent learners.

When we talk of high-quality early years practice we are referring to the quality of what is happening in early years settings every day. The importance of the day-to-day, the ordinary, rests in the fact that it is within the ordinary that the curriculum is made visible. It is through the ordinary experiences of the early years that children create the foundation on which the development (positive or negative) of emotional well-being, sound physical and mental health, social competence and cognitive skills are based. To unlock the full potential of this foundation, young children require well-informed adults who, particularly in early years services, are well trained so that their direct work with children, and their indirect work with them through support and guidance of parents and other professionals, can be as effective as possible. Practically, at the day-to-day level, this means providing enriching and challenging learning environments that recognise the developmental trajectories of children at different stages and along different paths of development. It also means creating an atmosphere of secure relationships in which children feel that they belong and are valued members of the space. The gain from such practice and provision can be seen in the run of the mill contentedness and satisfaction in both children and adults, and the foundational impact of such experiences on later learning, caring and solid citizenship. Swedish research (Sheridan 2011) reports that high-quality early years settings are characterised by learning environments rich in challenge and learning opportunities in which children actively participate. Communication between adults and children shares a similar focus and the adults interact with the children in the 'here and now' by being physically and emotionally present for the children. The adults focus on the interests, knowledge and experiences of the children within an agreed vision for the outcome of their work.

By contrast, low-quality preschools can be characterised by limitations of space and materials, poor interactions, communication and reciprocal encounters between the adults and children, and few opportunities for child participation. Although physically present, the adults in poor-quality early years settings appear to be more focused on keeping control and maintaining order than on engaging with the children or providing challenging and interesting learning opportunities for them.

THE ROLE OF INTERACTIONS IN DEVELOPMENT

Bruner (1996) stresses the importance of positive interactions in language and content-rich environments to empower humans to go beyond their potential. Such intense interactions are similar to the proximal processes proposed by Bronfenbrenner and Morris (1998) as the drivers of development. This raises the question: why are interactions so important to development?

Development is a process of continuous change that is self-maintaining, self-restoring and self-regulating. Early brain research indicates that the brain is only partially mature at birth and continues to develop over the first years of life. This makes it immediately susceptible to the ongoing influence of experiences of all types, and thus the quality of interactions impacts on development (Trevarthen 1992). Studies indicate that 'meaning-making' activity is enhanced by quality interactions. Results from observations of infant–caretaker interactions highlights the importance of joint attention to objects and events in assisting infants to come to attend to objects and recognise meaning-making and intention on the part of the other (Dunn 1987). This research suggests that the construction of knowledge does not simply involve a cumulative effect of multiple individual contributions, but rather it represents a stronger view of learning in which the actual act, the process of interacting itself, the shared meanings growing out of participation in shared activity, are important. Current research from developmental psychology confirms that it is not simply the opportunity for interactions but the nature and quality of the interactive process itself that is important. In particular, research highlights the value of dynamic, bidirectional social interactions as crucial to early development. The importance of bidirectional, transformational interactions in stable learning environments lies in their contribution to facilitating children to consider and explain their ideas to others, negotiate and argue a point and clarify their thinking, thus refining their social, cognitive and metacognitive skills, the skills of thinking about thinking. Findings suggest that early years programmes that have a strong emphasis, both curricular (content) and pedagogical (practice), on the nurturing of affective development positively influence children's overall development, including their academic cognitive development.

Social relationships seem to be central to the positive well-being of both the adults and children in early years settings. Positive learning environments are those that are warm and provide secure relationships to facilitate children's exploration, play and learning. This is as true for the child of five years of age as it is for the child of five months. Practitioners who provide for these learning opportunities rather than focusing too closely on the development of academic skills are supporting the development of fundamental aspects of learning. Positive and supportive adult–child interactions enhance children's security to explore and experience connectedness to peers and are important for well-being, flourishing and also for the development of literacy and numeracy dispositions and skills. Blakemore and Frith highlight the danger of introducing academic training too early and make the point that 'there is no biological necessity to rush and put the start of teaching earlier and earlier. Rather, late starts might be reconsidered as perfectly in tune with findings from . . . brain research' (2000:4).

Practice happens all the time: it is embedded from the beginning within the various levels of day-to-day activity; and it impacts on all children's developmental levels or dimensions. Holistic practice with children requires the attention of the adult *in context* to the whole child *in context*, highlighting the importance of being present in the now and not thinking of what you will be doing once this activity is over. A reflective practitioner is one who is always checking up on their practice and asking, 'Why am I doing this? Of what value is it to the child, the group, my colleagues, parents, community?' It is a willingness to acknowledge that working professionally in the early years involves recognising that there is always something more to learn about child development, learning environments and practice in general. The word 'why' is key in quality early years practice – both actually and metaphorically. It challenges practitioners to evaluate the quality and relevance of early years practice to children. It is through asking and answering the 'why' questions that practitioners begin to consolidate a shared understanding and language of early years practice.

What is the evidence?

In reflecting on why early years experiences are so important to a child's development we can consider research findings from a range of disciplines, including developmental psychology, education and neuroscience, which highlight the connectedness between various experiences of young children in different developmental domains such as the physical, linguistic, cognitive, emotional and social. The cumulative knowledge of decades of research has contributed to a greater understanding of development in the early years.[2] The USA's National Scientific Council on the Developing Child (NSCDC), in its report on *The Science of Early Childhood Development* (2007a), argues that research into early brain development clearly points to the importance of early life experiences and their impact on the basic architecture of the brain. The quality of these early experiences can determine the sturdiness or fragility of the foundations for learning and behaviour over time. The report points out that we now know that brains are built up over time, beginning before birth and continuing into adulthood.

> Scientists now know a major ingredient in this developmental process is the 'serve and return' relationship between children and their parents and other caregivers in the family or community. Young children naturally reach out for interaction through babbling, facial expressions, and gestures, and adults respond with the same kind of vocalising and gesturing back at them. In the absence of such responses – or if the responses are unreliable or inappropriate – the brain's architecture does not form as expected, which can lead to disparities in learning and behavior. (NSCDC 2007a:1–2)

A key ingredient in the process of brain development is the quality of early relationships between children and their parents and other significant adults. The 'turn-taking' or 'serve and return' relationships so commonly seen in the interaction between children and adults seem to have a critical role in brain development. Young children benefit most from these relationships when they occur within stable, caring and interactive learning environments. From the start, even very young children are equipped with the skills necessary to initiate and maintain communication; they naturally seek out and attract attention through their vocalisations, their facial expressions and gestures. Responsive adults will reply in kind with vocalisations and gestures of their own and children in turn reward such adult attention by responding, smiling or mimicking behaviour such as sticking out the tongue. We have long known that children who grow up in restricted or depleted environments, such as some institutional settings or chaotic and impoverished homes, show signs of developmental delay from very early on. We now know that this is in part because of the absence of close, stable relationships – the proximal processes described by Bronfenbrenner. The idea of the brain as a 'social brain' has been suggested as a way of strengthening our understanding of the importance of

---

2   Good links on this topic can be accessed at: http://developingchild.harvard. edu/resources/reports_and_working_papers/.

interactions and relationships to brain development, and it may be a useful concept for those working directly with young children as it provides a clear expression of the link between the environment (the space, materials, people and so forth) and the learning, developing child.

We also know that the brain is most flexible in the early years and therefore more responsive to a range of environmental and interactional influences. As the child grows older this flexibility diminishes and it is more difficult to change existing brain circuitry. Take language development, for instance. In the first months of life the baby will respond to a wide range of sounds and begins to differentiate and specialise in those sounds she is exposed to. At the same time as this discrimination and specialisation is happening, research tells us, the brain is already starting to lose the sounds of other languages. 'Although the "windows" for language learning and other skills remain open, these brain circuits become increasingly difficult to alter over time' (NSCDC 2007a:2).

Amazing development occurs in the first six years of a child's life. They move from the tiny babe-in-arms at birth through the physical development, from inability to move from one place to the next through crawling, toddling and on to the competent physical child we see at six years of age. Language development is also visible as we watch a child change from a being who has a limited range of sounds (the cry, the laugh, the coo), through to a two-year-old making sentences and on to a six-year-old with a vocabulary of some 1,500–2,000 words. We see the influence of good food, of exercise, of language opportunities in the children we know and those we work with.

What is less visible and even more amazing is the development of the brain. Research into the brain has found extensive evidence 'that early experiences determine whether a child's developing brain architecture provides a strong or weak foundation for all future learning, behavior and health' (NSCDC 2007b:3).

In summarising some of the central findings derived from research into early brain development five central points have been identified:

1   *Brains are built over time from the bottom up.* Early experiences have a strong influence on how a child's brain architecture develops and this, in turn, can influence the strength or weakness of the foundation for future learning, development and behaviour.

2   *The interactive influences of genes and experience shape the developing brain.* Interactions are central to this developing architecture. The active agent in the influence is the turn-taking, the 'serve and return' nature of interactive relationships. It is important, therefore, that the adult is attuned and responsive to the early signals from children. Young children need positive relationships, rich learning opportunities and safe environments in all their early years settings.

3   *The brain's capacity for change decreases with age.* Research suggests that the brain is most responsive to change during the early years, and so this is highlighted as a crucial period. However, we still have a great deal more to learn about the brain, how it develops and what role the environment plays.

4   *Cognitive, emotional and social capacities are inextricably intertwined throughout the life course.* As research grows, so too does our understanding of the complex, inter-related and dynamic nature of development. From a practice point of view we need to be aware that everything we do with and for children may have an impact, and so we need to be alert and present in our practice so that we can come to understand more fully how our practices are influencing children's development and learning across a range of dimensions.

5   *Toxic stress damages effective brain architecture, which can lead to lifelong problems in learning, behaviour and physical and mental health.* We know that children who grow up in poverty or in chaotic households need a great deal of support, directly and indirectly, to overcome the stresses they are living with. However, we must also recognise that while early years settings can provide a nurturing, safe and secure space for young children, and can provide a protective context within which they can develop and learn, such settings are only one of a number of supports that may be needed for such children. (NSCDC 2009)

The basic principles of neuroscience indicate that early preventive intervention will be more efficient and produce more favourable outcomes than remediation later in life. Supportive relationships and positive learning experiences begin at home and are also provided in high-quality early years environments. Babies and young children require stable, caring, interactive relationships with adults for healthy brain development. For those babies and young children experiencing severe poverty, abuse or stress, additional specialised and supportive interventions are needed to address, insofar as possible, the cause of the stress and protect the child from its consequences.

Brain research has also confirmed that the brain is a complex and interconnected organ. So it should come as no surprise that social, emotional and cognitive (or thinking) capacities are intertwined. Positive early experiences contribute to personal health and well-being and the development of social skills necessary to function in society. Both well-being and social competence contribute to a child's sense of self-confidence, which in turn contributes to their learning and their cognitive development. 'The emotional and physical health, social skills and cognitive–linguistic capacities that emerge in the early years are all important prerequisites for success in school and later in the workplace and community' (NCSDC 2007a:2). As one might expect, the evidence also indicates that stress associated with poverty, neglect, abuse or poor parenting can compromise the positive brain development so essential to later achievement and success. High-quality early childhood experiences in cases such as these can counteract – to some extent – the impact of negative stressors and set the child on a more positive developmental path. This happens not only as a result of direct impact on children but also indirectly through influences on parents and the home learning environment.

From this evidence it is clear that the early years of a child's life are crucial to brain development, which in turn influences the path and trajectory of a child's overall development and learning. Supportive relationships and positive learning experiences are key to this and so the role of early years practitioners cannot be overstated. Through quality practice, early years practitioners can provide learning environments that stimulate and challenge children and give them a secure sense of well-being and belonging and within which they can explore, play, learn, develop and strive to reach their full potential.

It is also important to understand that there is a distinction between the brain and the mind. While the terms are often used interchangeably, there is a difference: the brain is a physical organ; the mind is a philosophical concept. The mind manifests itself in our thoughts and words and is unlocked within the social world. Brooks makes the point that we are born into relationships and are created through relationships. Our physical brain develops within our own skull, but 'a mind only exists within a network. It is the result of interactions between brains, and it is important not to confuse brains with minds' (2011:43).

DEVELOPING AND LEARNING TO LEARN

What is it about positive brain development that influences an individual's learning and development, and why is it important to early years practice?

The skills necessary to control and co-ordinate information – so critical to success in life in general and school success in children in particular – are developed in the early years and provide the foundation for all later learning and development. These skills are called the *executive functions* as they are the functions we use to manage our behaviour, our emotions and our attention. Executive function involves both concrete behaviours and abstract concepts, and research indicates that children who have good executive functioning and self-regulation do better both in academic areas, such as literacy and numeracy, and in general social adjustment. The development of executive function skills depends on the biological maturity of the child and the process is heavily influenced by environmental experiences. It is through the quality of their early learning experiences that children have the opportunity to develop these functions, and the adults in their lives are of critical importance in facilitating this.

The elements of executive function are characterised in different ways, but they include: (a) working memory and recall; (b) activation, arousal and effort; (c) mental flexibility; and (d) self-control.

A *working memory and recall* are key components of executive function and involve problem solving, reasoning and planning. It is through our working memory that we make sense of things over time. It requires that we hold in mind what has happened and relate it to what is happening now. It assists recall. Those of you familiar with the HighScope model of early education will know that this is foregrounded through the *plan/do/review* process. Adults are expected to respond to children, give them the time to talk about their ideas and their plans, allow them the space to actively explore their environment, create opportunities for them to review their plans and encourage their thinking and recall. Working memory is also necessary to connect ideas, to link what you have done, heard or read with what you are doing, hearing or reading right now and to remember instructions and carry them out in the correct order. In addition, it is our working memory that helps us to understand cause and effect.

Activation, arousal and effort refer to the child's willingness and ability to get started at something, to pay attention to the activity and to put in the effort necessary to complete it. Such skills will only develop where the child is comfortable, feels secure and has a sense of belonging. Providing children with the opportunities, materials, time and space to make choices and decisions in their play and activities while facilitating them in thinking about what they are doing is a key role that the early years practitioner fulfils – it is the essence of quality early childhood education and care.

Mental flexibility includes being able to switch perspectives, to see things in a new light. It is being able to see opportunities and take advantage of them and being able and willing to change course if what you are doing seems wrong or is not working. It is this flexibility of mind that allows people think outside the box and to be creative. It also has important behavioural dimensions in that it helps us understand another person's point of view. Creating a context that allows children to explore objects and ideas from different perspectives requires careful planning and responsive practice.

Self-control is crucial to successful learning and development. It allows us to stay focused, avoid distraction and stay on task, and helps to limit and manage impulsive behaviour. Where children are impulsive they are less likely to persist at an activity and are also less likely to pay attention. From longitudinal research we know that this can lead to later difficulties in school and less success in adulthood. In a study that tracked a population of children from birth into adulthood, Moffitt and colleagues (2011) found that self-control, as measured by parents, teachers and self-report ratings during the first ten years of life, predicted physical and mental health, employment, financial security, substance use and criminal conviction (and lack of). Self-controlled children are less likely drop out of school, smoke or become teenage parents. Other studies have also found the early years settings that encourage the development of self-control and self-regulation are most effective in later school success (Blair 2002). Quite apart from these later impacts, children who have well-developed self-control are more likely to have enjoyable and satisfying everyday experiences; their childhoods are more likely to be happy and content than fractured and stressful.

We know that development progresses through feedback loops. The messages we get back from the environment (social, cultural or material) inform the view we have of ourselves, which influences the extent to which we see ourselves as masterful or helpless, trusted or mistrusted and so on. Poor executive function can lead to troublesome behaviour, while good executive functioning leads to greater co-operation, caring and responsiveness in children.

While understanding how our behaviour impacts so profoundly on children and at such a crucial and deep level is important, it is also a huge responsibility, and this can be daunting and paralysing. The thing is that even if we do not understand the impact of our practice, it still has an impact on the children: but knowledge helps us to consider our practice a little more carefully; it challenges us to consider the implications such knowledge has for our practice. In the first instance it allows us to recognise that feedback and the form that it takes has an influence on young children's confidence, mental flexibility and self-control. Through the provision of opportunities, materials, times and space to explore, play, take risks and rise to social and physical challenges in a setting that is secure and comfortable, children develop a sense of belonging, they feel that they are trusted participants in the learning environment and this in turn facilitates healthy development and learning.

Through observation, adults can see executive function at work in children's play when they talk themselves through an activity as they move objects around or place things in a particular order. The example below is an illustration of a young child at play. If you follow it closely you will be able to see the different elements of executive function in action and the practitioner's role in extending the opportunities presented.

Example: executive function

At planning time, Gabrielle says, 'I'm going to play with the doggies and Magnatiles in the toy area. I'm making a tall elevator.' At work time, Gabrielle builds with the magnetic tiles while playing with the small toy dogs, as she planned. She stacks the tiles on top of one another in a tower-like form – her 'elevator' – then places some dogs in it. The elevator then falls over. She repeats this several times but the elevator continues to fall over. Gabrielle then arranges the magnetic tiles into squares, connecting them to form a row. Gabrielle says to Shannon, her teacher, 'I'm making doghouses because the elevator keeps falling down.' Shannon says, 'I was wondering what you were building, because you planned to make a tall elevator going up vertically, and now you are using them to make doghouses in a long horizontal row. You solved the problem by changing the way you were building.' Gabrielle uses pretend talk while moving the dogs around. At one point she says, 'Mommy, Mommy, we are hungry' and opens one of the doghouses and moves the dog inside where a bigger dog is placed. Gabrielle says, 'Mommy says the food's not ready, so go play.'

While moving the dogs around, Gabrielle says to herself out loud, 'We have to find something to do until the food is ready.' Gabrielle says to Shannon, 'Let's pretend we are going to the park.' Shannon agrees and says, 'I'm going to slide down the slide three times and then jump off the climber.' As Shannon pretends to do this with one of the dogs, Gabrielle watches then copies her and says, 'My dog jumped higher than yours.' She then says, 'Mommy says we have to go home now. We need to move our dogs over there so they can eat.' The pretend play continues.

At recall time, Gabrielle is using a scarf to hide some objects she played with. When it is her turn to recall, she gives clues about what is under the scarf. She shows the group a couple of magnetic tiles and dogs. Shannon asks her what she did with these materials during work time. Gabrielle talks about the problem with the falling 'elevator' and then recounts the story about the doggies.

Source: Lockhart (n.d.).

In this example you will have noticed how, with the careful intervention of the early years practitioner, Gabrielle was made aware of the fact that she had solved a problem through her behaviour. Later in her play she was given the opportunity to see planning in action when Shannon, the early years practitioner, talked through her plans for sliding on the slide. Finally we see Gabrielle given the opportunity to recall and share her activity with others. Where playful everyday experiences are available in well-designed and interactive early years settings, children have the time, encouragement and the context within which to develop the dispositions and skills necessary to function competently and effectively at their own level. The presence of observant, attuned and engaged practitioners enriches their experiences and expands and strengthens their learning and development.

Executive functions in early childhood

Contemporary society is fast, complex and intertwined with information overload and multiple distractions. For positive early learning and development, young children need calm and predictable early experiences that give them the encouragement and the time to develop the necessary functions and skills for later success in the more frantic world. A key contribution of quality early years practice to these developments is the provision of unhurried learning environments where practitioners themselves are calm and understand and respect the central developmental features of early childhood that need to be developed and refined during this first stage of education. In her book *Mind in the Making: The Seven Essential Life Skills Every Child Needs* (2010), Ellen Galinsky elaborates on the idea of executive function in young children. The seven skills she identifies are:

1 focus and self-control
2 perspective taking
3 communicating
4 making connections
5 critical thinking
6 taking on challenges
7 self-directed engaged learning.

She makes a strong case for giving very careful attention to the role of early years experience in the development of these seven skills. She is anxious to make the point that there is a strong cognitive dimension to these skills and that they are important in their own right, not just as precursors to the development of other skills, such as literacy or numeracy skills. She dislikes the fact that they are often referred to as 'soft skills', a term often used to describe the less measurable skills developed in early childhood, and she fears that the term may undervalue them. She argues that these skills require intellect and are indeed cognitive skills as much as they are social and emotional skills. They can be considered the essential cognitive 'how' skills to the more traditional cognitive 'what' skills. The importance of these skills has been recognised and articulated by the United Nations in its General Comment No. 1, which describes the aims of education as including not only:

> . . . literacy and numeracy but also life skills such as the ability to make balanced decisions, to resolve conflicts in a non-violent manner and to develop a healthy lifestyle, good social relationships and responsibility, critical thinking, creative talents and other abilities which give children the tools needed to pursue their options in life. (2001: para. 9)

You can see from the above the contribution that quality, intelligent early years practice makes to children's development of these skills and how it is uniquely placed to assist in the development of these particularly valuable foundational aspects of learning.

Whether referred to as soft skills or life skills, they are learned, developed and refined during early childhood and they act as the basis for later learning and development. They are critical dimensions of a child's learning toolkit and children need time and appropriate early years experiences to strengthen and consolidate them. Armed with a well-formed and supported toolkit, young children are better placed to gain more from other educational contexts and later life than children who have not had those opportunities. The opportunities can be missed in situations where children's early learning experiences are chaotic, overly managed, too prescriptive or too academic. It is the responsibility of the adults in a child's early life to understand how these skills develop and to defend the need to attend to these over and above the more 'traditional' learning skills such as reading, writing and arithmetic. We now know from research that these latter, more formal school skills develop best when children feel confident about their own learning skills and interested in learning for its own sake. Such frames of mind are established in their early years.

Let us consider Galinsky's seven skills in more detail.

Focus and self-control

This is a central executive function, which Galinsky further breaks down into component parts: (a) focus; (b) cognitive flexibility; (c) working memory; and (d) inhibitory control. We can see this focus and self-control in action when we look at how closely young children, even very young babies, attend to an activity they want to master. Think of the fourteen-month-old trying to get food on to a spoon in order to eat it: with encouragement they will try, try and try again. In addition to focus and self-control we also see, in the older child, concentration – often evident in facial expressions or actions such as biting the lower lip as if to hold on until the task is successfully completed.

Cognitive flexibility refers to the ability to switch attention or change perspective from one thing to the next as necessary. It is important because it helps children function well in social situations as well as challenging cognitive activities. Working memory allows you to hold information in your head while you work with it or apply it. This capacity is central to, for instance, remembering stories told or read. It is to enhance the working memory that early years practitioners tell and retell stories and that children so enjoy hearing them again and again. Introducing 'mistakes' once the story is familiar and enjoyed can provide children with the opportunity to call on their memory and 'correct' the mistake. Inhibitory control refers to the ability to delay an action until it is appropriate, to manage impulses or feelings so that you can maintain attention on a particular task. Considered in its positive manifestation, it is what we call self-control.

Perspective taking

This develops over time and involves the ability to step into another's shoes, working out what others may be feeling. It is through perspective taking that children make judgements about what adults mean and so it is important in early years practice that adults are attuned to a child's level of understanding and are clear about the demands made. For instance, it is difficult for a three-year-old to know exactly what you mean when you ask them to 'be good'. Being good depends on the context and can mean different things at different times. It is unhelpful to children to make such general demands. To encourage a child to behave in a particular way you should attract their attention and be specific about what you want: 'Can you stay in your seat until . . . ?'; 'Sophie, will you listen to James first and then . . . ?' Galinsky points out that perspective taking uses a variety of executive functions, such as inhibitory control, cognitive flexibility and reflection (considering another person's view of things alongside your own). Disputes or arguments often come down to the fact that one person cannot or will not shift their perspective. We know from recent brain research and longitudinal studies into later school success that assisting children to develop perspective-taking skills, through providing a rich variety of different opportunities and allowing them the space to learn, is an important aspect of early years practice across the age range from birth through to six years.

Communicating

Communication – both verbal and non-verbal – happens all the time. Sensitive and attuned adults consciously strive to communicate clearly and to pick up on communication signals from children. This can be observed in very young children at, for instance, changing time, when a turn-taking, cooing session develops with the baby. The baby becomes animated, observant, participating in the game but also learning important things about communication such as the role of tone of voice, the importance of eye contact and the rhythm of turn-taking, which is a precursor to the rhythm of conversation. As well as the familiar aspects of language communication – understanding, speaking, reading and writing – communication also requires the development of understanding and selecting what is to be communicated or what aspect of a communication is important. These latter skills take time and are important forerunners to early literacy, for instance. The publication in 2011 of the national literacy and numeracy strategy, *Literacy and Numeracy for Learning and Life* (DES 2011), has made literacy and numeracy topical. The strategy sees early education as a critical period for developing the foundations for later literacy and numeracy learning. For the development of these foundations it is more important that young children become confident communicators, comprehending and speaking, during their early years experiences than that they develop the skills of reading or writing.

Making connections

A lot of learning is about making connections. At a very basic level, learning is about working out what is the same and what is different. Creativity comes about when unusual connections are made – and we can see many examples of that in young children's play when, for instance, they use materials in the 'wrong' way, when they experiment. In observing how children play, how in pretend play they can make objects represent different things, we are also observing how they are working things out, making connections that ultimately inform their understanding of the world. While initially making connections may be simply about working out what is the same and what is different, it also includes finding out how things relate to each other. As they grow older and into later preschool age, children can make multiple connections across objects, ideas and behaviours that call on executive functions such as working memory, inhibitory control and cognitive flexibility. Early years practitioners can contribute to these developments by allowing children the freedom and time to try out different connections and through their leadership in facilitating the development of confident, engaged, creative learners.

Critical thinking

Critical thinking is essential in seeking out knowledge and understanding and it is a skill that can be strengthened and refined. It is behaviour that poses questions such as 'What if . . . ?', 'Why not . . . ?' or starts activities with, 'Suppose I do this . . . ' It involves testing ideas, challenging answers, developing ideas about what causes this and not that to happen. It is a skill that facilitates the scientific method – an ordered way of seeking to understand the world which is as important in day-to-day life as it is for scientists.

Children need to be given the opportunities to engage in critical thinking; if they simply accept unquestioningly whatever they are told, they become mere performers, behaving in the absence of understanding rather than learning. Opportunities to engage in critical thinking (facilitated as necessary) guide children in their learning and they grow to recognise the importance of questioning, of striving towards full understanding. In practice, providing such rich learning opportunities demands a transformation in practitioners from the more traditional approaches in early years practice, where routines and activities are planned in advance for the children to 'do'. Based on our current understanding of child development and early learning, we now recognise that quality practice shares the learning experiences with children and is led more by the possibilities of the learning environment and the child's developing curiosity to explore and learn than by the transmission of facts or the training of specific skills. It is practice that recognises the greater understanding of the adult but that also recognises that we are all learning. Taking the time to follow the child's lead in questioning – even when it may seem irrelevant – can often bring them to a richer learning experience than those we prescribe in advance. Such practice requires that we trust that children can and do learn without being told what to do or being overly guided in their actions.

Taking on challenges

This is an important life skill. Throughout our lives we will be challenged, some of us more than others, and it is in our earliest years that we learn how to respond to challenge. Challenge is often a good thing. For instance, when he introduced the concept of the zone of proximal development (ZPD), Vygotsky encouraged adults to provide learning opportunities that lift children a little beyond what they can do easily. Challenging children in this way assists their progress along the developmental path. As adults we should not limit a child's opportunity to experience risk, to face physical and emotional challenges. Rather we should be alert to situations where some guidance is necessary and provide assistance to children when they need it. In this way we can encourage the development of personal strategies for managing challenges and the coping skills necessary.

Self-directed and engaged learning

Finally, where education, at any level, is successful we observe children in self-directed and engaged learning, which is as satisfying as it is useful. It is through this effective learning that we can all realise our potential and develop our individual talents and interests. This positive style of learning stays with us through life and can be called into action as each new situation and challenge arises. It is the type of behaviour we associate with educational success, but it also seems to be important to life success. It is professionally satisfying to observe children actively engaged in learning and, as they are busy doing, talking or thinking, we can take that time to observe them and to respond to them sensitively and effectively as necessary.

Working Memory	Inhibitory Control	Cognitive Flexibility
Adult: Can remember multiple tasks, rules, and strategies that may vary by situation	Adult: Consistent self-control; situationally appropriate responses (e.g. resists saying something socially inappropriate, resists 'tit for tat' response)	Adult: Able to revise actions and plans in response to changing circumstances

Working Memory (contd)	Inhibitory Control (contd)	Cognitive Flexibility (contd)
5–16 years: Develops ability to search varying locations, remember where something was found, then explore other locations (e.g. a game of Concentration or hiding a penny under one of three cups)	*10–18 years:* Continues to develop self-control, such as flexibly switching between a central focus (such as riding a bike or driving) and peripheral stimuli that may or may not need attention (road signs and pedestrians vs. billboards and passing houses)	*13–18 years:* Continued improvement in accuracy when switching focus and adapting to changing rules
4–5 years: Comprehends that appearance does not always equal reality (e.g. when given a sponge that looks like a rock)	*7 years:* Children perform at adult levels on learning to ignore irrelevant, peripheral stimuli (such as a dot on the side of a screen) and focus on the central stimulus (such as a picture in the middle of the screen)	*10–12 years:* Successfully adapts to changing rules, even along multiple dimensions (okay to shout in playground, not okay in school, okay sometimes in theater rehearsal)
3 years: Can hold in mind two rules (e.g. red goes here, blue goes there) and act on the basis of the rules	*4–5 years:* Reductions in perseveration (persisting with following a rule even when knowing that the rule has changed). Can delay eating a treat; also can begin to hold an arbitrary rule in mind and follow it to produce a response that differs from their natural instinct (sort colored cards by shape rather than color)	*2–5 years:* Succeeds at shifting actions according to changing rules (e.g. takes shoes off at home, leaves on at school, puts on boots for rain)
9–10 months: Can execute simple means-to-ends tasks and two-step plans; also able to integrate looking one place and acting (e.g. reaching) at another place	*9–11 months:* Able to inhibit reaching straight for a visible but inaccessible reward, such as a toy on the other side of a window, and instead delay a moment to recognize the barrier and detour around it	*9–11 months:* Develops ability to seek alternate methods to retrieve objects beyond directly reaching for what's in view
7–9 months: Develops ability to remember that unseen objects are still there (toy hidden under a cloth); learns to put two actions together in a sequence (remove cloth, grasp toy)	*8–10 months:* Begins to maintain focus despite distractions during brief delays in a task	
	6 months: Rudimentary response inhibition (able to not touch something instructed not to touch)	

Source: Center on the Developing Child (2011).

Positive executive functioning leads to more positive experiences and thence to more positive outcomes. On the other hand, poor executive functioning yields negative experiences and less positive outcomes. Two children can be similar in many ways but if one has poor executive function and the other has good executive function, developmentally they will pull apart from each other so that across a trajectory of time they are much further apart behaviourally than they were initially.

Poor executive functioning can be improved with safe, secure and stimulating environments. So how might that manifest itself in practice? Well, a child with poor executive functioning is likely to be impulsive, so introducing a pause before a particular activity or to get over some attention difficulty will help the child learn to manage this impulsivity. Positive feedback from the environment (particularly the adults) will reinforce the value of pausing, managing impulsivity, so that the overall effect is a sense of personal self-control. For example, children who are giddy or restless at times when you want their attention – for instance story time – can be encouraged to attend and listen if they are given a picture of an ear. The ear is associated with listening and so there is a concrete reminder for the child that it is listening time. Of course, for this to be effective there has to be something interesting and engaging in the listening activity. If it is forcing a child to be quiet and listen to something dull and/or boring it will be difficult to hold the attention of any children and there will be a general air of giddiness.

ENHANCING PRACTICE TO DEVELOP LEARNING

Scaffolding is a word widely used in the literature to describe effective teaching/learning interactions. Scaffolding is often used synonymously with the Vygotskian concept of the ZPD, although the two concepts developed independently of each other. The scaffolding metaphor captures the notion of the child as a constructor of knowledge and the construction is supported, or scaffolded, by the social environment within which such construction is occurring. Generally the adult is considered as the scaffold to the child's development. Berk and Winsler observe that:

> [S]caffolding connotes a warm, pleasant collaboration between a teacher and a learner while the two are engaged in joint problem-solving activity. During this collaboration the adult supports the child's autonomy by providing sensitive and contingent assistance, facilitating children's representational and strategic thinking and prompting children to take over responsibility for the task as their skill increases. (1995:31–2)

The importance of relationships and interactions in the process of development has been strengthened by research showing the powerful role played by the social context, even in the lives of very young children. Studies into collaborative learning in context and the importance of 'intersubjectivity', the ability to 'read other minds' (Bruner 1996) have informed a move towards a more respectful pedagogy, which sees the child as an active participant in the learning process. Bidirectional, transformational interactions have been defended for their contribution to facilitating children to explain their ideas to others, negotiate, argue a point and clarify their thinking. The concept of 'intersubjectivity' and joint activity becomes central. Collaborative learning between peers is considered particularly important in early childhood, when the collaborative opportunities in a safe environment enhance children's opportunities to refine their cognitive and metacognitive skills.

Sustained shared thinking is an interaction, which 'involves an adult being aware of the child's interests and understandings, and involves the adult and the child interacting together to develop an idea or skill' (Siraj-Blatchford *et al.* 2008:29). It has been linked to improved cognitive outcomes for children and is recognised as one of the key elements of quality early years practice. Early years professionals who are sensitive and responsive to children's cues are better able to engage in sustained shared thinking and are able to assess what type of assistance, if any, children need, and to ensure that their responses are accordingly child-centred. Sustained shared thinking underpins a range of techniques used in the education of young children, such as constructing understanding, philosophising, and scaffolding their learning, among others (MacNaughton & Williams 2009). Such a view recognises the young social child as capable of reasoning while making sense of the world, and presents the child as capable of higher-order functions such as thinking about thinking, connecting ideas through reflection, or 'going meta' (Bruner 1996:57).

While individual children need opportunities to explore, play and learn in an uninterrupted way, collaboration with peers and adults – as opposed to individual work – is also valuable because in practice it results in explaining one's thought processes and seeing things from another's viewpoint. These learning opportunities are important in encouraging the development of higher-order cognitive functions such as metacognition. Metacognition relates to the shared basis of learning in peer groups and 'learning communities', providing concepts such as socially shared cognition, distributed cognition and situated knowledge, which emphasise the collective nature of knowing. This attention to the shared or social nature of learning is consonant with the idea of the individual as a social learner even when interacting with objects or concepts.

One of the benefits of developing metacognitive skills – the skills of thinking about thinking – is that it assists in the development of cognitive self-regulation. Bronson (2001) argues that one of the central tasks of childhood is to develop the ability to regulate cognitive functioning, to exercise conscious control over attention and memory processes. Research is now suggesting that language and a language-rich environment can assist young children in developing self-regulatory skills. Bronson, capturing the dynamic to-ing and fro-ing of the developmental process, proposes that learning can lead, as well as follow, cognitive development when adults or more competent peers provide guidance in the form of structuring or 'scaffolding'. Experience in attempting to successfully carry out cognitive tasks is influenced by the environment and the responsiveness of those in the environment. In her concluding comments on the preschool child, she notes that 'environments that nurture self-regulation are orderly and consistent enough for children to understand the requirements for successful independent functioning within them' (Bronson 2001: 220).

Self-regulation also has an affective or emotional dimension. Goleman (1996) considers that school success is more dependent on emotional and social measures than on a child's fund of facts or ability to read. It is, he argues, more important in the long run for children to be interested; to know what kind of behaviour is expected and how to rein in the impulse to misbehave (self-regulation); to be able to wait, to follow directions, and to turn to adults and peers for help. This view is similar to that proposed by Maslow (1987). He characterised the 'self-actualised' child as one capable of tolerating uncertainty, of being problem-centred rather than self-centred and with a concern for the welfare of the wider world, an outside-looking rather than an inside-looking child who enjoys satisfying interpersonal relationships. Behaviours that assist children in achieving self-actualisation, or facilitate them on their journey, include: the ability to become absorbed, to concentrate; a willingness to try the new; a facility to listen to themselves as well as others; an honesty that allows them to be individual; a readiness to assume responsibility; and the ability to work hard and persevere. Also important to this process is a sense of belonging, the connectedness that assists in the development of well-being (Laevers 2002). The evidence from scientific research indicates that prioritising emotional and social development, particularly in early education, can assist children in their overall development in the present and into the future.

This review of the research findings informing our understandings of effective early years practice suggests that high-quality settings are those in which practitioners interact with children in a responsive and informative way, encourage verbal interaction and are not harsh with children. Development is enhanced if group sizes are small, settings are child-focused and well organised, with adults playing a facilitative role rather than a didactic one. Organisation and structure are important and are provided by adults who carefully plan and prepare the learning environment and who have high expectations of children in relation to social and linguistic development (Bowman, Donovan & Burns 2001; Schweinhart 2002). The evidence confirms that settings that facilitate more involvement with and attention to activities by children themselves result in the children learning more skills and concepts, including the kind of knowledge that is tested on achievement measures. In addition, children from such learning environments show more cognitive advance and have more verbal and social skills. It seems that allowing children the time and space to make decisions and take some responsibility for their own learning and actions may help them internalise control or engender 'the dispositions in children that enable them to achieve greater success' (Schweinhart, Barnes & Weikart 1993).

THE IMPORTANCE OF DISPOSITIONS

Individual learning power, or cognitive functioning, can be considered as having two dimensions: *capabilities* – skills and strategies; and *dispositions* – tendencies to learn and to learn from learning. This latter dimension includes the less measurable, but no less important, sides of cognitive behaviour such as the motivational, perceptual and affective. Understanding where motivation or inclination comes from, how the inclination to apply skills or knowledge develops and how this might be cultivated in early education is an important challenge as it can set the stage for future school success. The term 'affective' refers to emotion or desire, especially in influencing behaviour. It is derived from the Latin *affectus*, meaning 'disposition'. The affective dimension of a child's development influences the motivation or disposition to learn and it also shapes the sense of self as learner; the dimension of development, which predisposes the learner to apply the knowledge and the skills acquired with some understanding of their role in the process (Carr *et al.* 2010; Dweck 1999). Dispositions have been defined in a variety of ways, depending on the focus of the author.

In a comprehensive review of the definitional difficulties surrounding the concept of disposition, Katz (1993) highlights the ambiguous and inconsistent use of the term in educational and developmental studies. Arising from her review of the literature, she considers dispositions to be patterns of behaviour exhibited frequently and in the absence of coercion and that they constitute a habit of mind under some conscious and voluntary control that is intentional and oriented to broad goals. The concept of disposition has been considered 'messy' because it invokes a vague assortment of ill-defined or difficult to measure behavioural influences. Perkins *et al.* note that 'dispositions inevitably include reference to things that are genuinely hard to pin down: motivation, affect, sensitivities, values and the like' (1993:18). Carr considers dispositions to be a 'slippery' concept. She defines learning dispositions in the early years as 'participation repertoires from which a learner recognises, selects, edits, responds to, resists, searches for and constructs learning opportunities. . . . Learning dispositions are about responsive and reciprocal relationships between the individual and the environment' (2001:21–2).

The development in children of an identity as learner is seen as an important outcome of early education. It facilitates flexible, responsive learning to changing contexts and situations and rests comfortably with the contemporary emphasis on lifelong learning and learning how to learn. Katz (1995a) urges early years practitioners to consider developing the affective dimension of cognitive development by assisting the child to become a 'good learner' rather than focusing on their being a 'good person'. She is concerned that too much attention to becoming a 'good person' may encourage performance for praise rather than learning for personal satisfaction. The two identities of 'good person' and 'good learner' may become blurred unless practitioners are very clear in their communication with children in relation to their behaviour.

Informed and intelligent early years practice enhances the development of dispositions or 'habits of mind' as an explicit aspect of education alongside knowledge and skill. While more research is needed to come to a better understanding of how contexts and interactions facilitate the acquisition of dispositions, developing learning dispositions is generally considered an important aim of early years practice. Developing learning dispositions involves: encouraging a mastery, or learning, orientation; promoting metacognitive skills; developing cognitive and social self-regulation; providing for multiple intelligences; and fostering engaged involvement and emotional well-being.

Katz has suggested a number of reasons for including the development of dispositions as a goal in early education:

1   The acquisition of knowledge and skills alone does not guarantee that they will be used and applied; one must also have the disposition to use or apply.
2   Explicitly attending to the encouragement of learner dispositions is important because the instructional process by which some knowledge and skills are acquired may damage or undermine the disposition to use them.
3   When children's experiences are supported to manifest dispositions they become robust; without such supports they are likely to weaken or disappear.
4   The process of selecting content and practice strategies should include consideration of how desirable dispositions can be strengthened and undesirable dispositions can be weakened.
5   On the basis of evidence accumulated from research on mastery versus performance motivation, it seems reasonable to suggest that there is an optimum amount of positive feedback for young children above which children may become preoccupied with their performance and the judgement of others rather than involvement in the task.
6   Dispositions must be included in the evaluation and assessment of early years programmes.
7   Dispositions are not likely to be acquired through didactic processes, but are more likely to develop in young children as they experience being around people who exhibit positive dispositions. Therefore, practitioners and parents should become aware of what dispositions can be seen in them by the children for whom they are responsible. (Katz 1993:11–12)

Learning- or mastery-oriented children tend to exhibit positive learning dispositions and maintain persistence in the face of difficulty, locating any difficulty or problem in the context rather than within themselves. Quality early years settings provide extensive opportunities for learning and the practitioners are instrumental in shaping the dispositions through careful observation of children as they explore, play, interact with others and the environment, or sit quietly alone. Through such careful observation they identify the emerging dispositions particular to individual children at particular times and in particular contexts. Where feedback to children from the learning environment is clear, and explicitly articulates the features of the context, the task, the process and their function in it, it is most beneficial. It is important, however, to note that by the age of five young children exhibit a vulnerability to adult criticism and this has been associated with the development of a negative, 'helpless' learning orientation in older children. Thus practitioners must consider carefully how best to give feedback, particularly if the feedback is negative in nature. It is not about only praising children, it is also about being respectful and sensitive when correcting them or pointing out whatever difficulty there may be with their behaviour.

We know that early childhood education is one of the most important influencing factors for the development of the 'soft' and difficult to measure aspects of development such as aspirations, social skills, motivation and learner confidence – those aspects influenced by the developing executive functions. An emphasis on the affective dimension of learning also positively influences children's academic cognitive development. This approach yields foundational short-term benefits and sustainable long-term benefits across social and educational dimensions. Rather than attempting to provide a balanced approach to guiding academic skills and affective skills development in young children, it appears that it is more productive to foreground the affective, over the academic, dimension of development in early education. This approach is evident in New Zealand's early years curriculum Te Whariki, and it underpins the practices found in Reggio Emilia early years settings. It can also be seen in the Aistear materials.

A general disposition to learn, or mastery orientation, may be present in some form at birth in normal infants. Its manifestation is likely to change with development, to be related to the child's experience, and to be increasingly varied and differentiated across children with increasing age and experience. Dispositions are an integral part of the individual child and can be identified through observing children's choices, decisions and actions. To develop and function they require a balance between the inclination of the learner and the goals of knowledge, skills and abilities to be learned. This suggests an active role for the early years practitioner and the learning environment itself in the development of learning dispositions as well as in the encouragement of other skills and knowledge. This developmental view of dispositional learning is in keeping with our current understanding of the complexity and dynamic nature of learning and is the reason that consideration must be explicitly given to nurturing learning dispositions in early education, particularly as they appear to facilitate the later application of the literacy and numeracy skills and competencies valued by primary education. It helps explain why early years practice is specialised and focuses on developing and nurturing the less definable skills, such as motivation, organisation, inclination and attitude to learning. In attending to dispositional aspects of learning it is important to provide a context which is meaningful and relevant to the child through interactions and relationships aimed at nurturing the affective dimension of learning within a content-rich context. In this way it will impact on those 'basic skills' identified by policy-makers as so important to later school success.

In summary we can conclude that quality early years settings provide rich learning opportunities to assist the development of the executive functions underpinning positive development. The review of research highlights how important it is for early years practitioners to: facilitate the development of learning dispositions; encourage a mastery, or learning, orientation; promote metacognitive skills; assist the development of cognitive and social self-regulation; and foster engaged involvement and emotional well-being. The picture emerging is one of quality early years settings as dynamic learning environments rich in interactions and communication where learning and development occur in a complex, dynamic and shared context and not simply as a result of individual differences in ability or of a specific pedagogy.

While contemporary education policy emphasises the importance of children learning to learn and develop an identity as learner in their early education, policy also identifies specific outcomes for education that may compete with this. This tension can influence practice and the learning environment and may in fact be encouraging early years environments that facilitate a performance rather than a learning orientation. To be able to counteract this trend and resolve the tension, early years practitioners require a shared understanding of their role in the education of young children and a common language of professional early years practice. This can be aided by reference to the two frameworks of practice, Síolta and Aistear, which share a common view of early childhood and early years practice. They are considered in greater detail in the following chapters.

CHAPTER 3

Pillars of Practice: Introducing Síolta and Aistear

Good learning starts with questions, not answers. (Claxton 1990)

In her wide-ranging keynote address to the 2012 annual European Early Childhood Education Research Association conference, Margaret Carr called on us to consider the importance of democracy, dreaming and doubt on the learning journeys we all take. Stressing the importance of clear observations that are open to all that is to be 'seen', she gave many wonderful examples of how practice can respect, for instance, children's democratic participation.

In one example, Carr introduced us to a creative young artist whose work was on display in the early years setting and who was explaining it to an adult. As he was explaining a younger child from the setting came over and, unexpectedly, walked past the paintings and pulled them off the display stand. As one might expect, the young artist was upset. How to react? In this case the early years practitioner acknowledged the upset of the young artist and agreed it was reasonable. However, there followed some discussion about why the younger child behaved as he did and how he simply did not realise that he was 'destroying' the work of the older child. While the older child could understand this, he was still sad and thought something needed to be done. The adult agreed and asked for his ideas on what could be done. His suggestion on how to stop this happening again was to have the 'museum line' in the art display area of the setting. On further investigation by the adult it transpired that this was a reference to the line in museums and art galleries over which patrons are asked not to step – it keeps people at a short distance from the art, while still allowing them to view and discuss it. This suggested solution was introduced into the setting. In this example we see that the adult was respectful of both children, acknowledging the impulsiveness of the younger child while at the same time recognising the upset of the older child. Furthermore, the practitioner took the time to tease out how best to respond to the situation and both listened to and acted on the suggestion of the older child. Overall there was specific respect for the views of the children, which created a true sense of belonging for both children. This is a rich example of democratic practice in action, and it also gives us further insight into the type of practice in the setting. The conversation between the practitioner and the child in advance of the disruption suggests that the practitioner and the child were engaged in discussion over time and the practitioner took note of and recorded what the child had done and learned. Finally we can infer from the availability of the story that the information on this event was documented by the adult for sharing and future reference.

One way to identify opportunities for this level of engagement with children is through ongoing observation of their activity and play. Play is recognised as a key process through which children extend their learning development during early childhood in particular. Lester and Russell have argued, in their writings on the right to play and its importance to children, that:

> [P]lay is about creating a world in which, for that moment, children are in control and can seek out uncertainty in order to triumph over it – or, if not, no matter, it is only a game . . . it is primarily behaviour for its own sake, for the pleasure and joy of being able to do it. Yet play is more than mere indulgence; it is essential to children's health and wellbeing (Lester & Russell 2010:x)

While children are biologically equipped to play from birth, they need sensitive adults to guide them through their frustrations and share in their satisfactions (Bruce 2001). Effective play is promoted and nurtured by adults who provide quality learning environments (indoors and outdoors), objects, activities, time and encouragement. It is through their play that young children explore, create, imagine, experiment, manipulate, negotiate, problem-solve and consolidate their understanding of the world. Play provides a safe 'magic circle' (Huizinga 1938) within which they can struggle and strive and succeed; it is the space that allows them to explore feelings and to test their fears; it is through play that they come to experience the nature of materials such as water and sand, and begin to explore the foundations of science and mathematics. In the main, children are curious and interested in understanding the world around them and through their play they become competent and confident learners who are prepared to take risks and challenge themselves to learn more.

While adults prepare environments to encourage play, there are times when it may be appropriate for them to participate in play. Participating in play with children can provide valuable opportunities for practitioners to extend or elaborate a particular theme through guidance, the introduction of new themes or new materials. We saw an example of this in Chapter 2. Care needs to be taken, however, when considering participation in children's play and it is most successful where practitioners are invited into a play situation as a participant and respect the direction of the children so as to avoid intruding or interrupting the flow.

Observant and sensitive early years practitioners use play as a window into children's minds; into their interests, their skills and knowledge, their friendships and their level of development in different areas. Records of play observations can inform curriculum planning and development and allow practitioners to determine how best to meet the individual needs of children and what particular interests can be built on. Observations of group play can also highlight aspects of social interactions that may need supporting, strengthening or redirecting.

Gathering records and other documentation of learning, whether for learning, assessment or planning, is most effective when approached collaboratively rather than through isolated individual activity. While individual observations of individual children have a key role to play in certain aspects of early years practice (such as gathering specific developmental or social information), the more general day-to-day documentation in practice is a social activity and its value rests in that fact. When we talk about collaboration in this context it often includes (as in the example above) the active participation of the children themselves. Apart from the value of this collaborative engagement in relation to learning and to practice, it is also meeting the first goal of the National Children's Strategy (DoHC 2000), which is that children's voices will be heard. Realising the challenge to give voice to children, to hear them, in a democratic and respectful manner, can, particularly with very young children, be a challenge, but there are a growing number of methods and resources to assist. For instance, Carr has written extensively on how the visual – drawings, photos and video clips – can be more powerful than the traditional written documentation. There is a democracy in sharing photos of children with other children, their families and visitors to the setting; it is a really inclusive practice in which all children can participate at some level. Through such visual displays – which are shared and discussed – they see themselves as belonging to the place and recognise the past as part of their present.

Adjusting practice to encourage the active involvement of children with adults and other children can be unsettling because it alters the power balance in a setting. This does not shift the balance from adult to child, nor does it lead to a situation of chaos and inappropriate behaviour in the children; rather it facilitates a context where learning becomes more reciprocal, where children learn in an engaged way with adults and other children who respect each other and where adults are also open to learning. Such reciprocal practice makes visible for children their place in the setting and enhances their sense of belonging and self-worth. While observations of individual children are very useful in focusing on a specific issue, there is a danger that some observations of individual children may inadvertently omit or remove the context of the observation and compromise the quality of the interpretation and analysis. This may be problematic when seeking the meaning of actions or behaviours as learning is, in many instances, located within a social context. Too individual a focus can limit our true understanding of the real meaning behind the observation. There are strategies of recording that capture social context and can be used to overcome this. Small group observations and records capture the critical social/relational dimension of learning that we now know is so critical for young children.

CONSIDERING THE EARLY YEARS CURRICULUM

Conceptions about early learning are often captured in the values and principles that are provided to introduce curricular or practice frameworks. Traditional early childhood curricula often include the assumption that learning in early childhood is a preparation for future learning and is about 'acquiring the early rungs of a hierarchy of defined knowledge and skill, a process that begins the climb up the ladder to grown-up ways of thinking and learning' (Carr 1998:1). Such assumptions consolidate the view of the learner as an individual and learning as furniture of the mind. This is a limited and limiting view of early learning. New conceptions about the curriculum recognise that it is in early childhood that children get their first messages about themselves, about what it is to be a learner, about where they fit in a social context and about the expectations and constraints that an environment can place on them.

Looking at the early years curriculum from the point of view of the development of the child raises the question, 'What should be learned?' Carr suggests that the primary outcome for early education is adaptive learners who can effectively co-ordinate performance and learning goals, balancing the curriculum aims of belonging and exploration. Research has found two opposing learning characteristics in children as young as four or five years of age: a learning orientation or a performance orientation (Smiley & Dweck 1994).

- *Learning orientation* children strive to increase their competence, to understand or master something, to attempt hard tasks and persist despite failure or setback.
- *Performance orientation* children, on the other hand, strive to gain favourable judgements from others and avoid negative judgement of their competence. They are anxious to appear competent to the extent that they avoid harder tasks where the outcome is uncertain.

On balance, quality early years settings provide sufficient challenge and risk in an enabling environment to encourage young children to develop a learning orientation or disposition rather than the more limiting performance orientation. Realising an enabling curriculum in early years practice requires deliberate and thoughtful consideration by adults in order to establish a learning climate in which stereotypes are questioned, new challenges are tackled and it is standard practice to risk being wrong.

We saw in Chapter 2 that it is important to consider fostering dispositions as well as capabilities when seeking to understand the complex process of cognition and to adjust curricular aims and pedagogical practice in early education to facilitate the transfer of such learning to new learning contexts. Early education and care can develop and nurture those less definable skills, such as motivation, organisation, inclination and attitude to learning, that appear to facilitate the application of the literacy and numeracy skills and competencies valued by primary education. In attending to these dispositional aspects of learning, it is important to provide a context that is meaningful and relevant to the child as learner through interactions and relationships aimed at nurturing the affective dimension of learning within a content-rich context. In this way it will impact on those 'basic skills' identified by policy-makers as so important to later school success.

Emphasis on the dynamic nature of early education and the multi-layered effect of the processes on those involved, and on the processes themselves, has led to a move away from drafting the curriculum in the more traditional, prescribed manner of primary and secondary school curricula. In some countries this is being addressed by the emergence of national curricular guidelines or frameworks to support educators in their practice. In other countries, for instance the USA, there is no national curriculum, but professional bodies such as the National Association for the Education of Young Children (NAEYC) have developed national guidelines for practice (Bredekamp 1987; Bredekamp & Copple 1997). This trend is causing a move away from the more formal, didactic modes of instruction and a loosening up of centrally determined curriculum content. The result is greater attention to a pedagogical style that is child- and context-sensitive, emphasising the social, experiential and active nature of early learning. This approach is less content-bound in early education than in later stages of education, but to be effective and enriching in terms of development and learning the practice must be content rich. This move to understand and explain the dynamics of early learning presents a difficulty in separating pedagogy from curriculum content. They are both central elements of a continuous process in which each depends on the other.

Defining what exactly an early years curriculum is proves to be quite difficult (Goffin 2000). It can range from the highly prescriptive and detailed US intervention programme Direct Instruction System for Teaching and Remediation (DISTAR) (Marcon 1999) to the more general definition given in the New Zealand Te Whariki curriculum, which defines curriculum as 'the sum total of the experiences, activities and events, whether direct or indirect, which occur within an environment designed to foster children's learning and development' (Ministry of Education (New Zealand) 1996:10). In some cases an approach to early years practice can quickly become characterised as a curriculum. Such is the case with the fluid and emergent curriculum evident in the Reggio Emilia approach (Edwards, Gandini & Forman 1995) and the NAEYC document on developmentally appropriate practice (Bredekamp & Copple 1997). Research suggests that 'flexible curricula, built on inputs from children, teachers and parents, are more suitable in early childhood than detailed, expert-driven curricula' (OECD 2002:116).

Different curricular approaches to early years provision can reflect polarised views on the aim of such provision, with a strong focus on either an academic or an activity/play-based curriculum. As the name suggests, an academic programme is guided by the content of the curriculum and the expected outcomes. On the other hand, an activity- or play-based programme functions in the belief that learning occurs as a result of activity. One of the major problems resulting from the ongoing arguments over curriculum types, goals and methods is that both sides in the struggle may overlook curriculum and practice that have moved beyond this traditional dichotomy. The results of many studies suggest that both sides underemphasise and undervalue a third option – namely, considering an early years curriculum and pedagogy that address children's current interests and the progress of their intellectual development as distinct from both the direct instruction emphasis on academic learning and future outcomes and the child-initiated learning emphasis on children's play and self-initiated learning in the immediate present. This 'third' approach can be called the *process approach* and its essence is that the curriculum is located within a firm set of principles rather than guided by a set of short-term objectives or goals. These principles allow early childhood education and care to meet the immediate learning needs of the child and also allow the practitioner to plan for future development and learning in line with an individual child's own interest, experience and developmental level and in keeping with general curricular goals.

Katz and Chard (1994) consider that introducing formal academic or direct instruction in the early years may jeopardise the development of desirable dispositions. They argue that there is, in fact, no compelling evidence that early introduction to academic work guarantees success in school in the long term. On the contrary, there is reason to believe that, because of the dynamic nature of development, the cumulative effects of early introduction to academic work may act against development of desirable learning and thinking dispositions. For instance, while the early introduction of academic work may result in young children developing literacy and numeracy skills, it may also inhibit the development of the dispositions to become readers, scientists and appliers of mathematics. Katz (1993) notes that there is a significant and important difference between being able to read and being disposed to read, being able to listen and having a disposition to listen. Learning and disposition are interdependent; learning a skill or developing an ability may tend to make one more inclined to engage in that skill or ability and, conversely, the disposition to learn about something tends to lead to greater engagement and associated success. There is a concern that early years practitioners, while attending to the development of literacy and numeracy skills, may in fact underestimate the general cognitive abilities of young children and may focus on skills rather than extending and building on existing knowledge and willingness to learn. It may be that the expectations these practitioners have for young children's learning are, in fact, set too low. As we saw in the previous chapter, research supports the fact that young children are capable of developing higher-order thinking skills and the dispositions to apply this higher-order thinking. Cultivating the disposition to apply higher-order thinking challenges early years practitioners to consider how best to create learning environments that provide experiences that nurture the affective or emotional dimension of learning and support the development and application of learning dispositions.

We now have evidence of the importance to learning and development of interactions and reciprocal, respectful relationships. The dynamic process approach to early education offers more for children's positive development than either the academic or play-based approach alone. Research consistently shows that successful early education facilitates the child in active learning in learning environments that are well planned, where staff are well trained, confident and supported in their work. Interpretation has become central to both children and adults as they participate in the process of early education: children interpreting and making sense of the world; and adults observing, reflecting on and interpreting children's behaviour to plan the curriculum and assessment and guide their practice. From the pedagogical perspective, quality models of early education are characterised by underpinning principles that present a view of the child as an active partner in the integrated and ongoing process of learning, reflecting a strong commitment to developing the social and affective dimensions of learning as well as the more traditional emphasis on cognitive development. It is important that within this nurturing pedagogy early years practitioners do not ignore skills development or knowledge acquisition. Practice aimed at encouraging the development of learning dispositions and metacognitive skills cannot be content-free; indeed, it is essential that children's interactions with their environments are challenging and rich in both language and content. This can occur either directly, through the content of social interactions with an adult or advanced peer, or indirectly, through the carefully considered provision of materials, objects, activities and opportunities.

Discussions on content, particularly in relation to the older children in early years settings, often come round to a discussion on the importance to children of developing sound literacy and numeracy skills and how to balance this against the value of a play-based early years approach. Research suggests that practitioners may underestimate or be unaware of the broad prior knowledge children can bring to new experiences and learning. Such prior knowledge can provide a valuable basis from which to extend children's learning in subject areas such as science, technology, maths and literacy. However, to do so effectively, practitioners require confidence that they have a sufficient breadth and depth of personal knowledge and understanding in these subject areas. Hedges and Cullen (2005) argue that there are four themes to consider in high-quality early years practice: knowledge of pedagogy and philosophy; knowledge of learners; knowledge of context; and subject content knowledge. Where practitioners have confidence in the depth of their knowledge they are more aware of their own content gaps. In such cases practitioners are also more confident in acknowledging these gaps and admitting that there are things they too have to learn. In such learning environments practitioners are also more likely to welcome children's ideas, contributions and questions.

Too strong an academic emphasis has been criticised as being inappropriate for young children, as placing too much emphasis on the future and insufficient attention to the importance of day-to-day experiences or the natural curriculum (Siraj-Blatchford 2003) in their actual development. Activity-based curricula, on the other hand, attend more to the child's way of learning and emphasise principles rather than outcomes. Focusing on principles rather than outcomes allows for greater flexibility and responsiveness to the immediate learning context for the child and makes particular demands on the pedagogical skills and knowledge of the practitioner to enhance the opportunities for all young children to learn effectively during the early years.

Different systems of education are driven by different beliefs and values about early childhood, and their early years practices vary accordingly. Variations in curricula reflect the different values and understandings societies have concerning how and what young children learn. These values and beliefs inform the design of curricula, the location and support of services, the role of the practitioner and the degree of involvement of children in the process. In addition to values and beliefs, theories of child development also inform curriculum development and design and impact on practice. In developing Síolta and Aistear a number of exemplary early years approaches were studied. Below is a review of some of the quality curricular approaches that informed the guiding principles, themes and standards that go to make up the Irish curriculum frameworks.

Te Whariki

There is an international trend towards reconsidering early years curriculum and practice to ensure that it takes account of child development, contextual variables and the dynamic interactions that are the essence of early education. In New Zealand, Scandinavia and, more recently, Ireland, this is being addressed by the emergence of national curricular guidelines or frameworks to support practitioners. In the New Zealand curriculum framework, Te Whariki, the focus of early years practice is children's well-being; belonging, contribution, communication and exploration. Within defined learning areas, Te Whariki offers guidance in terms of principles and aims. It provides an integrated curriculum characterised by a tapestry, or weave, of increasing complexity and richness. Such an integrated approach also emphasises the importance of considering assessment as pedagogy. Following a period of extensive collaboration across the widely diverse cultural groups within the early education sector, the New Zealand Ministry of Education published what has become a highly regarded early years curriculum.

HighScope

A wide variety of programmes are run throughout the USA, but the HighScope programme is one of the best known and evaluated and it has been adopted by certain states as the state-wide curriculum. The original HighScope curriculum emerged from one of the earliest intervention programmes – the Perry Preschool Project – which was developed to provide quality early education services to children aged 2½ to five years from disadvantaged backgrounds. This project formed the basis of an influential longitudinal study, which is still reporting and has found long-lasting social and educational effects sustained over thirty years (Schweinhart 2006). The history of the development of the HighScope curriculum can be found at www.highscope.org (click on the Research link).

Reggio Emilia

One of the most influential early educational programmes to emerge from Europe is that developed by the Reggio Emilia municipality in northern Italy (Edwards, Gandini & Forman 1995). It is a publicly supported programme that has become known as the Reggio approach. Developed in the region of Reggio Emilia by Loris Malaguzzi, it acts as a proxy for the type of early education provided throughout northern Italy and, to some extent, throughout Italy as a whole (Corsaro 2003). Services offer full provision to children under six years of age in specially built settings and are staffed by multi-disciplinary teams. Children are grouped in mixed age groups with a key teacher for their entire period in the setting and there is close liaison between early education and the elementary system.

Norway

The policy on early education in Norway reflects a particular view of childhood common to most Scandinavian countries. Early childhood is considered a specific phase of life with 'high intrinsic value, and children's own free time, own culture and play are fundamentally important – the need for control and management must at all times be weighed against the children's need to be children on their own premises and based on their own interests' (Ministry of Children and Family Affairs (Norway) 1996). This view of childhood recognises the need for children to develop skills and learning appropriate for later schooling while conceptualising children as a competent learners, discovering and exploring their immediate surroundings and developing confidence in their own abilities.

PRINCIPLES AND POLICIES

In their various reviews of different early childhood education and care (ECEC) policies, the OECD has noted the concern that, where early years policy and practice focuses on preparing children for school, there is a risk that too much attention may be given to the teaching of specific skills and knowledge in the areas of literacy and numeracy (OECD 2001, 2006). It also points out that 'if countries choose to adopt a view of the child as full of potential and capable of learning from birth, and a view of childhood as an important stage in its own right, then ECEC provision can be concerned with both the present and the future' (2001:43).

The principles underpinning the New Zealand curriculum are presented as part of a complex weave of interacting elements, reflecting the diverse cultures and practices found in New Zealand and captured in the title of the curriculum, Te Whariki, which means 'a weave'. The New Zealand principles are brief and state that an early years curriculum should:

* empower children with the tools to capitalise on and extend their learning
* take a holistic approach to learning and development
* create systematic links to parents and the community
* encourage and provide responsive relationships.

These principles are then linked to aims addressing four interacting strands, each with identified goals. The aims are to facilitate:

1 the well-being of the children (nurture and protect)
2 belonging for children and their families
3 communication through reciprocal relationships at all levels
4 exploration that recognises active learning as the means for learning and constructing meaning.

Drawing explicitly on the work of Piaget and Dewey, these are the principles that guide practitioners in the HighScope curriculum:

1 Active learning – through which children construct knowledge that helps them make sense of their world.
2 Positive adult–child interactions – central to facilitating active learning.
3 A child-friendly learning environment – organised into specific interest areas containing a wide range of well-labelled materials to support children's interests.
4 A consistent, carefully managed daily routine that includes the 'plan–do–review' process, which enables children to express their intentions, carry them out and reflect on what they have done.
5 Team-based daily assessment to allow for individualised curricular planning. (Hohman & Weikart 2002)

In this approach, learning is conceptualised as developmental change and is characterised as a complex physical and mental process. The role of the adult is to support children in their learning through observation and interaction. The 'plan–do–review' method, developed by the HighScope team and central to their model of practice, was developed with the intention of facilitating the development of metacognitive and cognitive skills.

In keeping with the dynamic, integrated and interactionist approach to young children learning evident in the Reggio Emilia approach, it is not easy to find a list of principles underpinning their 'emergent curriculum'. However, in talking about the way in which the curriculum for early education emerges within the social constructivist tradition of development, Rinaldi makes the point that the primary principle guiding the work of Reggio Emilia is the image of the child:

> The cornerstone of our experience, based on practice, theory and research, is the image of the children as rich, strong and powerful. The emphasis is placed on seeing the children as unique subjects with rights rather than simply needs. They have potential, plasticity, the desire to grow, curiosity, the ability to be amazed and the desire to relate to other people and to communicate. (Rinaldi 1995:102)

CONTENT AND THE EARLY YEARS CURRICULUM

It is difficult to isolate the content of the Te Whariki curriculum as it is embedded within the principles and outlined in terms of short-term learning outcomes associated with each of the identified goals. The learning outcomes describe various skills, knowledge and attitudes recommended for children as they develop through the early childhood period. The framework offers guidance on how the outcomes link to essential skills and essential learning areas. Given the holistic nature of the underpinning philosophy guiding the New Zealand curriculum, the weave is crafted as a whole rather than being unravelled into specific aims, objectives and outcomes (Ministry of Education (New Zealand) 1996:93–8). The early years practitioner is challenged to weave together the various strands of talents and dispositions of the young child with the agreed areas of learning within a context that reflects the principles identified as central to a culturally authentic curriculum. The four guiding principles reflect a view that early years practice should respond to the complex and context-sensitive nature of development and the interactive nature of learning within and across contexts. The curriculum is designed to be empowering, holistic, transactional and ecological (Carr 1998:2). In practice, the learning and assessment of learning are integrated into the overall pedagogy, with teachers documenting development, assessing its meaning and deriving curricular guidance from reflecting on their engagement with the children and their evaluation of the considerable and varied documentation maintained.

It is in New Zealand that the concept of learning dispositions in early education has been most extensively elaborated and researched (Carr 1998; Carr *et al.* 2010). Carr has linked the development of certain learning dispositions to the Te Whariki curricular framework. These include:

- courage (and curiosity) to find something of interest here in the learning community (Curriculum Strand – Belonging)
- trust that this is a safe place to be involved, focusing one's attention and encouraging the playfulness that often follows from deep involvement over a period of time (Curriculum Strand – Well-being)
- perseverance to persist with difficulty or uncertainty (Curriculum Strand – Exploration)
- confidence to express an idea or a point of view (Curriculum Strand – Communication)
- responsibility for justice and fairness and the disposition to take on another point of view (Curriculum Strand – Contribution). (Carr 1998:4)

The content of the HighScope curriculum is presented in the form of fifty 'key experiences' or statements describing the social, cognitive and physical development of children between the ages of 2½ and five years. The 'key experiences' are clustered under topic headings reflecting their Piagetian origin: creative representation; language and literacy; initiative and social relations; movement; music; classification; seriation; number; space and time. The task of the adult is to provide an environment in which these key experiences can occur, to recognise and support them and then to build on them with the child.

There is no written curriculum for early education in Reggio Emilia. Rather, the focus of attention is on projects and activities, which act as the content around which early experiences are designed and extended. In the early years settings of Reggio Emilia, where children are educated together from birth to six, they speak of the 'hundred languages of children', meaning all the different ways in which children can communicate and through which they can express themselves (Edwards, Gandini & Forman 1995). Children do not spend time in formal classes developing literacy or numeracy skills. Rather, the interest and curiosity of the children are used by the practitioners as a key to their learning. The processes of exploration, experimentation, discovery, representation, transformation, interpretation, creation and evaluation are foregrounded for attention and expression by the practitioners, mostly via the use of project work through the arts. In order for practitioners to be able to respond appropriately to the children, they build in opportunities for reflection and maintain rigorous quantities of documentation, which they use as a basis for their reflection; a form of continuing professional development. Documentation and labelling also exemplify for children the practical application of literacy and numeracry skills in daily life. Practice decisions are made, not on the basis of a prescribed curriculum, but on the basis of evidence and experiences that have been analysed.

The important content of the Reggio Emilia approach is not that of the curriculum but that of the relationship. The content is not focused on routine and management but on the work in hand. Shared activities are considered valuable to both children and adults. The benefits of this approach are the active engagement of children in the learning process and the active engagement of the adult in teaching for learning. The content, to all intents and purposes, is the 'proximal processes' that are crucial to the development of generative dispositions in the child. The practitioner's role is key as there is no prescribed content: instead, whatever emerges from the task becomes a shared curriculum in which the problem has to be set and then solved. This approach allows for rich developments in skills and knowledge in a dispositional milieu which encourages learning dispositions that meet the values of the community.

In reflecting on the pedagogy of the Reggio approach, Katz notes the importance of creating a sense of belonging, of relationship, in young children and points to the rich content that such relationships can have. For relationships to be effective they must be about something, to allow for engagement, by the child and the adult, and feedback and guidance. Katz suggests six lessons for practice to be learned from Reggio:

1   Children and teachers together examine topics of mutual interest in depth and detail and using a variety of media and approaches.

2   When children are engaged in this way they attend to their work with great care. The work is a form of documentation of the process of their learning, which they evaluate, as well as the adults.

3   Early introduction of observational and representational skills is not detrimental to creativity.

4   The work in the projects provides rich content for teacher–child interactions.
5   Many features of the adults' behaviour convey to the children that all aspects of their work are taken seriously.
6   The driving force behind the programme's principles is community/family rather than industrial/corporate. (Katz 1995:36–7)

One of the most striking features of the Reggio approach is the willingness of the practitioners to learn, not just from each other, but also from the children. Reggio practice is not based on the notion of teaching as applied child development: it demands of practitioners a clear view of what interests children, what children are doing, what is being offered as their learning environment, materials, interactions and context. Practice is not the application of a curriculum within a particular pedagogical formula; it is responsive and fluid and acts as the basis for an emergent curriculum.

While there has been a lot of international interest in the Reggio approach, and many authors have written extensively about its principles and practice, Gardner, in his foreword to *The Hundred Languages of Children,* cautions that one cannot transpose something like the Reggio Emilia approach to another country without adapting it appropriately to that culture. He does, however, recognise the approach as valid and appropriate for young children and notes that Reggio Emilia 'epitomises . . . an education that is effective and humane: its students undergo a sustained apprenticeship in humanity, one which may last a lifetime' (Gardner 1995:xiii).

EARLY YEARS QUALITY AND CURRICULUM IN IRELAND

Early years settings in Ireland vary greatly in curriculum approaches and have developed rapidly over the last twenty years, often from very different beginnings. With the expansion of settings and the growing attention to early childhood as a key period of learning and development, a lot of attention has been drawn to the needs and rights of young children and to what constitutes effective, high-quality early years practice. Arising from this, two excellent practice frameworks have been developed and they can be used, together, to enhance and evaluate practice in early years settings. Síolta – the national quality framework – was published by the Centre for Early Child Development and Education (CECDE) in 2006 and in 2009 the National Council for Curriculum and Assessment (NCCA) published Aistear – the early childhood curriculum framework. However, because the documents were developed at different times and by two different bodies they are often considered in isolation. This is disappointing as the frameworks complement each other and act as an excellent basis from which to review setting practice, enhance knowledge and skills, maintain and sustain quality and monitor and evaluate progress. It is the aim of this book to facilitate readers in working with both frameworks to inform day-to-day practice in early years settings.

The two frameworks have different primary purposes: Síolta focuses on the overall quality within settings; and Aistear focuses on learning experiences. They are *complementary* in that both strive – through their different focus – to guide practitioners in providing high-quality learning experiences for children. Síolta offers support for creating and sustaining a quality context within which to provide the challenging, positive and enjoyable learning experiences outlined in Aistear. Both frameworks are developed for children from birth to six years old and are sufficiently broad to be applied in any early learning setting, from the home through to the infant classes of primary school. In addition, this age range is subdivided into the same bands in both frameworks: babies from birth to 18 months; toddlers of 12–36 months; and young children of 2½ to six years. It is an important aspect of Aistear that the age bands used to frame the curriculum overlap. This reflects a move away from the more traditional 'ages and stages' approach of the primary school curriculum (NCCA 1999) towards explicitly recognising and responding to the dynamic nature of development present in each individual child.

Both frameworks drew extensively on national and international research to derive their principles. Research informing each of the standards of Síolta that form the basis of the quality framework has been gathered into a research digest, which is available from the Síolta website (www.siolta.ie). In developing Aistear, the NCCA commissioned four background research papers to inform the creation of the framework. These can be accessed from the NCCA website (www.ncca.ie). In addition to considering national and international research, both frameworks also reflect the detailed consultation with the sector that was undertaken. Indeed, the development of Aistear included consultation with children as young as nine months through a research project entitled *Listening for Children's Stories: Children as Partners in the Framework for Early Learning* (NCCA 2007).

Like the international curricular approaches discussed earlier, Síolta and Aistear are underpinned by key principles or core beliefs about early childhood and young children. They present the vision or philosophy guiding the frameworks. Both frameworks have identified the principles that guided their planning and development. In Síolta the overarching vision for quality was captured by twelve principles, which underpin the standards of quality practice and the associated components. In their consultation Aistear also identified twelve principles and grouped them into three categories. These three categories provide a useful context within which to consider the principles in both frameworks. The first category of principles concerns *children and their lives in early childhood*. This category contains the principles concerned with valuing young children as unique citizens, recognising early childhood as a period in itself and stressing the importance of respect for equality and diversity in practice. The second category is *children's connections with others*. Under this category the principles included relate to the critical importance of relationships within and between children and the key adults in their lives. The final category concerns *how children learn and develop*. Given the focus of both frameworks, it is no surprise that this category includes a wide range of principles concerning play, active and holistic learning and development, pedagogy, communication, teamwork and meaningful experiences in rich learning environments.

THE TWELVE PRINCIPLES OF SÍOLTA

The value of early childhood	Early childhood is a significant and distinct time in life that m[ust be] respected, valued and supported in its own right.
Children first	The child's individuality, strengths, rights and needs are centrai in the provision of quality early childhood experiences.
Parents	Parents are the primary educators of the child and have a pre-eminent role in promoting her/his well-being, learning and development.
Relationships	Responsive, sensitive and reciprocal relationships, which are consistent over time, are essential to the well-being, learning and development of the young child.
Equality	Equality is an essential characteristic of quality early childhood care and education.
Diversity	Quality early childhood settings acknowledge and respect diversity and ensure that all children and families have their individual, personal, cultural and linguistic identity validated.
Environments	The physical environment of the young child has a direct impact on her/his well-being, learning and development.
Welfare	The safety, welfare and well-being of all children must be protected and promoted in all early childhood environments.
Role of the adult	The role of the adult in providing quality early childhood experiences is fundamental.
Teamwork	The provision of quality early childhood experiences requires co-operation, communication and mutual respect.
Pedagogy	Pedagogy in early childhood is expressed by curricula or programmes of activities which take a holistic approach to the development and learning of the child and reflect the inseparable nature of care and education.
Play	Play is central to the well-being, development and learning of the young child.

THE TWELVE PRINCIPLES OF AISTEAR

Children's lives in early childhood	Connections with others	Learning and developing
• The child's uniqueness • Equality and diversity • Children as citizens	• Relationships • Parents, family and community • The adult's role	• Holistic learning and development • Active learning • Play; hands-on experiences • Relevant and meaningful experiences • Communication and language • The learning environment

Given that both frameworks were developed in close consultation with the broad early years sector, it is no surprise to find that their principles are broadly similar and totally in harmony with each other.

Aistear is informed by an understanding of early childhood that considers children to be competent and confident learners and through four interconnected themes it provides a 'a key resource in ensuring children in early childhood settings are given rich and varied experiences to support and progress their learning and development' (Daly & Forster 2012:103). Each of the four themes has four aims, giving sixteen aims in all; each of the sixteen aims has six learning goals, so there are ninety-six learning goals with associated points for reflection and questions for practice.

Where Aistear focuses on the early years curriculum, Síolta focuses on quality early years practice. Quality practice is defined as 'the pursuit of excellence that has the capacity to transform' (Duignan 2012:91). The framework is designed around twelve principles that lead on to sixteen standards of quality. There are seventy-five components across all the standards, with Signposts for Reflection and 'Think Abouts' for practice.

Aistear describes children's early learning and development in terms of four interconnected themes. The first theme, *well-being*, considers how children develop to be happy, healthy and confident; *identity and belonging*, the second theme, explores how children form a positive identity of themselves in the world and how they evolve a strong and healthy sense of belonging to that world. The third theme is *communicating*, which is concerned with understanding how children share their experiences, feeling, fears, ideas and thoughts to others and how this extends and expands over time. The final theme is *exploring and thinking*, which considers how children make sense of their world and the objects and people in it. It is concerned with how children play, interact, investigate, question and test out their ideas. The four themes are linked to aims and learning goals and the interconnected whole is outlined in the diagram.

AISTEAR'S FOUR THEMES

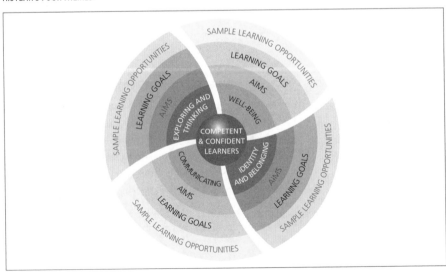

Although not designed to map directly on to one another, there are close links between the two frameworks. For instance, the themes from Aistear can be connected to various Síolta standards. The well-being theme can be associated with eleven of the Síolta standards; identity and belonging with ten; the communicating theme links to seven standards; and exploring and thinking is associated with six standards.

Realising Aistear in practice is guided by four central 'guidelines for good practice'. The four themes are seen as providing the 'what' of early years practice and the guidelines offer examples of the 'how'. The guidelines are:

- building partnerships between parents and practitioners
- learning and developing through interactions
- learning and developing through play
- supporting learning and development through assessment.

These are important headlines for good practice.

Building partnerships between parents and practitioners
At its most ordinary, this is about the way we work together – with our adult colleagues, with the children and with their families. It involves recognising and respecting differences of culture, opinion and values. It requires us to be responsible and respectful in our dealings with others. Through the illustrations provided we are invited to consider different situations, which offer possibilities and challenges. For quality practice it is important to balance professional understandings with sensitivity to individual situations and to other professional roles. Not all professionals recognise the uniquely powerful role that early years practitioners have in relation to young children and their families. They are, for example, often the first to notice changes in circumstances and may often be in a position to intervene early in a problem to the benefit of all. For this reason, among others, it is valuable to cultivate and sustain working relationships with other professionals and community leaders.

The most important relationships are those with the children and their families. Research suggests that parents are comfortable with early years practitioners in a way they may not be with other professionals. They recognise the shared interest in their child and they are, in the main, willing to hear about how their child is developing and learning. We also know from research that one of the most important influences on children's learning and development is the quality of the home learning environment (HLE) (Melhuish *et al.* 2008). Early years practitioners have a particularly rich opportunity to influence the quality of the HLE through talking with parents about the interests of their children and ideas about how to meet these interests in the home. Many parents of young children, particularly new parents, welcome suggestions about books, examples of simple activities, inclusion in events in the early years setting and links to information, seminars or talks on child development, learning or health – anything that may be of relevance to them and their children. This places quite a responsibility on those working in the field and it is a trusted position that needs to be cultivated in the best interests of the child.

Learning and developing through interactions

One point of common agreement among those researching and working in the early years is the critical role of meaningful relationships and interactions, not only in the development of young children but also for the professional satisfaction of early years practitioners. From a theoretical perspective we have seen that Bronfenbrenner has – in his much referred-to model of human development – identified these interactions, which he called *proximal processes*, as the engines of development. The daily activities of an early years setting, whatever it might be, form the context within which development and learning occurs. The nature of the interactions depends on a number of features associated with the interacting people and the environments they come from and those they share. To be effective, interactions need attention and reflection and they must occur on a fairly regular basis over an extended period of time. Time is particularly important, both in terms of extension over an extended period but also in terms of the moment, the present nature of time given meaningfully to interactions. It is with time that young children find the space to really explore their environment, express their concerns, show their delight and solve the exciting problems that the world and those in it present. For the early years practitioner it is key to recognise the treasure that time is to young children, to be prepared to allow for time in the daily routine in such a way that all children benefit.

Learning and developing through play

Irrespective of how one chooses to define play or seek to find its meaning, there is general agreement that the developing child – right from the beginning – needs the opportunities, both indoors and outdoors, to be active and playful. Play comes in many shapes: it can be adventurous, risky, communicative, solitary, enjoyable, involved, meaningful, sociable, interactive, symbolic, therapeutic and voluntary. It is through play that children create meaning and develop their understanding of the world and their place in it. It is also through play that they acquire and strengthen, among other things, their ability to share, to negotiate, to take turns, to self-regulate, to direct their curiosity, to handle emotions, to manage their behaviour and to behave according to the requirements of a situation or a particular context. Play is also a process through which practitioners can gain insight into the development and learning of individual children as individuals and also as group members.

Supporting learning and development through assessment

It is through assessment that we make judgements about all sorts of things. For the early years practitioner it is the mechanism we use to make decisions that inform our practice, planning and responses. In Aistear, assessment is defined as 'the on-going process of collecting, documenting, reflecting on and using information to develop rich portraits of children as learners in order to support and enhance their . . . learning' (NCCA 2009a:72).

It is difficult to assess development, and in early years practice assessment is a way of doing things. We make judgements, or assess, all the time – even when we do not realise it. In keeping with quality reflective practice, it is useful to stop yourself from time to time to see what judgement motivated a particular action or planning decision. When considering assessment it is useful to approach it as either 'assessment *for* learning' or 'assessment *of* learning'.

Assessment *for* learning is more common in practice with younger children. It informs the style of practice that nurtures and supports learning, it enhances planning for individual children but also for the group. Assessment *of* learning is the process we use for measuring what children know. In the early years this aspect of assessment may have limited value, although it can be helpful if there is a particular cause for concern and you want to develop an understanding of the child's normative development to inform planning for practice or intervention. Gathering materials for reflection and consideration assists the quality of the assessment and judgement you make of the children you work with. This is further enhanced if these reflections occur in the context of a critical friend or the team you work with. Procedures can be put in place to allow for collecting data, documenting processes or progress, reflecting on materials and using the findings from reflection and discussion to inform further practices. Within the Aistear framework a continuum of assessment methods is provided to assist practitioners to review and consider their practice. The methods range from child-led self-assessment through observation on to more adult-led assessment and are outlined in the figure below.

AISTEAR'S ASSESSMENT METHODS

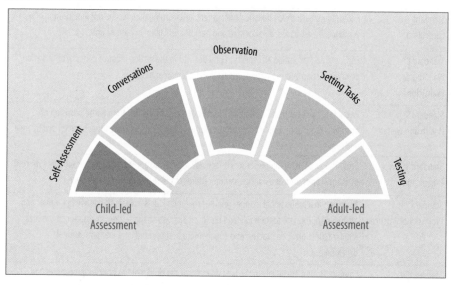

oth frameworks differs, reflecting their different points of departure. andbooks, takes its twelve principles and translates them into practice ixteen standards of quality.

SÍOLTA STANDARDS

Standard 1: Rights of the Child	Ensuring that each child's rights are met requires that she/he is enabled to exercise choice and to use initiative as an active participant and partner in her/his own development and learning.
Standard 2: Environments	Enriching environments, both indoor and outdoor (including materials and equipment), are well maintained, safe, available, accessible, adaptable, developmentally appropriate, and offer a variety of challenging and stimulating experiences.
Standard 3: Parents and Families	Valuing and involving parents and families requires a proactive partnership approach evidenced by a range of clearly stated, accessible and implemented processes, policies and procedures.
Standard 4: Consultation	Ensuring inclusive decision-making requires consultation that promotes participation and seeks out, listens to and acts upon the views and opinions of children, parents and staff, and other stakeholders, as appropriate.
Standard 5: Interactions	Fostering constructive interactions (child/child, child/adult and adult/adult) requires explicit policies, procedures and practice that emphasise the value of process and are based on mutual respect, equal partnership and sensitivity.
Standard 6: Play	Promoting play requires that each child has ample time to engage in freely available and accessible, developmentally appropriate and well-resourced opportunities for exploration, creativity and 'meaning making' in the company of other children, with participating and supportive adults and alone, where appropriate.
Standard 7: Curriculum	Encouraging each child's holistic development and learning requires the implementation of a verifiable, broad-based, documented and flexible curriculum or programme.
Standard 8: Planning and Evaluation	Enriching and informing all aspects of practice within the setting requires cycles of observation, planning, action and evaluation, undertaken on a regular basis.
Standard 9: Health and Welfare	Promoting the health and welfare of the child requires protection from harm, provision of nutritious food, appropriate opportunities for rest, and secure relationships characterised by trust and respect.
Standard 10: Organisation	Organising and managing resources effectively requires an agreed written philosophy, supported by clearly communicated policies and procedures to guide and determine practice.
Standard 11: Professional Practice	Practising in a professional manner requires that individuals have skills, knowledge, values and attitudes appropriate to their role and responsibility within the setting. In addition, it requires regular reflection upon practice and engagement in supported, ongoing professional development.
Standard 12: Communication	Communicating effectively in the best interests of the child requires policies, procedures and actions that promote the proactive sharing of knowledge and information among appropriate stakeholders, with respect and confidentiality.

Standard 13: Transitions	Ensuring continuity of experiences for children requires policies, procedures and practice that promote sensitive management of transitions, consistency in key relationships, liaison within and between settings, the keeping and transfer of relevant information (with parental consent), and the close involvement of parents and, where appropriate, relevant professionals.
Standard 14: Identity and Belonging	Promoting positive identities and a strong sense of belonging requires clearly defined policies, procedures and practice that empower every child and adult to develop a confident self- and group identity, and to have a positive understanding and regard for the identity and rights of others.
Standard 15: Legislation and Regulation	Being compliant requires that all relevant regulations and legislative requirements are met or exceeded.
Standard 16: Community Involvement	Promoting community involvement requires the establishment of networks and connections evidenced by policies, procedures and actions which extend and support all adult's and children's engagement with the wider community.

Source: CECDE (2006).

Aistear, on the other hand, takes its twelve principles and derives four overarching themes within which guidelines for practice are presented. Most of the Síolta standards can be related to Aistear themes and guidelines in a manner that facilitates working the two documents together in early years settings. Realising the potential of Aistear and Síolta for day-to-day practice in early years settings is best approached if the frameworks are considered together in the context of the everyday life of early years settings. While they focus on two different aspects of practice, together they can inform and expand our understanding of how to enrich and sustain the quality of our early years practice. The frameworks can be used as part of the daily routine as the basis for planning the learning environments, creating content- and language-rich spaces, providing a safe but risk-rich environment and as the context for posing questions to the children, yourself, those you work with and those you come into contact with.

In 2009 the NCCA published a short document outlining the similarities and differences between Aistear and Síolta. The NCCA considered the frameworks at different levels, from the purpose of the framework through the principles to the discrete elements in each. The report concludes that the frameworks are 'important milestones in early childhood care and education', which, if used together, 'present significant potential to support the development of practice for all adults who care for and educate children from birth to six in Ireland' (NCCA 2009c:15). The audit highlights the close connection between Síolta standards of quality practice and the various themes and guidelines in Aistear. The NCCA report goes on to point out that Aistear can be used to support all the Síolta standards, but 'it gives particular support in the case of standards related to the Rights of the Child, Environments, Parents and Families, Interactions, Play, Curriculum and Identity and Belonging' (NCCA 2009c:11).

The document further expands on the links between Síolta and Aistear with a selection of examples. Two examples of the links provided in the NCCA report are reproduced and discussed below to illustrate how settings can work with both frameworks to meet the aim of high-quality early years practice.

Example 1: Connecting Síolta Standard 1 to the Aistear framework

Síolta	Aistear
Standard 1: Rights of the child Ensuring that each child's rights are met requires that she/he is enabled to exercise choice and to use initiative as an active participant and partner in her/his own learning and development.	*Principle: Active learning* Active learning involves children learning by doing things. They use their senses to explore and work with the objects and materials around them and they interact enthusiastically with the adults and other children that they meet. Through these experiences, children develop the dispositions, skills, knowledge and understanding, attitudes, and values that will help them to grow as confident and competent learners.
Component 1. 2 Each child has opportunities and is enabled to take the lead, initiate activity, be appropriately independent and is supported to solve problems.	• Let me explore, try out, make mistakes, discover and create my own theories about how things work and why, so that I can be independent and self-reliant and can learn about the world I live in. (Principles and Themes) *Guidelines: Learning and developing through interactions* During early childhood it is important that children have opportunities to lead learning through self-initiated and self-directed learning, and to be involved in decisions about what they do. At other times, the adult leads through planned and guided activities and increases or lessens the amount and type of support as children grow in confidence and competence. (Guidelines on Good Practice)

Source: NCCA (2009c).

In this example Síolta's Standard 1 *Rights of the Child* is linked to the Aistear principle *Active Learning* and the Guideline on Good Practice *Learning and Developing through Interactions.*

It is proposed that Standard 1 is met by 'ensuring that . . . she/he is enabled to exercise choice and to use initiative as an active participant and partner in her/his own learning and development' (CECDE 2006:13[1]). This standard reflects the current understanding of child development that even the very youngest of children plays an active part in their development, influencing those around them to a greater extent than was previously understood. It also highlights the importance of interactions. The

---

1   For the purpose of illustration the *Full and Part-time Daycare User Manual* has been used as the source for examples throughout this book.

research section in Chapter 2 gives an overview of the exciting scientific research that is informing this greater understanding of early learning and development and the important role played by early years practitioners.

How should we adjust our practice to realise children's rights in our early years setting? To guide our thinking on this, Síolta offers three components alongside Standard 1. These components can be used to illustrate what the standard in practice might look like.

- Component 1.1: Each child has opportunities to make choices, is enabled to make decisions, and has her/his choices and decisions respected.
- Component 1.2: *Each child has opportunities and is enabled to take the lead, initiate activity, be appropriately independent and is supported to solve problems.*
- Component 1.3: Each child is enabled to participate actively in the daily routine, in activities, in conversations and in all other appropriate situations, and is considered as a partner by the adult. (CECDE 2006:14)

The Síolta manual further elaborates each of the components through the use of Signposts for Reflection and Think Abouts across the different age ranges. So, for Component 1.2 above, the Signpost for Reflection for working with children of birth to 18 months challenges the reader to consider, 'How do you ensure that the child is responded to quickly when she/he cries or otherwise indicates that she/he needs attention?' and the associated Think About for this component at this age proposes routines to ensure that the child gets regular and frequent individual attention (in addition to responses to distress or care needs) (CECDE 2006:15).

Using Component 1.2 above, the Síolta standard is linked to the Aistear Principle of Active Learning and the Guideline Learning and Developing through Interactions.

Active Learning: active learning involves children learning by doing things. They use their senses to explore and work with the objects and materials around them and they interact enthusiastically with adults and other children that they meet. Through their experiences, children develop the dispositions, skills, knowledge and understanding, attitudes, and values that will help them grow as confident and competent learners. (NCCA 2009a:10)

This principle is expanded in the Aistear document, with three instances of learning opportunities provided in the voice of the child.

- Let me explore, try out, make mistakes, discover, and create my own theories about how things work and why, so that I can be independent and self-reliant and can learn about the world I live in.
- Give me opportunities to use my different senses when I am learning.
- Support me in learning with and from adults and other children. Ask me about my discoveries and adventures; talk to me and help me to learn more. I learn a lot on my own but I also learn a lot when I can share my experiences with others.

In addition, this Síolta standard can be realised in the context of the Aistear Guidelines on Good Practice. The quote selected for inclusion in the NCCA guidelines reads:

> During early childhood it is important that children have opportunities to lead learning through self-initiated and self-directed learning, and to be involved in decisions about what they do. At other times, the adult leads through planned and guided activities and increases or lessens the amount and type of support as children grow in confidence and competence. (NCCA 2009b:28)

Throughout the example there is attention to how early years practice can be said to directly and visibly meet the rights of the child. It is providing the useful and available language of practice to articulate an abstract idea and one that is often hard to describe. It illustrates how the routine day-to-day practices of early years settings can be adjusted or modified, where necessary, to really engage with children as active and participating agents in their own learning and development.

Example 2: Connecting Síolta Standard 5 to the Aistear framework

Síolta	Aistear
Standard 5: Interactions Fostering constructive interactions (child/child, child/adult and adult/adult) requires explicit policies, procedures and practice that emphasise the value of process and are based on mutual respect, equal partnership and sensitivity. *Component 5.4* The adult interactive style is focused on process as opposed to outcomes. It is balanced between talking and listening, offers the child a choice of responses and encourages expanded use of language. It follows the child's lead and interests, and challenges the child appropriately.	*Guidelines: Learning and developing through interactions* Relationships are at the very heart of learning and development. Good adult/child interactions are respectful, playful, enjoyable, enabling and rewarding. These guidelines focus on four strategies: 1 Building relationships 2 Facilitating 3 Organising 4 Directing Children learn and develop by interacting with others. Adults who are respectful listeners and keen observers, who are prepared to negotiate, who change their practice, and who make meaning with children are those who are most responsive to them. They know the children well, are sensitive to their current level of understanding, know their interests and intentions, and pitch activities and experiences which are just beyond what they can currently do and understand so that they can extend their learning. Their interactions promote children's learning and development and help children to reach their potential. (Guidelines on Good Practice)

Source: NCCA (2009c).

In this example the Síolta Standard 5: *Interactions* is chosen and linked to the Aistear Guideline on Good Practice *Learning and Developing through Interactions.*

Standard 5 notes that 'fostering constructive interactions (child/child, child/adult and adult/adult) requires explicit policies, procedures and practice that emphasise the value of process and are based on mutual respect, equal partnership and sensitivity' (CECDE 2006:39). This is a far-reaching standard that recognises what we have learned from research – that it is the interactions that matter most in early years practice. How the adults in the setting interact with parents can have a profound influence on the extent to which a child can feel a sense of belonging. This is particularly important in settings where there are children from different backgrounds, whether the differences are economic, cultural or ethnic. This standard also calls on practitioners to respect children in interactions, to recognise them as partners. This does not mean that they have the same power as the adult; rather it means that the adult needs to be aware of the power they do have and use it in a responsive and empowering way with the children, recognising them as having a contribution to make to the moment.

To realise Standard 5 in practice requires careful attention to interactions at a number of levels. This standard has six associated components:

- Component 5.1: Each child is enabled to interact with her/his peers and with children of different ages in pairs, small groups and, to a lesser degree, in large groups.
- Component 5.2: Each child receives appropriate support to enable her/him to interact positively with other children.
- Component 5.3: The adult uses all aspects of the daily routine (both formal and informal) to interact sensitively and respectfully with the child.
- Component 5.4: *The adult interactive style is focused on process as opposed to outcomes. It is balanced between talking and listening, offers the child a choice of responses and encourages expanded use of language. It follows the child's lead and interests, and challenges the child appropriately.*
- Component 5.5: Interactions between the adults within, and associated with the setting, act as a model of respect, support and partnership for the child.
- Component 5.6: There is a clear written policy and associated procedures which underpin interactive practice taking place within the setting. (CECDE 2006:40).

In the example above, the Síolta standard is linked to the Aistear Guidelines on Good Practice through Component 5.4.

In the Síolta manual the Signpost for Reflection for Component 5.4.9 for working with children aged 12–36 months asks the reader to consider, 'How do you draw on the child's previous learning to support "meaning making"?' One of the associated Think Abouts includes reflection on children's previous learning (e.g. rhymes, stories, people, family, etc.) (CECDE 2006:44).

Component 5.4 is linked to the Aistear Guideline: Learning and Developing through Interactions, which reads:

Relationships are at the very heart of learning and development. Good adult/child interactions are respectful, playful, enabling and rewarding.

The guidelines here focus on four strategies:

Building Relationships	Facilitating	Organising	Directing
Children learn by being with others. This strategy includes methods which the adult uses to build relationships and to create an environment in which children feel secure and confident enough to take risks, to explore, to take part in challenging experiences, and to direct and co-direct their own learning.	Children learn by being involved in making choices and decisions, and by feeling in control. Learning is enjoyable and rewarding for them when they challenge themselves and when they can use and build on their existing knowledge, understanding and skills. They enjoy learning through child-initiated activities. This strategy includes methods which the adult uses to encourage children to take the lead or to share the lead with adults.	Children learn in a well-planned and well-resourced environment. The environment represents all children in the setting and makes learning challenging and fun. This strategy includes methods which the adult uses to create and maintain such an environment, including reflecting on the learning that is occurring in the environment and planning ways to enhance it.	Children learn through planned and guided activities which build on their interests and experiences. This strategy includes methods which the adult uses to focus on children's learning and to develop particular dispositions, values and attitudes, skills, knowledge, and understanding.

Source: NCCA (2009b).

Children learn and develop by interacting with others. Adults who are respectful listeners and keen observers, who are prepared to negotiate, who change their practice, and who make meaning with children are those who are most responsive to them. They know the children well, are sensitive to their current level of understanding, know their interests and intentions, and pitch activities and experiences which are just beyond what they can currently do and understand so that they extend learning. Their interactions promote children's learning and development and help children to reach their potential (NCCA 2009c:14).

In this example the Síolta standard is linked directly to a good practice guideline and the reader is introduced to the four strategies underpinning the guideline: building relationships; facilitating; organising; and directing. In practice these strategies are finely balanced, from the child leading learning at the building relationships end of the continuum, through to more adult-led learning, where the practitioner is directing. Achieving the balance will depend on many factors and on weighing up the tension between 'offering children opportunities to choose activities that are meaningful to them with the responsibility of practitioners to ensure that specific learning outcomes are achieved' (Stephen 2010: 24).

If practice is making the curriculum visible in the day-to-day life of the setting, what are the implications of the Learning Goals of Aistear and the Standards and Competencies of Síolta? The NCCA report comparing Síolta and Aistear took a Síolta standard as the basis for considering comparisons between the two frameworks. Unlike that report, this book has chosen to link the two frameworks through illustrations from practice. This is deliberate as it is from within the practice of early years settings that both frameworks come alive. The illustrations, drawn from the Aistear document, serve as examples to suggest how best to approach integrating both frameworks. They are intended as a prompt to practitioners to select their own practice examples; it is likely that a richer integration of the frameworks into practice will emerge when samples of actual practice are used as the basis for exploring and reflecting on both Síolta and Aistear.

In each of the following four chapters a particular Aistear theme will be selected to guide our critical review of a number of practice illustrations. Elements from both frameworks will be woven into the analysis. This will provide an integrated and cohesive context within which to raise practice and quality issues for discussion and application to early years settings. It will also provide the basis for a shared language of practice made visible, which will strengthen practice among individual practitioners, within early years settings and across the profession in general.

CHAPTER 4

Well-being

Well-being changes as we move through life, which is why a child's version of it cannot be the same as an old person's. (Chopra, n.d.)

The concept of well-being and children's well-being in particular has emerged as an important policy item nationally and internationally. Kickbusch sees children's well-being as 'a key dimension of sustainable development and social resilience; it is about our present and our future', and she argues that 'children's well-being must be introduced as a central building block . . . not only as an investment in future adults but as a pledge to the children of today' (2012:9, 13). She identifies three reasons for action on children's well-being:

> *Children's well-being* – a happy, secure and flourishing childhood – is a value in its own right.
> *Children's well-being* is about the moral imperative of social justice and equitable life chances – it contributes to a better and more just society and to well-being for all.
> *Children's well-being* is about our present and our future, as individuals and as societies. It supports long-term social and economic development. It promotes life course physical, emotional, mental and spiritual health – what some define as the development of the whole child. (Kickbusch 2012:13)

This last point – relating well-being to the whole child perspective – reflects the Irish policy commitment outlined in the National Children's Strategy (NCS), which notes that:

> The Strategy seeks to establish this 'whole child' perspective at the centre of policy development and service delivery. The 'whole child' perspective recognises the capacity of children to interact with and shape the world around them as they grow up. . . . Children not only benefit from but actively contribute to the mix of relationships, mutual support networks, local knowledge and know-how that make for vibrant communities. (DoHC 2000:10–11)

While seeking the global improvement of children's well-being requires a significant shift in political priorities, there is potential at a local level for early years settings to play an important and immediate role in the well-being of children from the earliest age. In a review of the literature on well-being, Costello notes that 'it is important to focus on the well-being of the infant, as this can have crucial bearing on the well-being and development of the child as s/he grows older. Aspects of the infant's life relating to his/her well-being include the physical health of the mother during pregnancy, receipt and quality of child care, the presence of cognitive stimuli and maternal time use' (1999:7). This view is supported by the review of research presented in Chapter 2.

Settings can support children's well-being by providing safe and secure environments of learning where the four pillars of education as defined by UNESCO (Delors 1996) – *learning to know, learning to do, learning to live together and learning to be* – can be provided for in a responsive and reflective way. In fact, well-being is central to learning and learning is central to well-being; they are closely interconnected. We know from research and practice that the process of learning and the context within which it is facilitated can enhance a child's sense of mastery and capabilities, thus strengthening the child's sense of well-being.

It is difficult to define well-being; it is a concept that has a plurality of understandings reflecting different perspectives at different times and in different contexts. Broadly speaking, well-being is characterised by the absence of distress and the presence of a sense of happiness, of contentment. Well-being has a subjective component – how we feel about ourselves and/or our lives contributes to our overall well-being. UNICEF (2007) has identified well-being as a key to the realisation of children's rights, and most discussions of well-being emphasise that the quality of relationships is a central component of well-being, particularly so in relation to children. The National Economic and Social Council (NESC) report on well-being points out that not only are relationships central to child development and well-being, they are also valued by children themselves. The NESC report stresses the importance of democracy and values underpinning dimensions of children's well-being and notes that Aistear 'offers potential to promote active citizenship and values of social solidarity' while also pointing out that it 'needs to have greater priority within the education system' (NESC 2009:76).

Practice that is sensitive to children's developing well-being facilitates opportunities for children to actively engage with people, objects and materials, enables them to exercise their democratic rights through being heard and allows them participate – insofar as they can – in planning and reviewing decisions that impact on them and their experiences. The whole child approach (DoHC 2000) to children's well-being requires attention to the inclusion of children's views. One of the key components of well-being in the early years is the quality of early years practice in the early years settings children attend. Clearly the extent to which practice can include children's views will be different for infants of six months and an active three- or six-year-old. Nonetheless, awareness of the need to think about this and discuss with colleagues how it might be achieved will increase the likelihood that children's voices will be heard more widely and meaningfully in early years settings. There are some wonderful international studies illustrating what might be called democratic practices in early childhood, including the work of Singer and de Haan (2007) and Carr *et al.* (2010), who use observation and technology to record, discuss and elaborate on children's activities. As well as collecting such rich material they also find creative ways to present the material gathered to colleagues and use the material as a basis for engagement with children about their learning and development.

In the introduction to the theme of well-being in Aistear (NCCA 2009a) the distinction is drawn between psychological well-being (feeling and thinking) and physical well-being (health and mental health). 'Children . . . become positive about themselves and their learning when adults value them for who they are when they promote warm and supportive relationships with them' (NCCA 2009a:16). Well-being fosters a positive outlook and is important for overall positive development and learning precisely because it gives children a sense of their own importance and helps them appreciate that they have control over their own lives, development and learning. Building from this basis, Aistear goes on to point out that '[P]hysical well-being is important for learning and development as this enables children to explore, to investigate, and to challenge themselves in the environment' (NCCA 2009a:16). A central point in this approach is the recognition that one's sense of well-being is critically influenced by the context within which it develops. For instance, in environments that are critical, unsupportive or impatient with children it is difficult for them to attain either psychological or physical well-being; indeed children in such environments may come to feel worthless and unloved. From such a perspective it is difficult for children to become excited by possibilities, or curious to explore the environment and learn more about the world and their place in it. Adults play a key role in providing a truly rich, stimulating and secure environment guiding children towards 'being flexible and having a positive outlook on learning and on life . . . [and] . . . to become resilient and resourceful and to learn to cope with change and situations in which things go wrong' (NCCA 2009a:16). Positive well-being is the basis of mastery, of the sense that one has of a certain degree of control over things, a willingness to try without an unrealistic fear of failure. Such a sense of well-being provides a good place within which to grow and learn.

We know from research with schoolchildren that a majority of Irish children and young people consider themselves to be happy and healthy (Nic Gabhainn and Sixsmith 2005). Results from this creative study on children's observations of well-being suggest that, despite discrete differences across age and gender, there is a common understanding of well-being. The study showed that children understood the complexity of well-being and the various factors impacting on it. Not unexpectedly, interpersonal relationships were found to be central to children's understanding and sense of well-being, along with the value they place on actively doing things. At all different phases of the study the participating children discussed 'how relationships (with people and animals) and the activities within or context of those relationships gave them a sense of belonging, being safe, loved, valued and being cared for' (Nic Gabhainn and Sixsmith 2005:64). This reflects an explanation of well-being that captures feeling good: being happy and able to live life to the full. The focus of responses on animals and places as well as people illustrates the extent to which children interact with the natural world around them as well as the interpersonal. It also broadens our understanding of the impact of interactions to include interactions with objects and materials as well as animals and people.

We know less about the understandings very young children have of well-being because it is difficult to access their views on such an abstract concept. Taking a lead from the voice of children reported above, we can, however, identify what makes young children happy and content and able to live life to the full. This can guide us in creating situations to allow them illustrate this in their own way. In an effort to access the views of very young children on this abstract topic a study was carried out in 2011 for the organisation Start Strong. Called 'If I had a Magic Wand', the project worked with a number of early years settings to unlock the wishes of young children. They recorded the findings by compiling a selection of the drawings made to illustrate the wishes and recording the words of a sample of the children that captured the main themes. The e-book derived from the project can be accessed at www.startstrong.ie/contents/213.

Not surprisingly, the study found that it is the simple things that children wish for that make them happy. It also found that children enjoyed being in early years settings. Key themes emerging from children's ideas and images included:

- the value children place on being able to shape their own daily activities
- the centrality of play in young children's lives
- the importance of opportunities for children's creativity and imagination
- young children's wish to be outdoors and engage in physical activities
- the pleasure and interest for young children in being with animals
- the importance to children of having their families around them. (Start Strong 2011:6–7)

These findings highlight the value that children place on their own active role in making their wishes come true, their attention to play, the importance of the outdoors and of relationships. And we know from research that all these factors contribute to the well-being of children and can be linked to a basic human flourishing. It is interesting to observe how closely children's wishes and dreams reflect the four necessary elements to flourishing that Gaffney (2011) has identified. She notes that to flourish as individuals we need *challenge*; some call or demand on us to do something, to get over an obstacle, to engage with some life task, to make something happen. We also need what she terms *connectivity*; that is, being attuned or connected to what is happening inside us but also outside us. Connectivity orients us to the challenges and prepares us to deal with them. *Autonomy* – feeling free to move and to act in pursuit of a particular challenge – is also important. This gives us the energy to get going and sets the direction of our task.

Finally she observes that we need to *use our valued competencies*; we need the experience of using our talents, especially the strengths we most value in ourselves (Gaffney 2011:6). At some level young children know what is helpful to their own positive development, flourishing and well-being and they reflect this in communicating through their wishes and their drawing. How we can assist human flourishing is a topic addressed by Martha Nussbaum in her book *Creating Capabilities: The Human Development Approach* (2011) and the relevance of her ideas to the early years is considered by Taylor (2012) who concludes that her approach has a valuable practical application in framing early years practice towards enhancing young children's well-being and flourishing.

To foster and support children and their well-being we need to assist the development of flexibility, self-control and self-discipline in young children while encouraging curiosity, exploration and creativity. We know from research that this happens best in high-quality interactive environments where practitioners are confident and knowledgeable, where practices are well informed and relaxed and children are supported, safe and healthy. And this research knowledge has guided the development of the two key practice documents developed for the Irish context – Síolta and Aistear. The development of Síolta was guided by a vision in which all young children were afforded equity of access to early education opportunities that enrich their lives and contribute positively to their optimal well-being, learning and development. Aistear recognises the importance of quality in practice and points out that children 'need to feel valued, respected, empowered, cared for and included' (NCCA 2009a:16).

Picking up on much that research has found, the introduction to the well-being section of Aistear notes that '[W]ell-being focuses on developing as a person . . . [C]hildren's relationships and interactions with their families and communities contribute significantly to their sense of well-being' (2009a:16). The importance of relationships and interactions cannot be overstated. Children can develop well if they are in close relationships with adults and other children who love, value, respect and care for them, even in the absence of much of the materials we associate with early years practice. The socio-personal context is empowering and inclusive and assists children in strengthening their sense of self-worth and giving them a sense of mastery – so critical to later skills and success.

For the adult to be an effective support and model for children it is important to be actively present in all engagements with them – as individuals and as a group. Being present to the children does not mean always doing things with them or organising activities for them. Rather, being present means being alert, attuned, vigilant, aware and engaged in the process of early years practice. It means that while engaged in early years practice we should attend to the 'now', recognise that this moment is the present moment, the moment in which we should be present rather than planning what we are going to do at future moments. Adults need to exhibit adaptability and flexibility, be ready to catch the learning moments as they come along. They should also model in practice those characteristics they want to see developing in young children, such as resilience, resourcefulness, coping strategies for change, resolutions when things go wrong. We all develop and sustain our own self-image through our understanding of how others see us and value us and to children the adults in their world are the key models from whom to learn.

In addition to relationships and the particularly powerful influence of the adult on well-being, there is also the element of physical well-being. Children need the opportunities to experience challenge and risk in an unobtrusively safe environment. Settings must also be healthy and safe for all those present. Balancing environments that meet the safety and health requirements of very young children as well as toddlers and slightly older children, who delight in walking and running around, takes careful thought, particularly when settings are facilitating mixed age opportunities, which can be so valuable to children in their development. Providing for the well-being of children in early years settings can take many different forms and will depend on the age of the child, the type of setting and the particularities of any given day.

The next section of this chapter will take a closer look at well-being in the context of the Aistear Guidelines for Good Practice in association with Aistear Aims and Learning Goals for different age groups in different settings. It will link vignettes from the Aistear document with Síolta Standards, Competencies and Standards for Reflection with a view to illustrating how to use both practice documents as a resource by students and practitioners in daily practice through drawing on what is happening day-to-day in settings. This is intended to assist in realising Aistear and Síolta in daily practice in a way that makes it part of the daily routine and language of reflection and review. As noted earlier, the shared language of Aistear and Síolta has emerged from extensive consultation with and feedback from practitioners and parents in Ireland as well as from national and international research and has been informed by practice evidence. This shared language can form the basis for building and sustaining a strong professional identity for Irish early years practitioners.

The table outlines the four Aistear aims for well-being and expands them by reference to twenty-four learning goals.

AISTEAR'S AIMS AND LEARNING GOALS: WELL-BEING

Well-being	
Aims	**Learning goals**
Aim 1 Children will be strong psychologically and socially	In partnership with the adult, children will 1 make strong attachments and develop warm and supportive relationships with family, peers and adults in out-of-home settings and in their community 2 be aware of and name their own feelings, and understand that others may have different feelings 3 handle transitions and changes well 4 be confident and self-reliant 5 respect themselves, others and the environment 6 make decisions and choices about their own learning and development.

Aim 2	In partnership with the adult, children will
Children will be as healthy and fit as they can be	1 gain increasing control and co-ordination of body movements
	2 be aware of their bodies, their bodily functions, and their changing abilities
	3 discover, explore and refine gross and fine motor skills
	4 use self-help skills in caring for their own bodies
	5 show good judgement when taking risks
	6 make healthy choices and demonstrate positive attitudes to nutrition, hygiene, exercise, and routine.
Aim 3	In partnership with the adult, children will
Children will be creative and spiritual	1 express themselves creatively and experience the arts
	2 express themselves through a variety of types of play
	3 develop and nurture their sense of wonder and awe
	4 become reflective and think flexibly
	5 care for the environment
	6 understand that others may have beliefs and values different to their own.
Aim 4	In partnership with the adult, children will
Children will have positive outlooks on learning and on life	1 show increasing independence, and be able to make choices and decisions
	2 demonstrate a sense of mastery and belief in their own abilities and display learning dispositions, such as determination and perseverance
	3 think positively, take learning risks, and become resilient and resourceful when things go wrong
	4 motivate themselves, and welcome and seek challenge
	5 respect life, their own and others, and know that life has a meaning and purpose
	6 be active citizens.

Source: www.ncca.biz/Aistear/pdfs/PrinciplesThemes_ENG/PrinciplesThemes_ENG.pdf

The illustrations of learning experiences presented are samples of practice taken from different settings. They form the basis from which links are made across both Síolta and Aistear to allow for exploration of the values underlying the specific illustration and how the practice can be enriched or extended. The illustrations are presented and discussed in the context of the four Guidelines for Good Practice identified in Aistear (2009a):

1 Building partnerships between parents and practitioners.
2 Learning and developing through interactions.
3 Learning and developing through play.
4 Supporting learning and development through assessment.

To inform and enhance your own practice you should capture and record examples of practice from your own setting and use these as the basis for exploring what aspects of Aistear and Síolta are being met and how, under particular themes, your own practice could be enriched. Any sample of early years practice taken from your own setting experience as a student on placement or as a practitioner can act as a source for considering how Síolta Standards are met and how Aistear Themes are incorporated into existing practice. At the same time the exercise provides a rich resource for reflecting on, discussing and evaluating practice on an ongoing basis with a view to constant improvement.

BUILDING PARTNERSHIPS BETWEEN PARENTS AND PRACTITIONERS

Illustration 1

- Aim 1 and Learning Goal 3
- Age Group: Toddlers and young children
- Setting: Home and sessional service (playgroup)

Mina greets the children and their parents as they arrive at the playgroup every morning. She finds these few minutes of contact invaluable. Parents can let her know if they would like more time to chat about their children and she arranges a time to suit. At the beginning of the year she also lets them know that she can be contacted by phone every day from 1 p.m. to 1.30 p.m. if they have any concerns, or just want to chat about how their child is getting on in the playgroup. She reminds them of this regularly, and many of them find it reassuring that they can keep in touch like this. Some children are brought by relatives or childminders and this form of contact is invaluable for their parents as they can ring Mina during their lunchtime.

Mikie (two years and eleven months) started in the playgroup a month ago. His mam, Lucy, is very shy and Mina makes a special effort to have a chat with her once a week. Mina shows Lucy something, such as a photograph of him playing or a picture that Mikie has made. She uses this to encourage Lucy to talk about Mikie. She asks about things he likes to do at home and she offers ideas to Lucy to help extend what he is learning in the setting.

(?) *Reflection*: What strategies could I use to help parents to feel more confident in talking to me about their children? (NCCA 2009b:16).

Under the theme of well-being, this vignette meets Aistear's Aim 1: 'Children will be strong psychologically and socially', particularly through Learning Goal 3: 'In partnership with the adult, children will handle transitions and changes well' (NCCA 2009a:17). Of course, how these aims and goals are met will depend on the age of the child and the length of time they have been attending the setting. For very young children the tone of engagement with the adult is key as they have few other signals to guide them in their understanding of safety and security. Older children can often take a lead in the greeting situation, particularly if they want to talk about, or show, aspects of the setting or the work to others from outside the setting.

Practices such as that described in the example above also meet a number of Síolta standards. Take Standard 3: Parents and Family – 'Valuing and involving parents and families requires a proactive partnership approach evidenced by a range of clearly stated, accessible and implemented processes, policies and procedures' (CECDE 2006:31). In terms of the components under Standard 3, the greeting strategy meets Component 3.1: 'Staff and parents have both formal and informal opportunities for communication and information sharing about the child' (CECDE 2006:32). These opportunities are more than simply a smile and a 'Good morning' – they are a rich foundation for facilitating links to the home learning environment (HLE), following up on aspects of individual child development, checking on family factors that may be impacting on the child and giving parents/significant adults the opportunity to raise issues of relevance to the child's life.

This greeting practice also meets aspects of Síolta Standard 5: Interactions – 'Fostering constructive interactions (child/child; child/adult; adult/adult) requires explicit policies, procedures and practice that emphasise the value of process and are based on mutual respect, equal partnership and sensitivity' (CECDE 2006:39). Standard 5 has six components for consideration and Component 5.5 – 'Interactions between the adults within, and associated with the setting, act as a model of respect, support and partnership for the child' (CECDE 2006:40) – is met through appropriate greeting practices. In the Signposts for Reflection the ideas behind the standard are extended with questions that can be considered in relation to the particularities of individual settings. They ask at 5.5.1, for instance, 'how do your interactions with parents model friendly respect and partnership?' and at 5.5.4, 'Are there opportunities for the child to observe adults modelling positive interactions?' These are extended into some Think Abouts, including 'Co-operation and showing kindness'. Component 5.5 also links back to Standard 3 through Component 3.3: 'Staff are responsive and sensitive in the provision of information and support to parents in their key role in the learning and development of the child' (CECDE 2006:34), which prompts one to consider how best to communicate sensitive information. This provides an obvious direction to Standard 12: Communication – 'Communicating effectively in the best interests of the child requires policies, procedures and actions that promote the proactive sharing of knowledge and information among appropriate stakeholders with respect and confidentiality' (CECDE 2006:87). To explore in more detail what this might mean in real-life practice one can consider the most appropriate component to the practice illustration under consideration. In this instance the most relevant one seems to be Component 12.2: 'the setting is proactive in sharing information, as appropriate, in the best interests of the child, with other stakeholders' (CECDE 2006:89). The questions deriving from this component would be around what is meant by 'as appropriate' in terms of the illustration used – or in terms of an example from your own practice.

Illustration 2

- Aim 4 and Learning Goal 6
- Age Group: Young children
- Setting: Home and infant class (primary school)

Joan and Con have three children at primary school. They are both active members of the Parents' Association (PA) and take turns going to meetings. They have built good relationships with the teachers and other parents since their first child started school. A new housing estate has been built locally and the number of children attending the school has increased greatly. The PA and the school staff recently helped to organise an open day for parents of new children. Patrick, whose daughter Bláithín started junior infants this year, went along. The PA is also developing an outdoor play area for the infants, which includes a place for planting. Con suggested to the teachers that Patrick might be interested in getting involved in setting up the outdoor area. Patrick looks after his children each weekend since he and his wife separated. He is a part-time builder. Patrick is delighted to be asked and especially so when the teacher suggests that the children might help him out. His daughter Bláithín is delighted about this. Patrick feels that he is contributing positively to his child's learning and development and is also benefiting the school community by using his skills.

Over the next few weeks Patrick, the class teacher, the children and some other parents enjoy working together and have the play area ready for the sun in June!

 Reflection: Are there ways in which I can encourage dads to become more involved in their children's learning and development? (NCCA 2009b:22).

This example, under the theme Well-being, meets Aim 4: 'Children will have positive outlooks on learning and in life', particularly through Learning Goal 6: 'In partnership with the adult, children will be active citizens' (NCCA 2009b:17). There is a great deal of material for reflection in this particular example. It is carefully drawn to include aspects of contemporary life and it proposes an involvement of a number of adults in the main activity. It also introduces the idea of a parents' association – something not typical in the wider early years sector in Ireland. Through such an association, engagement with parents takes on a fairly formal role and can be managed and monitored. The activity of developing part of the outside area as a planting garden is one of many outdoor situations where fathers can be included, often a difficulty for settings to encourage. It is also interesting to note that the practitioner is actively involved in the activity and encourages the children to participate – it is not just a father working away on his own. It also reminds us of the rich learning possibilities nature can provide. This example links back to a number of key issues in Aistear, but it also links to a number of Síolta standards.

In the first instance the example can be seen to meet aspects of Standard 2: Environments – 'Enriching environments, both indoor and outdoor (including materials and equipment) are well-maintained, safe, available, accessible, adaptable, developmentally appropriate and offer a variety of challenging and stimulating experiences' (CECDE 2006:19). In this context the creation of an outside planting garden meets, among others, Component 2.3: 'The indoor and outdoor environment is well maintained and ensures comfortable and pleasant surroundings for children and adults' (CECDE 2006:20). That the children participate in the development of the garden alongside the adults helps them develop a sense of ownership and belonging. In addition, it provides the practitioner with many possibilities to document learning and create later opportunities for children to reflect on their role in creating the space and caring for it.

The example also meets aspects of Síolta Standard 1: Rights of the Child – 'Ensuring that each child's rights are met requires that she/he is enabled to exercise choice and to use initiative as an active participant and partner in her/his own development and learning' (CECDE 2006:13). In particular, it is relevant to consider Component 1.2: 'Each child is enabled to participate in the daily routine, in activities, in conversations and in all other appropriate situations, and is considered a partner by the adult' (CECDE 2006:14). The engagement with parents meets certain aspects of Síolta Standard 16: Community Involvement – 'Promoting community involvement requires the establishment of networks and connections evidenced by policies, procedures and actions which extend and support all adults' and children's engagement with the wider community' (CECDE 2006:105). While this standard looks from the setting out into the community, the activity of including parents through the PA in creating an outdoor garden area meets Component 16.3: 'The setting is connected and integrated with the local, regional and national community' (CECDE 2006:106). In the Signpost for Reflection associated with this Component (16.3.3), practitioners are asked to consider, 'What resources and amenities in your local community do you use regularly to enrich and enhance children's experiences in your setting and engagement with the environment?' (CECDE 2006:108). This reflection could assist the practitioner in the example above to consider the parks and natural environment around the setting in discussing the plans for the planting garden and to draw attention to the links from the setting out and from the community in. This extension of an activity to meet a variety of aims enriches practice for all in that it can excite adults and broaden the sources of their ideas while at the same time extending children's sense of identity and belonging, giving them an idea of how their space can influence the quality of their own immediate community.

LEARNING AND DEVELOPING THROUGH INTERACTIONS

Illustration 3

- Aim 4 and Learning Goal 2
- Age Group: Toddlers
- Setting: Sessional service (naíonra)

Christy (almost three years) has mild cerebral palsy. His parents speak English as a first language at home. They want Christy to have the opportunity to learn Irish as a second language and so they arrange for him to attend the local naíonra.

At the naíonra staff gather information on a daily basis about each child and use this to plan and support him/her. Niamh, Christy's key worker, is a native Irish speaker. She uses facial expressions, gestures and other non-verbal cues to help him understand the Irish language as she uses it to communicate with him. Niamh understands Christy well. She knows the things he can do, the things he finds challenging, and his understanding of words and phrases in Irish. Niamh focuses on helping him develop a range of skills, including his language skills. As Christy's learning progresses, Niamh is there to support him, and offers him choices about what he is doing. She always asks before doing things for him because every day he is becoming more independent. One day she asks if he needs help picking up the blocks as sometimes he finds it hard to grasp things. Christy exclaims, 'No, I do it.' Niamh acknowledges his wish to work independently and repeats his intention using correct vocabulary and grammar, 'I will do it myself'. She gives Christy the time he needs and encourages him, as it takes a great deal of effort on his part to get all the blocks into the bucket. Niamh photographs Christy beside the blocks, prints the photograph and displays it on the wall with the caption, 'Christy is helping to tidy up.' On Friday Christy shows it to his Granda, who collects him.

(?) *Reflection:* Do I give enough time and space to children to set their own learning goals? (NCCA 2009b:41).

This vignette is set in an Irish-medium setting, the naíonra, and illustrates the fine balance that practitioners need to maintain when working in bilingual situations. It also introduces the challenges of working with young children who have additional needs. It illustrates Aistear's Aim 4: 'Children will have positive outlooks on learning and life' through Learning Goal 2: 'In partnership with the adult, children will demonstrate a sense of mastery and belief in their own abilities and display learning dispositions, such as determination and perseverance' (NCCA 2009a:17). In particular,

̖nis short piece introduces a child with a mild disability who has the disposition to tackle a task; the practitioner, Niamh, understands the need to give him the time, space and encouragement to do so. She strengthens her encouragement by taking a photograph and displaying it so that Christy himself can show it to his Granda – thus bringing his success beyond the setting and the particular event into his home life. Although the setting is a naíonra, this vignette shows how a good practitioner will judge what is the key issue to attend to at a particular time. In this instance she models the correct way of saying the sentence and does so in Christy's own mother tongue rather than introducing a new dimension of second language to a task that is clearly important to Christy and is going to take some time and attention. She can attend to developing his vocabulary in Irish at other times.

The Aistear Aim and Learning Goal underpinning this example can also be considered by reference to different Síolta standards of quality practice. In the first instance one can see that it links to Standard 1: Rights of the Child – 'Ensuring that each child's rights are met requires that she/he is enabled to exercise choice and to use initiative as an active participant and partner in her/his own development and learning' (CECDE 2006:13). The practitioner in the example is sensitive to the role that Christy is playing in extending his skills and she facilitates this with patience. The component most related to this example is Component 1.1: 'Each child has opportunities to make choices, is enabled to make decisions, and has her/his choices and decisions respected' (CECDE 2006:15). This respectful response to the child enhances his sense of self and also his sense of control over his world, building his sense of well-being and contributing to him developing a strong sense of mastery – so critical to positive learning and development. There are three Signposts for Reflection associated with Component 1.1 and for a child of Christy's age Signpost 1.1.3 has particular relevance for the reflective practitioner: 'How do you foster each child's sense of control over her/his daily experiences and activities?' (CECDE 2006:15).

In addition to Standard 1, the vignette also links to Síolta Standard 7: Curriculum – 'Encouraging each child's holistic development and learning requires the implementation of a verifiable, broad-based, documented and flexible curriculum or programme' (CECDE 2006:55). You can see how in her response to Christy – expanding his words into a grammatically correct sentence and allowing him time, with encouragement, to gather up the blocks – Niamh has taken her lead from him and uses the event as a learning opportunity to enhance his communication. This links to the third component of the six components offered under this standard: Component 7.3 – 'The curriculum/programme is reflected in and implemented through the child's daily routine, spontaneous learning opportunities, structured activities and activities initiated by the child' (CECDE 2006:58). The Signpost for Reflection most relevant to the example is 7.3.7, which asks, 'In child-initiated activity, what strategies do you use to incorporate your curriculum/programme goals?' This signpost allows the practitioner to think explicitly about what aspects of the setting's curriculum or programme her actions have addressed . . . and if there is no clear answer it challenges her to think about what could have been done better. For this reason it is useful to take a small number of selected examples of your daily practice, search out the Aistear Aim and Learning Goal each reflects and see how this, in turn, links to Síolta Standards for Quality Practice. It is also a useful technique to use as the basis for team reflections on overall practice.

Illustration 4

- Aim 1 and Learning Goal 1
- Age Group: Babies
- Setting: Full- and part-time daycare (crèche)

Diane is the manager of the baby room in a crèche. She and her assistant Monique give special attention to structuring the environment for the six babies in their care. They talk to the parents, observe and talk to the babies, and plan accordingly. Diane and Monique check regularly that everybody is safe and happy. They provide toys, natural materials, and items from home of different textures, colours, shapes and sizes in order to stimulate the babies' senses. They display photographs of the babies and their families on the walls with the babies' names and words like 'mammy' and 'daddy' beside them. Some babies have photographs of their pets on the wall too. The double doors to the garden are often open and there is a ramp for babies who want to crawl outside. The less mobile babies are often placed near the window so that they can watch what is going on outside. There is a garden seat, as well as roll-along toys, rugs, and a variety of other toys and equipment to play with. All the toys and equipment are routinely checked for safety and added to regularly so that each baby's interests are extended. Diane and Monique position themselves near the babies at all times, and use a key worker system so that each baby is cared for by the same person as much as possible.

 Reflection: Do I make children feel welcome and motivated to explore and discover? (NCCA 2009b:42)

This example is developed under Aistear's Aim 1: 'Children will be strong psychologically and socially' through Learning Goal 1: 'In partnership with the adult, children will make strong attachments and develop warm and supportive relationships with family, peers and adults in out-of-home settings and their community' (NCCA 2009a:17). While highlighting the importance of safety and the ratio of adults to babies in out-of-home settings, this example also shows how to create an environment with safe risk opportunities available to those babies who can take them. The example also shows how we can arrange settings to provide direct access to the outdoors for those babies mobile enough to access it.

In considering the standards of quality practice that might inform this example, we can see that it can be linked to Standard 6: Play – 'promoting play requires that each child has ample time to engage in freely available and accessible, developmentally appropriate and well-resourced opportunities for exploration, creativity and "meaning making" in the company of other children, with participating and supportive adults and alone, where appropriate' (CECDE 2006:49). While the seven components all have relevance to the example, Component 6.2: 'When the child is engaged in play/exploration, the equipment and materials provided are freely available and easily accessible to her/him' (CECDE 2006:51) is a key one. Signpost for Reflection 6.2.5 is also relevant to this example and the age group covered: 'how does the child who is not mobile access the available equipment and materials?' In addition to the relevance of the play standard, the illustration also allows consideration of Standard 11: Professional Practice – 'Practising in a professional manner requires that individuals have skills, knowledge, values and attitudes appropriate to their role and responsibility within the setting. In addition, it requires regular reflection upon practice and engagement in supported, ongoing professional development' (CECDE 2006:81). The example given above refers to the room manager and her assistant, and we can see that their roles are closely combined but clearly defined, which allows for effective support to the six babies in the baby room. It also mentions a review of the equipment to ensure that it continues to be safe for use.

Under this standard I have selected Component 11.3: 'The setting supports and promotes regular opportunity for practitioners to reflect upon and review their practice and contribute positively to the development of quality practice in the setting' (CECDE 2006:84), as this aspect of professional practice cannot be overstated. The Signpost for Reflection most closely related to this notion is 11.3.2, which asks, 'How often is time scheduled in your setting for group reflection and discussion about practice?' After each day we should be able to look back, individually or as a team, and explain why we behaved in particular ways with a particular child or group of children, materials or elements of the curriculum. And in our reflection it is important that we are open to changing our practice as necessary. As with all the examples provided as illustrations here, there are other standards and components that could also be considered.

LEARNING AND DEVELOPING THROUGH PLAY

Illustration 5

- Aim 2 and Learning Goal 3
- Age Group: Toddlers
- Setting: Sessional service (special preschool), and full- and part-time daycare (nursery)

The toddlers in the nursery spend a lot of time outdoors all year round. Some of the children who are quite shy and timid inside become much more active and enthusiastic outside. They run, climb the ladder, go down the slide, kick a football, play in the outdoor café, get fuel for their vehicles at the pumps, play with the water and sand, and cycle their tricycles. The staff members play Hide and Seek with them, organise races, play football, join them for a latte in the café, and chat about what they are doing and learning. On cold days they all dress up warmly in their coats and hats before going outside, and on wet days they splash in the puddles in their wellies and listen to the rain fall on their tinfoil-covered umbrellas.

Daniel (almost three years) attends a special preschool three mornings a week. He joins the children in the toddler room in the nursery on the other two days. He can't move any of his limbs so is reliant on the staff to carry him outside. He squeals with delight when they lift him up in the air and when they put him on the slide. The staff talk to Daniel, building up and reinforcing his language, spatial awareness and physical skill, saying, for example, 'Now, Daniel, you are up, up, up . . . Now down, down, down.' They place Daniel on the ground and put a ball beside his head. He gets great pleasure from moving the ball slowly with his head and getting right under the bench. They say, 'Well done Daniel . . . under, under the bench.' These physical experiences help Daniel's gross motor development and enable him to understand spatial concepts like over/under, up/down, and in/out. The other children regularly run over to Daniel and gently push the ball to him or wave at him. He smiles and giggles when they do this.

(?) *Reflection:* Do all children in my setting have opportunities to get involved in and enjoy play? (NCCA 2009b:60)

This is an extensive illustration but it is important as it captures the complex reality of the various experiences staff have to deal with in early years settings, particularly when considering the well-being of children with differing abilities. Aistear's Aim 2 reads: 'Children will be as healthy and fit as they can be', and this is the core of this illustration. It is amplified by Learning Goal 3: 'In partnership with the adult, children will discover, explore and refine gross and fine motor skills' (NCCA 2009b:17). In particular, it describes how the outdoor environment can provide a rich source of enjoyment while at the same time providing ample opportunities for the development of gross and fine motor skills. However, it also points to the varied ways in which some children will attend a setting (while others may be there every day for the full session) and the implications of this for practice. In addition it is a good example of how to introduce mathematical language in gentle play with Daniel – the repeating of words such as 'up/down, over/under' in the routine activities they include him in.

This illustration clearly links to Síolta's Standard 6: Play – 'Promoting play requires that each child has ample time to engage in freely available and accessible, developmentally appropriate and well-resourced opportunities for exploration, creativity and "meaning making" in the company of other children, with participating and supportive adults and alone, where appropriate' (CECDE 2006:49) and offers a rich description of the exuberance of outdoor play in good weather and bad. The example refers to staff members playing with children and organising activities. While this provides a valuable example of rich, inclusive practice there should also be freedom and time for children to play alone or together in small groups. Component 6.7: 'Opportunities for play/exploration are devised in conjunction with planning for curriculum/programme implementation, and are adapted to meet changing learning and development requirements' (CECDE 2006:50) is relevant to the illustration as it refers to the curricular aims that can guide practice. In their playful interactions with Daniel, the staff choose their words carefully in an effort to assist him develop an understanding of positioning. The Signpost for Reflection most relevant here is 6.7.1: 'How does planning for learning through play accommodate the individual child, setting, local context and specific needs?' (CECDE 2006:54).

Síolta Standard 5: Interactions – 'Fostering constructive interactions (child/child, child/adult, adult/adult) requires explicit policies, procedures and practice that emphasise the value of process and are based on mutual respect, equal partnership and sensitivity' (CECDE 2006:39) – offers a valuable context within which to reflect on the way opportunities were made by the practitioners in the illustration to offer the more able-bodied children the opportunity to interact with Daniel in a way that was respectful of him but not contrived. Clearly some careful consideration was given on how this could happen because the staff realised how important it was for all the children, including Daniel himself. This illustrates Component 5.2: 'Each child receives appropriate support to enable her/him to interact positively with other children' (CECDE 2006:42) and the Signpost for Reflection 5.2.2, 'What is your role in supporting the child to interact with other children?' (CECDE 2006:42). This simple question is at the heart of high-quality early years practice and one you should be asking yourself every day.

Illustration 6

- Aim 3 and Learning Goal 3
- Age Group: Young children
- Setting: Sessional service (playgroup)

The children in the playgroup are outside on a frosty morning. Two boys, Fiachra and James (both four years), discover a large spider's web. They call the playgroup assistant, Zola, over to have a look at it. They are fascinated by the different colours. Zola explains that it is the sun's reflection on the frost that is doing this. Zola is French and she tells them that the French word for spider's web is toile d'araignée. They laugh at each other's attempts to say it! She asks the boys if they would like to take a photograph of the web and they race inside to get the camera, each trying to go faster than the other. Zola uploads the photograph to the computer. The boys study it, trying to work out how the spider made the web. The boys tell Zola that they want to make a web too. They assemble a range of materials including glue, paper, markers, string, knitting wool, and tinfoil. They spend a long time making their webs and proudly take photographs of them. 'Ils sont magnifique! Quelles couleurs!' ('They are brilliant! What colours!'), Zola says.

After lunch the boys run out to see the web but have trouble finding it because the ice has melted. They are disappointed. During circle time the group have a discussion about how ice and snow melt and how the ice melting made it difficult for Fiachra and James to find their web. The following day another child brings in a DVD about a spider. They all watch it. Over the following weeks some children do projects on spiders while others investigate ice.

 Reflection: How often do I encourage children to get involved in projects on things that interest them? (NCCA 2009b:61)

On reading the above example of practice you can see the value of listening carefully to children, following their lead and extending their learning and understanding, while at the same time allowing them the freedom to follow up on their activities. It also illustrates how you can use your own background and experience to introduce a new dimension – in this case a different language – which also broadens children's horizons. The example is presented under Aistear's Aim 3: 'Children will be creative and spiritual', and Learning Goal 3: 'In partnership with the adult, children will develop and nurture their sense of wonder and awe' (NCCA 2009b:17). It describes how very simple things in nature are recognised as wonderful by children and can open the door to new learning; it also reminds us as adults to keep our eyes open to the wonders that children find.

This example describes good practice in relation to responding to child-initiated activities outdoors in the context of a curriculum aim and can be linked to Síolta's Standard 7: Curriculum – 'Encouraging each child's holistic development and learning requires the implementation of a verifiable, broad-based, documented and flexible curriculum or programme' (CECDE 2006:55). In particular it can be related to Component 7.3: 'The curriculum/programme is reflected in and implemented through the child's daily routine, spontaneous learning opportunities, structured activities and activities initiated by the child.' It is a good example of how observant practitioners can take a lead from children's spontaneous learning to introduce additional learning opportunities and expand their development and learning. The Signpost for Reflection chosen for illustration here is 7.3.2, 'What aspects of the curriculum/programme lend

sponding to spontaneous learning opportunities which occur during
, and to the ever-changing nature of the child's activities?' (CECDE

...er practitioners an opportunity to further reflect on a particular sample of their practice (or, in this case the illustration above), Síolta has cross-referenced a number of components to others in the overall framework. In this instance Component 7.3.2 is cross-referenced to Component 6.5 of Standard 6: Play – 'Promoting play requires that each child has ample time to engage in freely available and accessible, developmentally appropriate and well-resourced opportunities for exploration, creativity and "meaning making" in the company of other children, with participating and supportive adults and alone, where appropriate' (CECDE 2006:49). The key Signpost for Reflection under Component 6.5: 'Play opportunities provided for the child encourage her/him to explore, to be creative and to use her/his previous learning to make new meanings relevant to this illustration' is Signpost for Reflection 6.5.3: 'How are you adding to the learning potential of those opportunities in the way you interact with the child'? (CECDE 2006:53). We can see that in the example above the children are freely playing outside in the frost and come upon a spider's web; clearly the staff are around but they are not interfering in the children's activities; they are engaged and observant and available to the children so that when they call to Zola she comes over, showing interest. Having listened to the children, she has an idea that furthers the interests of the children and extends their horizons both linguistically and in terms of their own observation skills, creative abilities and fine motor skills.

SUPPORTING LEARNING AND DEVELOPMENT THROUGH ASSESSMENT

Illustration 7
- Aim 4 and Learning Goal 2
- Age Group: Babies
- Setting: Full- and part-time daycare (crèche)

Miriam, the crèche room leader, is encouraging Liam (ten months) to crawl. She knows he can do it because his mum has told Miriam about him crawling at home. For some reason he rarely crawls while in the crèche. Miriam places the sorting cube, which Liam loves to play with, out of his reach. It is near him, but he will have to move closer to get it. Within a few seconds he shows his frustration, yelling and shaking his hands. He looks at Miriam as he yells louder. Miriam crawls to the toy and encourages him to crawl too: 'Let's crawl together, will we?' She places the cube a little closer to him, all the time modelling crawling and encouraging Liam to have a go. He loses interest and picks up a spoon close by and bangs the floor with it. After lunch, as Miriam plays with another baby in the room, she observes Liam making one or two false starts at crawling. She moves a little closer so she can observe him better. He moves on to all fours and reaches forward while balancing himself with the other hand to grab the cube. Eventually, he makes it and Miriam claps her hands as he reaches the cube. Meanwhile, Lisa, the room assistant, records the achievement on video while Miriam observes and stays ready to assist Liam if necessary. Miriam claps her hands and congratulates Liam on his achievement. Liam claps too and laughs loudly. He proceeds to play with the cube. Miriam shares the footage on the video recorder with Liam's parents that evening and notes his achievement in his Record of Care. Over the coming days Miriam provides lots of opportunities that encourage Liam to crawl, and by the end of the following week he is delighted with his new mobility and the options for exploration that it brings!

 Reflection: How can I use observations to greater effect in supporting and encouraging children to set their own learning goals? (NCCA 2009b:88)

There are a number of key things to note about the illustration above. In the first instance, there are clearly good staff–parent communication procedures in place: Miriam is aware of Liam crawling at home, and this encourages her to provide crawling opportunities in the setting. This is further illustrated by the reference to sharing the video footage with Liam's parents later in the day. There is also good communication between both adults in the setting, as evidenced by the speedy use of the video to record the crawling event. This example is given under Aistear Aim 4: 'Children will have positive outlooks on learning and life' and is an element of the fourth practice Guideline: supporting learning and development through assessment. It links directly to Learning Goal 2: 'In partnership with the adult, children will demonstrate a sense of mastery and belief in their own abilities and display learning dispositions, such as determination and perseverance' (NCCA 2009b:17). In keeping with the well-being theme, under which this illustration is provided, this learning goal is about striving to ensure that practice explicitly values children, respects them and provides environments that include and empower children to achieve, even in small ways. Recording occasional examples of positive behaviour and achievements offers opportunities to engage with parents about their own child's learning and development and also contributes to the child's sense of belonging in the setting.

In the Síolta framework there are standards of quality practice that are particularly relevant to this illustration, for instance Standard 14: Identity and Belonging – 'Promoting positive identities and a strong sense of belonging requires clearly defined policies, procedures and practice that empower every child and adult to develop a confident self- and group-identity, and to have a positive understanding and regard for the identity and rights of others' (CECDE 2006:95). It is interesting to note that this standard has relevance to both children and adults in the setting – research has shown that adults working in early years settings need to feel valued and respected if they are to be able to create an environment that can provide this sense of belonging and respect. The component chosen to expand on this point is Component 14.3: 'The setting promotes positive understanding and regard for the identity and rights of others through the provision of an appropriate environment, experiences and interactions within the setting' (CECDE 2006:99) and the Signpost for Reflection that can act as the basis for self-reflection and team reflection is 14.3.3: 'In what way does the setting promote high self-esteem among the children?' (CECDE 2006:100). Following on from this signpost, one is directed to Standard 1: Rights of the Child – 'Ensuring that each child's rights are met requires that she/he is enabled to exercise choice and to use initiative as an active participant and partner in her/his own development and learning' (CECDE 2006:13). There are three components associated with this standard and it is Component 1.2 that is most relevant to this example: 'Each child has opportunities and is enabled to take the lead, initiate activity, be appropriately independent and is supported to solve problems' (CECDE 2006:15). It is worth pointing out that the child in the example is only ten months old, and yet the practitioners in the setting are well able to allow him sufficient independence and time to achieve the next developmental step without undue interference. Despite leaving the child to his own devices, they are clearly engaged with the activity, and this is reflected in how Miriam observes Liam quietly but is able to respond positively when the crawling begins. You can extend consideration of this example of practice through Signpost for Reflection 1.2.3: 'How is the child provided with opportunities within the daily routine to use her/his initiative and to be appropriately independent?' (CECDE 2006:16); and this in turn directs the reader to Standard 7: Curriculum – 'Encouraging each child's holistic development and learning requires the implementation of a verifiable, broad-based, documented and flexible curriculum or programme' (CECDE 2006:55).

The seven illustrations given in this chapter are presented to highlight the close connection between Aistear and Síolta and to provide suggestions on how to take examples from your own daily practice and reflect on them both individually and collectively as a team. While these illustrations have presented opportunities to link specific samples of daily practice with the standards of Síolta and the learning goals of Aistear, they do not directly present ideas for achieving the aims of Aistear under the theme of Well-being. Attention to actual practice can be found in the Aistear (2009a) document in a series of Sample Learning Opportunities on Principles and Themes. The suggestions are set out according to age groups and provide useful ideas on how to really look at your own practice and check it for its potential to expand and enrich young children's communication skills, so crucial to early learning and development.

Below are the main practice styles suggested for maximising children's learning opportunities under the theme Well-being. The content of the situations derives from the children and the adults and will be unique to each opportunity that presents. When considering how to carry through these suggestions you will be greatly assisted by applying your knowledge and understanding of child development, relevant research and the processes that assist learning and development most appropriately for individual children. The ages act as a guide, but they are overlapping in order to capture the reality that children have different developmental trajectories across aspects of development.

- When working with babies – birth to eighteen months – practitioners should:
  - engage with babies in a consistent, calm, caring and respectful manner
  - enable babies to explore and manipulate objects in a multi-sensory way so that they can smell, taste, hear, see, touch, reach, grasp, lift and drop objects
  - encourage babies to do things for themselves, encourage their initiatives and choices and react positively to their endeavours so that they develop positive dispositions to learning
  - nurture babies' sense of wonder
  - facilitate repetition and challenge so that babies can master and extend what they are doing, while encouraging them to take risks
  - help babies to respect themselves and others.
- When working with toddlers – twelve months to three years – practitioners should:
  - ensure that toddlers get adequate rest, nutrition and stimulation
  - provide toddlers with a well-structured and orderly environment and a predictable but flexible routine
  - enable toddlers to become independent
  - encourage toddlers to solve problems and to think about different ways of doing things
  - provide lots of opportunities to strengthen toddlers' muscles, to refine skills and enhance hand–eye co-ordination
  - collaborate with toddlers in experiencing and caring for the environment
  - encourage toddlers to act on their curiosity, to take risks, to concentrate and to be resilient.
- When working with young children – 2½ years to six years – practitioners should:
  - help young children to predict and cope with changes, transitions and stressful life events
  - approach conflict situations calmly, model positive behaviour and create opportunities for children to share and take turns
  - promote good health and encourage children to make healthy choices
  - listen to and discuss things in depth with children
  - plan quiet times and set up space for thinking and reflecting
  - explore and promote the concept of citizenship and social justice with children and respect them as young citizens
  - appreciate children's efforts, identify their individual strengths and abilities and help them to cope and to try again when they experience failure.

(NCCA 2009a:18–23)

SUMMARY

In this chapter we considered the theme Well-being, what it means in terms of early years settings across a range of age groups and how practice can facilitate the development of well-being. Irish research shows that even very young children have some sense of the factors that contribute to their well-being and, not unexpectedly, we see how important relationships are to its development. Drawing on illustrations from Aistear we have seen how examples of practice can be interrogated and reflected on in terms of Aistear aims and learning goals within the context of achieving a sample of the quality standards proposed in Síolta. This was followed by some headline examples of practice, which can be applied in the context of particular practice examples from your own settings and experiences.

You will notice that the focus in these practice examples is on the practitioner and child/children relationship, the quality of listening and communicating and the provision of opportunities from within the ordinary and the lived experiences of the children and adults that make up the learning environment. The opportunities require the practitioner to be attuned and sensitive to the learning possibilities that arise in the most ordinary of events. They challenge you to take your time, to give plenty of time and to use time carefully. Many opportunities present themselves for capturing the learning moments that arise when individual children are concentrating on a task or when a group of children are playing a game, solving a problem or messing about. Most of all, the examples reflect the democratic nature of excellent early years practice, a practice that respects all children, that celebrates difference, that listens to children and hears them, that engages children in conversations, facilitates conversations between children and that provides a context where they develop a strong sense of well-being in keeping with their own lives and the world in which we all live.

CHAPTER 5

Identity and Belonging

In a globalised world, local culture must be the anchor of identity. (Nsamenang 2008)

In formulating an approach to identity and belonging, the NCCA notes that identity comprises characteristics, behaviours and understandings that children may have either as individuals (*I am Mary*) or shared with others (*I am a girl*). 'Shared identities enable children to develop a sense of belonging or a close relationship with or affinity to a particular group' (NCCA 2004:2). In considering the implications of this for early years practice, Síolta notes that 'promoting positive identities and a strong sense of belonging requires clearly defined policies, procedures and practice that empower every child and adult to develop a confident self- and group identity and to have a positive understanding and regard for the identity and rights of others' (CECDE 2006:95).

Children come to early years settings with their identity already in development. They come with personalities, capabilities, behavioural patterns, likes and dislikes. They also come with the influences of family and significant others. They have an emerging sense of belonging to their immediate environments. *Identity* is a personal attribute, a sense of uniqueness and of individuality; *belonging*, on the other hand, refers to a social attribute, a sense of being part of a community. Achieving a balance between the two so that children feel part of a shared, social environment or community, while at the same time having a strong sense of themselves is part of the process of development. Through showing awareness, interest and respect for individual children, their families and different cultures, languages and abilities, early years practitioners can help facilitate these important developments. To be able to achieve this it is helpful for practitioners to explore their own attitudes and values as these will affect practice and influence children as surely as their behaviour does. Developing self-awareness and personal insights into our own value system will enhance the overall inclusiveness of an early years setting.

Under Article 8 of the UN Convention on the Rights of the Child, children have a right to an identity. The Article reads:

1   States Parties undertake to respect the right of the child to preserve his or her identity, including nationality, name and family relations as recognized by law without unlawful interference.

2   Where a child is illegally deprived of some or all of the elements of his or her identity, States Parties shall provide appropriate assistance and protection, with a view to re-establishing speedily his or her identity. (UN 1989)

Positive identity is realised through strong and trusting early relationships. It is through interactions and the quality of relationships that practitioners can realise the child's right to an identity. How you relate to children, name them, label their belongings and talk about them will send messages to them about how they are considered by you and the extent to which their identity is respected. Where most children come from the same background there is less difficulty, but with increased immigration in Ireland we have children coming to early years settings with, for example, names that may be unusual; it is important that early years practitioners make the effort to pronounce and spell names correctly and help others in the setting to do the same.

While belonging is different from identity, they are interconnected, and a sense of belonging helps to strengthen a child's personal identity. In their report 'Enhancing a sense of belonging in the early years', Woodhead and Brooker note that:

> [W]hile there is no explicit right to belonging named in the UNCRC it is a concept that is implicit to realising many of the key rights articulated within the convention. If a child is not helped to feel part of a community or group then she/he will feel insecure or an outsider, and it is difficult for them to develop positively. (2008:3)

Woodhead and Brooker draw our attention to the fact that children's well-being and happiness in their day-to-day life depends to a large extent on their sense of belonging. It is difficult to realise the right of identity if you do not feel part of the early years setting you attend. Healthy belonging is characterised by reciprocity: it is two-way. Where children, even very young children, experience strong, positive relationships and feel respected for their views and feelings they do realise their sense of belonging. Woodhead and Brooker further note that 'belonging is the relational dimension to personal identity, the fundamental psycho-social "glue" that locates every individual (babies, children and adults) at a particular position in space, time and human society and – most important, connects people with each other' (2008:3).

Belonging is a sense that grows out of secure and dependable relationships and strong connections with parents, siblings and others. In the normal course of events children develop a sense of pride in being part of their family, part of their early years community. This is built up by receiving respectful and genuine attention to and praise for effort and ideas as well as achievements, which assists them to develop a pleasure and satisfaction in their own persistence, exploration and learning. This all builds into the positive development of their dispositions, skills and knowledge as they develop and grow. And this sense of mastery and control of themselves and the world in which they live and are valued comes from being valued as a member of the different groups of which they are a part. We all thrive and flourish in environments where we recognise that we are valued.

Your role as an early years practitioner is to build on the child's sense of identity and belonging and to strengthen both. Under the heading of Identity and Belonging we have an opportunity to consider the question of our own values and views of young children in practice. It is a particular challenge to the early years practitioner who may work with infants, toddlers and young children from diverse backgrounds and with different experiences of advantage or disadvantage. In working to achieve and maintain quality practice it is really important that practitioners have a clear understanding of the implications that their views and their values have for their practice. If working in an early years setting rather than in a home environment, it is important that the team discuss this among themselves and come to an agreement on the values underpinning their practice and see how this is realised in the daily practices with children, families and with colleagues. The attitudes and values we bring to a setting will influence our behaviour and the way we relate to children and their families. It will also affect the way we work with other adults in the setting. We can view children from different perspectives and this will influence how we plan for, interact with and assess children. Some will see children as dependent on adults; others will see them as competent and independent learners. There are a number of resources that can provide a basis for such consideration, including *Diversity and Equality in Early Childhood: An Irish Perspective* (Murray and Urban 2012).

Aistear has identified Identity and Belonging as a central theme underpinning its aims and learning goals and it recognises relationships as playing a key role in building one's identity. Children's experiences of a positive sense of identity and belonging is supported in environments where they experience respect, approval, encouragement; where they feel and believe that they matter, that they are important, that their views and opinions are heard and appreciated. The role of the early years practitioner in creating such an environment is critical – and it often involves very careful analysis and consideration of individual children and the other environments in which they live and develop. Where there is too big a gap between home experiences and experiences in an early years setting, it is difficult for children to feel confortable, to feel part of the new community. Indeed, it is just as important to a child's developing sense of identity that their families, their culture and beliefs, their way of living, their language are seen to be valued as much as the child is. Positive messages give confidence to children, which in turn assists them in their growing sense of belonging.

The Research Digest informing Síolta Standard 14 on Identity and Belonging defines 'identity' as 'a general term for how people think about themselves . . . [their] physical appearance, personality, ability, age, gender or ethnic group' (CECDE 2007:2). It goes on to point out that a child requires a secure personal identity that can act as a reference point for their own tolerance of difference and their understanding and acceptance of differences.

Identity formation is dynamic and is constantly evolving; it is influenced by how we interpret how others view us, even from a very young age. Research has found that children do note differences and their response to difference is influenced by the reactions of others to difference. Research by Connolly, Smith and Kelly (2002) has found that children as young as three years are influenced by their immediate cultural environment, that they notice similarities and difference and react in ways that match those of their immediate environments, both home and early years settings.

Early years practitioners are among the first new people children meet and thus carry a particular responsibility in helping children settle in to the new cultural milieu, to develop a sense of belonging in the felt knowledge that they are valued in and of themselves and that, in turn, their own background and family life is respected and valued. I use the term 'felt knowledge' as it is rare that children actually reason about their sense of belonging, but they certainly feel it; and attuned and sensitive practitioners can pick this up. The child is more likely to feel a sense of belonging if the culture of the early years setting is in harmony with the culture of the home and shares similar interests and approaches to children. For this reason it is important that practitioners actively work to create a sense of harmony between the two environments where young children spend so much of their time.

Our current understanding of child development is moving towards the view that adults can actively assist children in becoming aware of their own understanding of how they think and how they organise knowledge and information. Through informed practice they can assist children in learning how to learn, in recognising themselves as competent and masterful learners who can explore and problem-solve and are sufficiently self-aware to seek assistance when necessary. Bruner contends that it is as important for the child 'to be aware of how she goes about her learning and thinking as she is about the subject matter she is studying. Achieving skill and accumulating knowledge are not enough' (1996:64). The affective and cognitive abilities described can be developed through attending to the quality of interactions, communication and relations between individuals and their social environment. This, in turn, can reinforce the development of a sense of personal identity and belonging, connectedness and community identity; critical foundations for later educational and social success.

In practice we can assist and strengthen the development of a child's sense of identity by really getting to know each individual child, their likes and dislikes, their fears and their dreams. This can be done through a willingness in the setting to exchange experiences, discover similarities and differences, and to explore more thoroughly the differences and use them as an instrument for creating an inclusive and caring early years environment for all those participating. In our increasingly diverse society it is insufficient to simply focus on the similarities between children – 'Sure, we're all the same really' – particularly where there are manifest differences. Far better to acknowledge and celebrate diversity and recognise that we too are part of the diversity and that for young children from a minority culture you may actually represent what is different or diverse from them!

Diversity is a space that includes us all. Recognise what you don't know about cultures and languages and show a willingness to learn. Give positive messages with a respectful and balanced use of your knowledge. Embrace the wide range of individual differences you come across, be aware of your own views, allow yourself to be shocked or discomfited and then reflect on this, alone or with others. Don't wait until you find yourself in a difficult position: rather, try to imagine different scenarios and be prepared. Working through this within a group or a team is very helpful. Whether or not you have a range of cultures and languages in your early years setting it is valuable to broaden children's horizons and exposure to difference and there are many books, pictures and materials that can be used.

Murray and O'Doherty (2001), in their report on implementing the anti-bias curricular approach (Derman-Sparks & ABC 1998, 2010) identify the following four goals, which they argue settings should consider when planning for equality and diversity:

1   Nurture each child's construction of a knowledgeable, confident self-concept and group identity.
2   Promote each child's comfortable, empathic interactions with people from diverse backgrounds.
3   Foster each child's critical thinking about bias.
4   Cultivate each child's ability to stand up for her/himself and others in the face of bias.

These four points offer a useful checklist against which to reflect on the extent to which you are including and valuing all the children in your setting and assisting children to respond respectfully to differences.

In Ireland, policy and practice documents relating to children articulate a view of them as active agents in their own learning and acknowledge them as strong, competent 'meaning makers' (CECDE 2006; NCCA 2009a). But is this simple rhetoric, or has it really had an impact on how we work with the young children who attend the various early years settings available to them and their families? In Chapter 1 we mentioned how damaging 'taken for granted' understandings of words and concepts can be to responsive, reflective and intelligent practice. As reflective and professional practitioners it is important to discuss with peers and colleagues what exactly it means to respect children as individuals and competent learners, and how this impacts on practice in early years settings. What does it look like? Respect for children as competent learners who are curious and anxious to explore and understand their world is a key attribute for effective practice. Where adults believe that children are dependent or weak and need to be taught how to behave, the children themselves will recognise this and they may behave and perform as required. However, where adults have a faith in children's competence and willingness and have high and realistic expectations, children rise to the opportunities provided to extend their learning.

Central to the success of practice is the quality of your relationships and interactions with children and the extent to which you facilitate and encourage positive interactions between children. Practitioner engagement must be genuine and authentic. It is an essential characteristic of the professional early years practitioner.

There are two dimensions to engagement with children. On the one hand there is engagement at an emotional level – we genuinely feel for the children we work with, we sympathise, empathise and are joyful with them. On the other hand there is the intellectual dimension to engagement, and this involves respect for their efforts and their views – it is not about being amused by their cute little mistakes or their unrealistic efforts to achieve something. Rather it demands that you take them seriously and respect their efforts, try to understand their mistakes and guide them in their efforts to achieve through drawing on your understanding of their development. Taking time to listen to children and giving them time to talk, modelling patience and respect in your interactions all contribute to an environment where children feel safe and, within this space, children learn to cope with challenges and overcome difficulties; they develop a sense of mastery and a learning disposition. Give them a sense of importance with responsibilities that are real and authentic and they will take on those roles and responsibilities with pride. Create risky but safe opportunities for them so that they are really challenged and can overcome a real difficulty, barrier or problem. Such opportunities are rich in possibilities and can be used by practitioners to achieve a range of learning goals in the short, medium and long term.

In your practice, when thinking about identity and belonging, try to encourage interactions and assist children in managing their behaviour and their responses to difference, whether it is a cultural difference, a new experience, a challenging view or an unexpected behaviour.

Where there is a diverse group of children with a variety of cultures and linguistic backgrounds, the strength of parental involvement in the setting becomes crucial to enhancing children's sense of community and belonging while at the same time recognising and respecting their individual identities. Families may feel nervous about sharing the care of their young children and may even feel alienated in early years settings – even when you feel you are very welcoming. Not only is it helpful to involve parents in the daily life of the setting, it has also been found that assisting the development of parental/family networks can aid the cohesion of a community and consolidate the sense of belonging within diversity. While family networks may arise spontaneously, this is in fact rare; and practitioners in early years setting can certainly facilitate it by providing opportunities for families to meet each other, share ideas or solve problems.

What does belonging look like? Some elements of belonging that have been identified include feeling secure, feeling suitable, feeling like a fish in water, feeling recognised and feeling able to participate (Woodhead and Brooker 2008). To take an example: most settings have a greeting procedure, which can depend on the size of the setting and the number of children arriving at particular times. What is central to good practice is that the adults in the setting recognise the importance of this transient link to other adults in the lives of the children and are vigilant in their efforts to maintain contact with them. This should be done in a way that includes the child and t account of the particular characteristics of the family. Some settings nominate a ke worker to pay particular attention to a small group of children and take responsibility for engagement with their families, among other things. There are many examples of inclusive practices emerging from the literature and what we know about how other countries adapt to the arrival of children from different cultural and ethnic backgrounds. One such example is the Family Wall (Murray and Urban 2012): images and words appropriate to each child and family are captured as a point of reference and belonging for the child and a point of discussion and reflection for other children and adults in the setting.

Early years settings can offer supportive and secure contexts within which children can develop their sense of personal identity and provide an inclusive atmosphere in which children's sense of belonging can be enhanced. Practitioners contribute to these developments through proactive practice, which encourages children and families to participate in the life of the setting. For this to be successful the practitioner needs to actively promote inclusion and partnerships and create opportunities that take account of the needs of parents and family members. Simply inviting participation, without considering what form it might take or how it might be sustained, may disempower parents. Such situations fail to recognise and acknowledge that families are 'experts of experience' in relation to their children and that they can contribute valuable insights and knowledge about their children.

An early years setting in Berlin (Wagner 2008) found that using the Family Wall was a powerful way to include families from diverse backgrounds. The photographs used were selected and brought in by the parents and children and displayed in a part of the setting easily accessible to all. The pictures showed that all children had families and that they were of many different types. The wall provided a point of discussion between children and also information for practitioners. Wagner cautions that practitioners need to be sensitive to any unintended pressures that the activity may present and notes that in one instance a single mother included a photo of a male friend – not someone with a particularly close relationship to her child – so that her child would not feel so different from families where fathers were portrayed. Wagner also described a setting activity, used at a parent's meeting, called Name Stories, in which parents were asked to explain the story behind the name they chose for their child, and what the name meant. The parents felt the exercise was so good and informative that they wanted to keep a record of it and so they each agreed to write down the story of their child's name in a letter and place it in an envelope. The envelopes containing the letters were then presented in the form of a multilingual poster, where parents and visitors could choose ones to read. 'The name stories send a message that every child is important and that every family has a story to tell and a contribution to make to our community' (Wagner 2008:22).

The table outlines the four Aistear aims for Identity and Belonging and expands on them by reference to twenty-four learning goals.

G GOALS: IDENTITY AND BELONGING

Identity and Belonging	
Learning goals	
Aim 1 (partially obscured) ideentities and will feel respected and affirmed as unique individuals with their own life stories	In partnership with the adult, children will 1 build respectful relationships with others 2 appreciate the features that make a person special and unique (name, size, hair, hand and footprint, gender, birthday) 3 understand that as individuals they are separate from others with their own needs, interests and abilities 4 have a sense of 'who they are' and be able to describe their backgrounds, strengths and abilities 5 feel valued and see themselves and their interests reflected in the environment 6 express their own ideas, preferences and needs, and have these responded to with respect and consistency.
Aim 2 Children will have a sense of group identity where links with their family and community are acknowledged and extended	In partnership with the adult, children will 1 feel that they have a place and a right to belong to the group 2 know that members of their family and community are positively acknowledged and welcomed 3 be able to share personal experiences about their own families and cultures, and come to know that there is a diversity of family structures, cultures and backgrounds 4 understand and take part in routines, customs, festivals, and celebrations 5 see themselves as part of a wider community and know about their local area, including some of its places, features and people 6 understand the different roles of people in the community.
Aim 3 Children will be able to express their rights and show an understanding and regard for the identity, rights and views of others	In partnership with the adult, children will 1 express their views and help make decisions in matters that affect them 2 understand the rules and the boundaries of acceptable behaviour 3 interact, work co-operatively, and help others 4 be aware of and respect others' needs, rights, feelings, culture, language, background, and religious beliefs 5 have a sense of social justice and recognise and deal with unfair behaviour 6 demonstrate the skills of co-operation, responsibility, negotiation, and conflict resolution.
Aim 4 Children will see themselves as capable learners	In partnership with the adult, children will 1 develop a broad range of abilities and interests 2 show an awareness of their own unique strengths, abilities and learning styles, and be willing to share their skills and knowledge with others 3 show increasing confidence and self-assurance in directing their own learning 4 demonstrate dispositions like curiosity, persistence and responsibility 5 experience learning opportunities that are based on personal interests, and linked to their home, community and culture 6 be motivated, and begin to think about and recognise their own progress and achievements.

Source: www.ncca.biz/Aistear/pdfs/PrinciplesThemes_ENG/PrinciplesThemes_ENG.pdf

In the practice illustrations that follow, the theme of Identity and Belonging is considered across a variety of settings with a sample of children of different ages. These illustrations are intended as a starting point from which you can begin to take examples of your own day-to-day practice and reflect on them, alone or with colleagues, in the context of both Aistear and Síolta. This can form the basis for regularly reviewing your own practice and questioning the ethos of practice in your setting, and it can also provide a language within which you can consider the practice of others and explain your philosophy of practice as necessary. It should also present you with new questions and challenges, which in turn can enrich your practice, its effectiveness and your own professional satisfaction.

BUILDING PARTNERSHIPS BETWEEN PARENTS AND PRACTITIONERS

Illustration 1

- Aim 1 and Learning Goal 5
- Age Group: Young children
- Setting: Home and infant class (special primary school)

Paul (five years) has moderate general learning disabilities. He goes on a bus every morning to attend Holy Angels' Special School seventeen miles from home. His parents rarely visit his school because it is so far away, so they and his teacher use a daily diary to keep each other up to date on how Paul is getting on. This means that his parents can talk to him about what happens at school and can reinforce his learning at home. It also means that his practitioners are able to take what happens at home into account, as Paul has difficulty communicating this himself.

Paul was very excited recently when his family got a new puppy. His mam wrote about this in his diary. His teacher used this information when planning his activities for the week. Paul screeched excitedly when Miss O'Malley[1] knew the name of the puppy and he seemed to really enjoy it when she read him a story about a sheepdog working on a farm.

 Reflection: What special arrangements can I put in place to share information with parents I don't often see? (NCCA 2009b:18)

In addition to the illustration above Aistear also includes a sample extract from the diary to illustrate how information is passed between the home and school and incorporated into the daily plan for Paul (see NCCA 2009b:18).

This example takes its lead from the Identity and Belonging aims and learning goals. Specifically it refers to Aim 1: 'Children will have strong self-identities and will feel

---

1   In Aistear illustrations referring to primary school classrooms, the teachers are referred to in a more formal manner than in other early years settings.

respected and affirmed as unique individuals with their own life stories' (NCCA 2009a:26). We know from research that if we can strive to achieve this aim for all the children we work with we will be strengthening them in their views of themselves and improving the likelihood that they will be fulfilled and successful children in their immediate lives and into their future. There are six learning goals associated with this aim, and in this example we are guided to Learning Goal 5: 'In partnership with the adult, children will feel valued and themselves and their interests reflected in the environment.' There are additional demands on early years practitioners when working with children who have additional needs. The illustration above exemplifies ways in which the practitioner can work with parents to give the child a sense that they belong to the community of the setting and that their experiences at home as well as in school matter to others.

This ability to be responsive to the individual aspects of each child's life while working in a group is a key element of quality practice. This example directs us first to Síolta Standard 3: Parents and Families – 'Valuing and involving parents and families requires a proactive partnership approach evidenced by a range of clearly stated, accessible and implemented process, policies and procedures' (CECDE 2006:31). The case described clearly indicates how important it is to find ways – sometimes creative ways – to ensure that every effort is made to engage with all families and significant others in a child's life. Of the four components under this standard I have chosen to consider Component 3.2: 'There are a variety of opportunities for parents to be involved in activities within the setting, taking into account the range of parents' interests and time-constraints' (CECDE 2006:32). Under this component there is only one Signpost for Reflection and that is to consider, discuss and review your settings procedures for parental involvement. Signpost for Reflection 3.2.1 reads, 'How is parental involvement supported and encouraged within your setting?' In the example above, the parents live at a distance from the school and Paul is collected from home in the morning and brought to the school. Using a diary as a means of communicating is very important – but it is only useful if you have already developed a good relationship with the parents and respect and respond to the points they make while ensuring that the notes you send back are clear and accessible to the parents.

A second Síolta standard that is applicable to this example of practice is Standard 14: Identity and Belonging – 'Promoting positive identities and a strong sense of belonging requires clearly defined policies, procedures and practice that empower every child and adult to develop a confident self- and group-identity, and to have a positive understanding and regard for the identity and rights of others' (CECDE 2006:96). It is no surprise that Standard 14 is addressed here, given that all the Aistear examples in this chapter refer to the Aistear theme Identity and Belonging.

Under this standard there are three components, and the most relevant of these to the illustration above is Component 14.2: 'The setting promotes a confident self- and group-identity through the provision of an appropriate environment, experiences and interactions within the setting' (CECDE 2006:77). While many of the Signposts for

Reflection are relevant for consideration, perhaps 14.2.2 is the most relevant: 'How do the experiences you provide for the child promote a confident group- and self-identity?' In the example the practitioner chose to read a farm story including a reference to a dog and Paul 'seemed to really enjoy it' (NCCA 2009b:18). If one were to consider ways in which the illustration could be extended to meet further aspects of this standard, the practitioner could have chosen to read a story to the whole group arising from the knowledge she had that Paul had a new puppy. In this way both the individual's and the group's identity could have been addressed.

Illustration 2

- Aim 2 and Learning Goal 3
- Age Group: Toddlers
- Setting: Home and sessional service (playgroup)

Joseph (two years and eleven months) and his family are Travellers. They recently moved to the area and Joseph's mammy, Kathleen, enrolled him for two mornings a week at the local playgroup. The manager, Joan, meets with Kathleen and explains how the service works and shows her the different rooms and the outdoor play area. Joan asks Kathleen about Joseph and his likes and dislikes. She explains that she knows very little about Traveller culture and traditions. Joan asks Kathleen to tell her a little about their way of life and the Traveller traditions that are important to her. Understanding these will help the staff to support Joseph. Kathleen tells Joan that as a family they generally travel in their trailer during the summer months and settle in one area for the rest of the year. She also explains that most Travellers are not as nomadic as they used to be. Kathleen says that Joseph loves animals, especially horses and dogs. She tells Joan that she doesn't want Joseph to be discriminated against because he is a Traveller. She is worried because her older children had negative experiences in other settings.

In preparation for Joseph's arrival, and with Kathleen's help, Joan gets some books and jigsaws that depict Traveller life today. She organises displays of animals for Joseph to look at when he arrives. She tells the children that a new boy is joining them. A few days after Joseph's arrival Joan talks to the children about their homes. She uses wall displays to reinforce some of the points they talk about. These include pictures of the children's homes such as trailers, flats and terraced houses. They use these to talk about 'where we live'. The children bring photographs of their families and homes, and make lollipop stick models of them using junk materials, fabrics, wool, glitter, fancy paper and card. They display these beside their photographs. Over the coming days they enjoy sharing stories about their families, pets and outings. Joan observes the children during their activities and ensures that Joseph is included and that he is beginning to form friendships. She updates Kathleen regularly on how he is settling in.

 Reflection: How much do the children and I know about each other's family life and community? (NCCA 2009b:23)

This example is used to assist us in considering how to include children from cultures that differ from our own. It illustrates the importance of taking time to talk with parents and to find out some key points of interest about the child, while at the same time not intruding too much into their privacy. It also points to the value of recognising what we don't know and finding ways to find out so that we too can learn in the process of preparing for new children. The example links to Aistear Aim 2: 'Children will have a sense of group identity where links with their family and community are acknowledged and extended' (NCCA 2009a:26) and to Learning Goal 3: 'In partnership with the adult, children will be able to share personal experiences about their own families and cultures, and come to know that there is a diversity in family structures, cultures and backgrounds' (NCCA 2009a:26). It is important to understand that the example illustrates how to respond initially to the arrival of a child with a different cultural background, and the activities described refer to settling-in activities. To really meet this aim and learning goal, adults need to be constantly alert to the possibilities for including relevant examples from all the cultures represented in a setting in all activities, materials and curricular areas. It will be an ongoing learning experience for all, including the adults.

This point creates a link to Síolta Standard 11: Professional Practice – 'Practising in a professional manner requires that individuals have skills, knowledge, values and attitudes appropriate to their role and responsibility within the setting. In addition, it requires regular reflection upon practice and engagement in supported, ongoing professional development' (CECDE 2006:81). This standard recognises the value of continuing professional development, which can be in the form of self-directed reading, team meetings and discussion, attendance at seminars, conferences, or training and education to achieve a credited award. There are five components under this standard and it is the last, Component 5, that is most relevant to this illustration: 'Adults demonstrate sensitivity, warmth and positive regard for children and their families' (CECDE 2006:85). This component challenges practitioners to consider why this is important and how it can best be achieved. The Signposts for Reflection include 11.5.1, 'How are individual children's efforts and ideas acknowledged and encouraged?', and 11.5.2, 'How do you communicate this information to parents and families?' (CECDE 2006:85). Guided by this component we are directed to consider Standard 5: Interactions – 'Fostering constructive interactions (child/child, child/adult and adult/adult) requires explicit policies, procedures and practice that emphasise the value of process and are based on mutual respect, equal partnership and sensitivity' (CECDE 2006:39). Of the five components, Component 5.3 is of particular relevance. It reads, 'The adult uses all aspects of the daily routine (both formal and informal) to interact sensitively and respectfully with the child' (CECDE 2006:43). Signpost for Reflection 5.3.3, 'How do you show the child that you enjoy developing your relationship with her/him through sensitive and responsive interactive play?', provides a useful context within which to consider how to expand your inclusionary practices to ensure that you are working effectively with all the children in your setting.

Finally, this example can also be considered under Síolta Standard 3: Parents and Families – 'Valuing and involving parents and families requires a proactive partnership approach evidenced by a range of clearly stated, accessible and implemented processes, policies and procedures' (CECDE 2006:31). Settings need to be proactive in including parents of children from different cultural backgrounds in their work, and there are often unexpected barriers to this, to which practitioners need to be sensitive. These barriers may relate to language, but they can also be about perceptions. It is important to make your setting as welcoming as possible to all, and this means altering it to accommodate change as necessary. Component 3.3: 'Staff are responsive and sensitive in the provision of information and support to parents in their key role in the learning and development of the child' (CECDE 2006:34) expands on this point and asks further, 'How do you provide information for parents?' (3.3.1). This Signpost for Reflection, and others, highlights the need for a regular review of information so that it is meaningful to all parents.

LEARNING AND DEVELOPING THROUGH INTERACTIONS

Illustration 3
- Aim 1 and Learning Goal 6
- Age Group: Babies
- Setting: Home

Mommy is at home with baby Aoife (sixteen months). It is wintertime. She is about to dress Aoife so that they can walk to school with her older daughter Lorraine. Aoife leads Mommy to where she spotted a pair of summer shorts the day before and indicates that she wants to put them on. Mommy tries to explain that the shorts aren't suitable for a cold winter's day. She makes 'brrr' sounds and rubs her legs to warm up. She points to warmer clothes, smiles and nods, and explains that these will be cosy and warm for Aoife today. Then Mommy offers Aoife the choice of wearing her navy jumper and jeans or her purple tracksuit. Mommy observes Aoife's reaction and as soon as she shows an interest in the tracksuit Mommy responds: 'So, you would like to wear your tracksuit today, Aoife. Oh, it will keep you nice and warm, I wish I had a fleecy one like this.' Aoife then smiles and nods her head. When they are outside, Mommy repeats the 'brrr' sounds and describes how cold it is. Aoife's smile tells Mommy that she understands.

 Reflection: What opportunities can I use to give children choices within reasonable limits? (NCCA 2009b:40)

Aistear and Síolta were both designed for use by and with parents in the home as well as specifically for practitioners in other early years settings. This example focuses specifically on the home and locates itself under Aistear Aim 1 and Learning Goal 6. Aim 1: 'Children will have strong self-identities and will feel respected and affirmed as unique individuals with their own life stories' (NCCA 2009a:26) and Learning Goal 6: 'In partnership with the adult, children express their own ideas, preferences and needs and have these responded to with respect and consistency' (NCCA 2009a:26) highlight the importance of respecting children's preferences – even if the children are very young and their preferences are expressed non-verbally – while at the same time having regard to the necessities of the situation, in this case the need to dress up in cold weather even if the child's preference is for summer clothing. The mother in this example acknowledges the child's preference for inappropriate clothing and encourages the child to attend to more appropriate clothing while offering a choice. In this way she allows the child some control over the clothes she wears and reinforces the appropriateness of the selection of a tracksuit.

The Síolta standards that support this as an example of quality practice include Standard 5: Interactions – 'Fostering constructive interactions (child/child; child/adult; adult/adult) requires explicit policies, procedures and practice that emphasise the value of process and are based on mutual respect, equal partnership and sensitivity' (CECDE 2006:39) – even though parents are unlikely to have written policies and procedures. In particular it is the fourth component that relates most accurately to the example: Component 5.4: 'The adult interactive style is focused on process as opposed to outcomes. It is balanced between talking and listening, offers the child a choice of responses and encourages expanded use of language. It follows the child's lead and interests, and challenges the child appropriately' (CECDE 2006:44). The key point is about respect and balance – respect for the child's preference with a balance that takes account of the greater experience of the adult in a manner that is respectful to the child. This is also in line with Standard 1: Rights of the Child – 'Ensuring that each child's rights are met requires that she/he is enabled to exercise choice and to use initiative as an active participant and partner in her/his own development and learning' (CECDE 2006:13) and in particular Component 1.1: 'Each child has opportunities to make choices, is enabled to make decisions, and has her/his choices and decisions respected'

(CECDE 2006:14). In reading through the Signposts for Reflection under this component I have chosen 1.1.3: 'How do you foster each child's sense of control over her/his daily experiences and activities?' to provide a context for greater review and discussion on this topic, so important for those working with young children under three years. The reference to 'a sense of control' reflects the importance of interactions that assist the development of this skill, recognised as one of the central elements of executive function, which we know is crucial to adaptive behaviours that underpin successful social, emotional and intellectual development.

Illustration 4

- Aim 3 and Learning Goal 6
- Age Group: Toddlers
- Setting: Childminding

Jean, a childminder, works four days a week looking after four children, two school-going age and two pre-school age. She is playing in the garden with two sisters, Aoife (two years and nine months) and Siobhán (nearly four years). Jean steps in to help the sisters sort out their problem about sharing the dolls' clothes, as Aoife is becoming very frustrated. She asks the girls what the problem is and then asks for suggestions on how to deal with it. After some discussion the girls agree to divide the clothes between them. Jean stays with the girls and talks to them about what they are doing. She encourages them to help each other and she asks Siobhán to help Aoife put the socks on her baby doll. Jean suggests that they might pack the clothes and take the dolls on a holiday in the lovely sunny weather. Jean brings out the baby bath and the girls pretend it's a swimming pool for the dolls in sunny Spain. She encourages and acknowledges their efforts at playing together and they have great fun, ending up having a water fight between themselves and Jean!

 Reflection: How can I help children to work together in solving problems and resolving conflicts? (NCCA 2009b:49)

There are a number of important points to note in this example, including: the value of mixed age groups playing and learning together; the guiding role that adults can take; and the value of allowing for messy play – particularly in outdoor play. This illustration is presented as exemplifying key points of Aistear's Aim 3: 'Children will be able to express their rights and show an understanding and regard for the identity, rights and views of others' (NCCA 2009a:26) and Learning Goal 6: 'In the partnership with the adult, children will demonstrate the skills of cooperation, responsibility, negotiation and conflict resolution' (NCCA 2009a:26). The illustration provides an example of how to help children develop negotiation skills, to stand back from a problem and consider how they might address it. With the guidance of a respectful adult who models different possible solutions, children can sharpen their problem-solving and negotiation skills in a safe and supportive environment.

There are a number of Síolta standards that could be considered in line with this particular example, for instance Standard 5: Interactions – 'Fostering constructive interactions (child/child; child/adult; adult/adult) requires explicit policies, procedures and practice that emphasise the value of process and are based on mutual respect, equal partnership and sensitivity' (CECDE 2006:39). A number of components could be selected for reflection, and I have chosen Component 5.6: 'There is a clear written policy and associated procedures which underpin interactive practice taking place within the setting' (CECDE 2006:46) by way of example. There are six Signposts for Reflection and all are key to the illustration above: Signpost 5.6.3 – 'What procedures have you put in place to deal with unacceptable behaviour from the child?' – provides a number of Think Abouts that could usefully guide individual reflection and team discussion on practice in this area.

Standard 2: Environments – 'Enriching environments, both indoor and outdoor (including materials and equipment) are well-maintained, safe, available, accessible, adaptable, developmentally appropriate and offer a variety of challenging and stimulating experiences' (CECDE 2006:19) is also relevant to the example. Of particular importance is Component 2.7: 'There is an appropriate amount of equipment and materials within the setting (both indoors and outdoors) for use by individual children and groups of children' (CECDE 2006:27); and Signpost for Reflection 2.7.2: 'How do the equipment and materials ensure that the changing learning needs of each child are met?' is particularly useful for expanding reflection. Standard 6: Play – 'Promoting play requires that each child has ample time to engage in freely available and accessible, developmentally appropriate and well-resourced opportunities for exploration, creativity and "meaning making" in the company of other children, with participating and supportive adults and alone, where appropriate' (CECDE 2006:49) is also a valuable standard under which to consider the example, particularly given the role of the adult in guiding and extending the play opportunities for the two sisters through the provision of additional material and an idea for extending the play. Under Standard 6, Component 6.3 – 'The opportunities for play/exploration provided for the child mirror her/his stage of development, give the child the freedom to achieve mastery and success, and challenge the child to make the transition to new learning and development' (CECDE 2006:52) – allows for considering a number of elements of the illustration above. Signposts for Reflection 6.3.2, 'What range of opportunities are you providing for the child so that she/he can fully explore this type of play?', and 6.3.3, 'How are these opportunities giving the child a sense of control and of being competent?' challenge practitioners to review practice and consider how practice can be improved.

LEARNING AND DEVELOPING THROUGH PLAY

> ### *Illustration 5*
>
> - Aim 1 and Learning Goal 6
> - Age Group: Babies
> - Setting: Childminding
>
> Tess (fourteen months) is a shy little girl who is very sensitive to noise. She becomes upset easily and doesn't like to play with toys that pop up or that make music. She is also very apprehensive about being around other children. Her childminder, Anna, is aware of this and has made a cosy corner for Tess that is away from noise and bustle where she can play happily with books, blocks and soft toys. Gradually Anna introduces Tess to new, more interactive toys. If this upsets Tess Anna puts them away and reassures her. She also supports her in interacting with the other baby she looks after, fifteen-month-old Amy. Sometimes Anna sits with Tess and Amy in the cosy corner. Anna introduces a teapot and cups to the girls and they pretend to have a tea party together. The girls pretend to drink from the cups and Anna gives Teddy some tea too. Tess imitates her and then offers her cup to Amy. Anna pours some more tea for the girls and she talks softly about what is happening. Sometimes Tess shows her enjoyment by smiling and displaying positive body language; at other times she begins to cry and indicates that she wants to play on her own.
>
> *Reflection:* How can I help children who are shy or quiet to engage and play with others? (NCCA 2009b:62)

In this illustration we are presented with a situation that requires a good deal of sensitivity to the child while at the same time recognising the value of interactions to learning and development. It is presented under Aistear's Aim 1: 'Children will have strong self-identities and will feel respected and affirmed as unique individuals with their own life stories' (NCCA 2009a:26) and Learning Goal 6: 'In partnership with the adult, children express their own ideas, preferences and needs and have these responded to with respect and consistency' (NCCA 2009a:26). You might notice that Illustration 3 is presented under the same aim and learning goal. This is not unexpected, as it deals with babies in a home-like setting, but the difference here is that the example is illustrating 'Learning and development through play' rather than 'Learning and developing through interactions'. In line with this, different standards of quality practice are presented for consideration and reflection.

Síolta Standard 13: Transitions – 'Ensuring continuity of experiences for children requires policies, procedures and practice that promote sensitive management of transitions, consistency in key relationships, liaison within and between settings, the keeping and transfer of relevant information (with parental consent), and the close involvement of parents and, where appropriate, relevant professionals' (CECDE 2006:91). This standard refers to a number of different types of transition; in the example above the practitioner is managing transitions within the setting – encouraging Tess to move into social situations with another young child and to begin to play with noisier, more interactive toys. This standard has four components and it is the first that seems most appropriate to the example: Component 13.1: 'Smooth transitions are facilitated and promoted through the provision of consistent key relationships within the setting' highlights the importance of the adult and her style of interaction (CECDE 2006:93). Anna's presence and availability to Tess is central to the development of her confidence; at the same time she remains available to other children in the setting and this is captured in the Signpost for Reflection 13.1.1, 'How does the setting support consistent key relationships for children?', along with the Think About, 'Ensuring sensitivity to the child's needs at transition times throughout the day'. This Think About guides the reader to Standard 5 and Component 5.3, reflecting the importance of interactions. Standard 5: Interactions – 'Fostering constructive interactions (child/child; child/adult; adult/adult) requires explicit policies, procedures and practice that emphasise the value of process and are based on mutual respect, equal partnership and sensitivity' (CECDE 2006:39). Of the components associated with this standard it is Component 5.3, 'The adult uses all aspects of the daily routine (both formal and informal) to interact sensitively and respectfully with the child' (CECDE 2006:43), that is most relevant. In addition there are components in Standard 7 that are important to consider. Standard 7: Curriculum – 'Encouraging each child's holistic development and learning requires the implementation of a verifiable, broad-based, documented and flexible curriculum or programme' (CECDE 2006:55) directs reflection to the curriculum/programme of a given setting. In the example above there is a routine outlined and it is clear that Anna is working to a particular vision for children and to a curricular framework. Under this standard there are six components and it is Component 7.6: 'Planning for curriculum or programme implementation is based on the child's individual profile, which is established through systematic observation and assessment for learning' (CECDE 2006:61) that is most useful for reflection on practice, and the Think Abouts associated with Signpost for Reflection 7.6.1: 'What are the different elements of your system of child observation and assessment?' offer practitioners a valuable sample of key practices that can inform and improve practice.

Illustration 6

- Aim 4 and Learning Goal 3
- Age Group: Young children
- Setting: Infant class (primary school in the Gaeltacht)

During a series of drama lessons a group of children in junior and senior infants and their teacher, Múinteoir Síle, set up a market stall in the pretend play areas. Many of the children visit the local farmers' market on Saturday mornings with their parents and mention it during news time. Múinteoir Síle gets play props, including writing materials and money, empty food containers and jars. She clears the display table and uses this as a counter. The children take on different roles and ask Múinteoir Síle to be a customer. Over the next few days they bring one-, two-, five- and ten-cent coins to school for buying the produce. The play develops during the week as groups of children set up more specialised stalls. Space in the classroom for stalls begins to pose a problem. Múinteoir Síle suggests that they could rearrange the tables and chairs to make room. Excitedly, the children help her do this. Planning permission to extend the market is now in place! More and more stalls begin to appear as children make produce from play-dough and bring empty food cartons from home. They set up a stall selling their own paintings and flowers they are growing. They bring old toys and books from home and sell them to each other. They take turns playing customers and stall owners. Múinteoir Síle helps them to make signs for the different stalls. Some children make signs that show the price of their merchandise.

Múinteoir Síle sends a note home telling the parents what the children are doing and invites them to visit the children's market when they drop off or collect the children. She videos some of the play episodes. On another day she uses the market to pose a problem for the children; she wonders aloud how she can use the coins she has to pay for a 5¢ plant (junior infants) or a 10¢ plant (senior infants). With each child handling, observing and exploring real coins (1¢, 2¢, 5¢ and 10¢), she encourages the children to explore the combinations they could use to pay for the plants.

 Reflection: How can I use pretend play to a greater extent to develop children's literacy and numeracy skills? (NCCA 2009b:64)

This is a complex example of a complex situation. In the first instance it is located in a school setting and it incorporates a mixed age group of children, which could cover ages from four to six years. In addition, there are many possibilities to guide learning across a range of curricular aims such as motor development, various literacy and numeracy skills, alongside creativity across a range of arts. The example can only illustrate a small sample and for this reason it would be worth taking time to consider it in more detail and identify where and how other learning opportunities could be developed. The illustration is presented under Aim 4: 'Children will see themselves as capable learners' and Learning Goal 3: 'In partnership with the adult, children will show increasing confidence and self-assurance in directing their own learning' (NCCA 2009a:26).

The practitioner in the example stands back a great deal and only becomes involved to offer suggestions that the children can then consider or solutions they can apply. The example can be linked into the Síolta Standard 7: Curriculum – 'Encouraging each child's holistic development and learning requires the implementation of a verifiable, broad-based, documented and flexible curriculum or programme' (CECDE 2006:55). Given the setting for this example, we can assume that the practitioner is implementing Aistear principles in the context of the primary school curriculum and this would be seen as a 'verifiable, broad-based, documented and flexible curriculum'. Under this standard it is Component 7.1 – 'It is evident that the child's learning and development are holistic experiences and processes, that play is central to integrated learning and development and to curriculum/programme implementation' (CECDE 2006:57) that offers rich opportunities for reflection and review. Given this I have selected two different Signposts for Reflection under this component. At 7.1.2 we are asked to consider, 'In thinking of a child engaged in a particular activity, which aspects of learning and development are being integrated?' A selection of possible aspects for further development/learning is provided and offers a good basis from which to explore the illustration in more detail. Signpost for Reflection 7.1.9 is also useful; it asks us, 'Is the curriculum/programme you are implementing likely to result in you approaching the child's learning and development from a "subject" based perspective or from a "thematic" perspective?' In this particular example there is the opportunity to consider an integrated approach that addresses some of the subjects in the primary curriculum within the context of the thematic activity that is described.

In addition to Standard 7, the illustration can also be considered in relation to Standard 11: Professional Practice – 'Practising in a professional manner requires that individuals have skills, knowledge, values and attitudes appropriate to their role and responsibility within the setting. In addition, it requires regular reflection upon practice and engagement in supported, ongoing professional development' (CECDE 2006:81). Under this standard, Component 11.2 – 'All adults subscribe to a set of core principles, which inform all aspects of their practice in early childhood care and education settings' (CECDE 2006:83) – is a good basis from which to reflect on the principles that might be underpinning the curriculum that is guiding the example above, particularly in respect of dimensions of identity and belonging. Taking this example it is also useful to consider practices in your own setting and compare the issues that arise.

STRUCTURED LEARNING AND DEVELOPMENT THROUGH ASSESSMENT

Illustration 7

- Aim 3 and Learning Goal 3
- Age Group: Toddlers
- Setting: Sessional service (playgroup)

Patrick, Zyta and Johnny (each almost three years) are making a big tower. They talk to Aileen, the playgroup leader, about it and occasionally invite her to add a block or two to their construction while warning her to be careful! Johnny explains that they made it because he and Patrick (cousins) stayed in a big hotel on their holidays that was like a tower. 'It's 'normous [enormous] tower, isn't it, and we made it all by ourselves,' Patrick notes, looking at Aileen. Zyta draws Aileen's attention to the coloured blocks they used in the tower and comments: 'It's got loads o' [of] colours like red and green and orange and . . . and it could win a big medal.' Johnny adds, 'We did a good job.' Aileen suggests she could photograph the children with their tower. Using the digital camera, computer and printer, Aileen makes three copies of the photograph, and offers the children the opportunity to include them in their portfolios. Alongside the photograph, she writes each child's comment about the tower. The children tell Aileen that they'd like to add the photographs and comments to their learning portfolios. Meanwhile, Aileen makes some notes in her practitioner's file about each child's concentration on detail in building the tower and their ability to work together.

Through previous observations and conversations with Zyta, Aileen knows she is competitive and likes to be 'the best'. While Zyta's reference to getting a medal here reinforces this assessment, Aileen records how working collaboratively with Patrick and Johnny seemed to lessen her wish for Aileen to comment on how 'good' the tower was and what a great job she had done in building it. Aileen makes a note on her weekly plan to create more opportunities for co-operative learning for Zyta.

 Reflection: Do I create a climate in which children feel confident to make decisions about what should go in their learning portfolios? (NCCA 2009b:82)

Coming under the assessment guideline, it is no surprise that this illustration focuses on the use of pedagogical documentation in the form of Aileen's practitioner's file and the children's learning portfolios. The example comes under Aim 3: 'Children will be able to express their rights and show an understanding and regard for the identity, rights and views of others' and Learning Goal 3: 'In partnership with the adult, children will interact, work cooperatively and help others' (NCCA 2009a:26) and gives a detailed illustration of how three children can work together and call on the expertise of the practitioner as necessary. It also shows how the practitioner can assist the co-operative work and add to the pleasure of the experience through recording it: the recording offers material for the children's learning portfolios while also giving Aileen the opportunity to observe their actions closely and make notes to inform her future practice.

This example illustrates a number of the Síolta standards. To begin with, Standard 1: Rights of the Child – 'Ensuring that each child's rights are met requires that she/he is enabled to exercise choice and to use initiative as an active participant and partner in her/his own development and learning' (CECDE 2006:13) explicitly captures the importance of recognising and respecting the rights of the child if their rights are to be realised in early years settings. Exploring this standard in more detail we see that it has three components and for the purpose of this illustration I have chosen to draw attention to Component 1.1: 'Each child has opportunities to make choices, is enabled to make decisions and has her/his choices and decisions respected' (CECDE 2006:15). Signpost for Reflection 1.1.3 is worth considering in greater detail: 'How do you foster each child's sense of control over her/his daily experiences and activities?' In the Think Abouts associated with this signpost we are asked to consider a variety of different points, such as the extent to which we provide opportunities for the child to make decisions or to review their own plans and activities. Standard 14: Identity and Belonging – 'Promoting positive identities and a strong sense of belonging requires clearly defined policies, procedures and practice that empower every child and adult to develop a confident self- and group-identity, and to have a positive understanding and regard for the identity and rights of others' (CECDE 2006:95) is also relevant to this example as it captures the importance of the adult in creating a sense of belonging and group identity while at the same time recognising characteristics of individual identity (as in the case of Zyta). Component 14.2: 'The setting promotes a confident self- and group-identity through the provision of an appropriate environment, experiences and interactions within the setting' (CECDE 2006:97) allows us to reflect on how this is achieved in the setting above, and the Signposts for Reflection offer different ways in which such quality practice can be sustained and expanded. Finally, Standard 5: Interactions – 'Fostering constructive interactions (child/child; child/adult; adult/adult) requires explicit policies, procedures and practice that emphasise the value of process and are based on mutual respect, equal partnership and sensitivity' (CECDE 2006:39) is also relevant to this illustration and it provides a number of important components, including Component 5.4: 'The adult interactive style is focused on process as opposed to outcomes. It is balanced between talking and listening, offers the child a choice of responses and encourages expanded use of language. It follows the child's lead and interests and challenges the child appropriately' (CECDE 2006:44). This component has a wide range of important Signposts for Reflection; however, I will reference only one here. Signpost for Reflection 5.4.17 poses the following question: 'In your interactions with the child, what process characteristics do you emphasise?' and offers a selection of Think Abouts that offer a good basis for personal reflection on practice and for team discussion on both practice and curriculum or programme.

While the illustrations above have presented opportunities to link specific samples of daily practice with the standards of Síolta and the learning goals of Aistear, they do not directly present ideas for achieving the aims of Aistear under the theme of Identity and Belonging. Attention to actual practice can be found in a series of Sample Learning Opportunities in the Aistear document. The suggestions are set out according to age groups and provide useful ideas on how to really look at your own practice and check it for its potential in supporting children to develop a strong sense of personal identity and belonging. Below I present the main practice styles suggested for maximising children's learning opportunities under the theme Identity and Belonging. The content of the situations derives from the children and the adults and will be unique to each opportunity that presents itself. When considering how to carry through these suggestions you will be greatly assisted by applying your knowledge and understanding of child development, relevant research and the processes that assist learning and development most appropriately for individual children. The ages act as a guide, but they are overlapping in order to capture the reality that children have different developmental trajectories across aspects of development.

- When working with babies – birth to eighteen months – practitioners should:
  - closely observe babies, know their personalities well, respect and respond to their individual needs and preferences, and build on care practices from home
  - support babies' emerging sense of identity
  - provide opportunities for older siblings, peers and babies to see one another and to be together at different times during the day, optimising opportunities that will enable them to interact and communicate
  - provide babies with experiences of the outside world.
- When working with toddlers – twelve months to three years – practitioners should:
  - play with and observe toddlers and take account of their interests, needs, rights and wishes
  - spend one-to-one time with toddlers to make them feel special and valued
  - use resources and materials that reflect toddlers' families, genders, abilities, backgrounds and cultures
  - facilitate activities that encourage toddlers to interact and play with others
  - support toddlers in beginning to manage their behaviour appropriately and to know what behaviour is acceptable
  - ensure that both boys and girls are encouraged to explore, take risks, enjoy challenge and to take on caring roles.

- When working with young children – 2½ years to six years – practitioners should:
  - support young children to think about themselves, who they are, and their strengths, interests and abilities
  - create multiple opportunities for young children to talk, listen and be heard whenever possible with peers, with adults or in small groups
  - use pretend play and support children to empathise with others and see things from another's point of view
  - adapt routines to cater for individual needs, interests, preferences and capabilities
  - create a language environment that reflects the languages of all the children and adults in the setting
  - develop young children's awareness of the community in which they live.

(NCCA 2009a:27–32)

SUMMARY

The focus of this chapter was practice in a variety of settings with particular attention to how these settings met the ambitions of the Aistear theme of Identity and Belonging. The chapter highlighted the distinction between identity and belonging while at the same time emphasising their interconnectedness. It also discussed the need to actively respect diversity and pointed to the fact that we are all part of the diversity of the community to which we belong and we all strive to maintain our identity therein. The importance of reflecting on our personal responses to difference was noted and the value of exploring such responses with colleagues was mentioned. Some practical examples of how to enhance children's developing sense of personal identity and belonging were suggested.

You will notice that the focus of the learning opportunities and practice examples presented is on the practitioner and child/children relationship, the quality of listening and communicating and the provision of opportunities from within the ordinary and the lived experiences of the children and adults who make up the learning environment. The opportunities require the practitioner to be attuned and sensitive to the learning possibilities that arise in the most ordinary of events. They challenge you to take your time, to give plenty of time and to use time carefully. There are many opportunities presented for capturing the learning moments that arise when individual children are concentrating on a task or when a group of children are playing a game, solving a problem or messing about. Most of all, the examples reflect the democratic nature of excellent early years practice, a practice that respects all children, that celebrates difference, that listens to children and hears them, that engages children in conversations, facilitates conversations between children and that provides a context where they grow and belong and develop a strong personal identity in keeping with their own lives and the world in which we all live.

CHAPTER 6

Communicating

Oh the comfort, the inexpressible comfort of feeling safe with a person, having neither to weigh thoughts nor measure words, but pouring them all right out, just as they are – chaff and grain together. (Craik:1859)

Human beings are born with the desire and the ability to communicate in many different ways about our ideas, feelings and opinions, and about facts. Communication is a two-way process of giving and receiving information. Children communicate from birth and they do so both verbally and non-verbally. They communicate their feelings, their wants, their ideas, their fears and hopes and they do so through their body language, particularly when very young, and later through sounds, talking, crying, laughing. They also communicate through expression, dance, drama, gesture, information and communication technology (ICT) and in some cases through Braille or sign language. The many ways in which children communicate is captured evocatively in the title of a book written about the preschool practices of Reggio Emilia – *The Hundred Languages of Children* (Edwards, Gandini & Forman 1995).

The act of communicating 'involves giving, receiving and making sense of information' (NCCA 2009a:34). The ability and facility to communicate is essential to learning and development and careful communication helps children 'learn to think about and make sense of their world' (NCCA 2009a:12). To learn how to communicate through language, children need to develop in a social context with other language users. We know from studies of children brought up in the wild (feral children) that in the absence of human language as a source they do not acquire appropriate language skills, even though they do find ways to communicate. The adults in the lives of young children are a particularly important source of guidance on how, what, when and where to communicate. Children who grow up in bilingual or multilingual environments communicate successfully in all the available languages as long as they have good models in each language. As well as environmental factors, children's own abilities influence the development of their communicating skills. For early years practitioners it is important to understand the unfolding of communication skills in children so that you can adjust your own communicating style to meet the individual needs of a particular child or group of children. This also assists in identifying any early signs of language difficulties or delays. It is, however, important to bear in mind that children's developmental paths can vary a lot in early childhood, so not all children will be at the same stage of development on all dimensions. Where you do suspect a difficulty or a delay, particularly if you are considering outside help for the child, it is useful to collect clear evidence to support your concern and discuss your views with a colleague before deciding on a final course of action.

Communication has an important interpersonal dimension and a content dimension. At the interpersonal level the adult models the behaviour appropriate to communication, such as eye contact, active listening and attentive responses. At the content level the early years practitioner selects the level of detail, the choice of words, the type of information and the extent of new vocabulary to introduce and bases this on knowledge about the child or children. In early childhood the learning environments that children inhabit – the adults, other children, objects, materials and space therein – provide the source of these interpersonal and content dimensions. Effective early years practice requires that practitioners build up the content from within the context. It is the role of the early years practitioner to work with the children to make meaning from the 'dictionary of experiences' (Rinaldi 2006) available and to make the most of this. This will provide children with the opportunity to reflect, infer, hypothesise and understand. The style of the language used by the adult is also important. Rather than saying, 'Oh, that's lovely' in response to some activity or process, you show more engaging communication if you say, '*You* did this and it is . . . '. This approach can be used with children of all ages and it shows an interest in the child and their activity and further supports the child's sense of belonging. It can also help develop a child's vocabulary and draw attention to more advanced grammatical structure.

Good practitioners recognise the important role they play in supporting young children in the development of their communication skills. Through timely responsiveness to the gestures of a baby they are helping the child learn the basis for communication. The baby learns that certain gestures or vocalisations yield a response and that the response may be either positive or negative. Picking up a child who reaches out to you, looking directly at her, smiling and chatting as you do so, conveys a positive reaction and sends a clear message to the child that she is cherished, she is important and she belongs. Older children want to talk, to share their ideas, their discoveries and their queries, and to do so they need time. Practitioners who find the time, who make eye contact, are helping the child to recognise active listening and are signalling to the child that they and their opinions, ideas or questions matter. Conversations can be extended by careful open-ended questions and vocabulary can be extended when you provide new or additional words to help a story flow.

It is also important to understand non-verbal communication, and children may need help in recognising and reading such signals from others. An attentive adult will find opportunities to explain body language so that children become more attuned to the breadth and meaning of communications. When communicating with young children – even very young children – practitioners can also take opportunities to help children name their feeling. A crying baby can be consoled in a soft voice, which explains to them that 'You're hungry' or 'You're tired.' Older children can use the names you put on their feelings – 'You're sad,' 'You're happy' or 'You're angry' – to help develop their own understanding of emotions and to move on. Extending communication skills can also occur where practitioners act as a good role model and make conscious attempts to narrate or talk through their (or children's) routine activities, for example 'I'm preparing the table' or 'I'm tidying up.' By providing opportunities for pretend play you also help the development of communication, as children often find a voice with other children in the safety of play. Through careful observations of such play activities it is possible to learn a great deal about how skilled children are at communicating. Finally, practitioners must be clear and distinct when requesting children to carry out some task or activity. Be sure to catch the child's attention through touch or eye contact and then make the request in simple sentences to assist their understanding.

The quality of communication influences the quality of children's learning. For instance, the quality of communication in joint attention to an activity can enhance the experience: joint attention is 'an encounter between two individuals in which the participants pay joint attention to, and jointly act on some external topic' (Schaffer 1992:101). Joint activity of this sort is recognised as a valuable site for learning in the early years. Siraj-Blatchford and her colleagues, in studying quality joint activity between early years practitioners and children, identified 'sustained, shared thinking' as having a particularly powerful impact on children's development and learning. The term 'sustained shared thinking' captures the idea of time being important to the process, time being given to engage meaningfully in the joint activity. It is characterised as 'an effective pedagogic interaction where two or more individuals 'work together' in an intellectual way to solve a problem, clarify a concept, evaluate activities or extend a narrative (Siraj-Blatchford & Manni 2008:7). Thus communication that takes place to facilitate sustained shared thinking, the questioning, the adapting, the negotiation, enhance the development of the executive functions which form the basis for positive learning and enhance the dispositions to learn. Clear and attuned communication that is respectful in both directions offers a fertile space for the development and refinement of executive functions.

COMMUNICATING WITH PARENTS

In the early years setting practitioners have a dual role: the direct impact on the child in the setting from day to day; and the indirect impact on the child through supporting parents in understanding their children's development. A quality learning environment for children is enriched where there is a good relationship between the home and the setting. This provides a reasonably stable context within which children can strengthen their learning and development across multiple environments. It also assists children to develop and broaden their sense of identity and competence and overall sense of belonging. Communicating with parents about why quality early years experiences are so important to their children's development and learning, and helping parents recognise what such experiences look like in early years settings are important tasks for practitioners, particularly as many parents are unaware of the significance of quality to their children's development.

We know from the work of Bronfenbrenner and others that the most central influence on the child is that of their immediate environment, the microsystem, which is any individual setting, for example the home or the early years setting. The people in these settings have the most immediate effect on the child, and if the relationships within and across these immediate settings break down it can cause the child difficulty. The relational network with others, consisting of linkages between any of the various settings in which the child spends time, is particularly important, and can exert an influence over the child in subtle ways, for example if early years practitioners and parents have differences of opinion on the education of the child. Consistency and continuity between the two settings is in the best interest of the child and requires that both work in partnership with the interests of the child at the forefront of their minds. The visible inclusion of their family in the early years setting, and positive interactions between practitioners and parents, creates a sense of inclusion as well as of belonging; it strengthens the link to activities that could be followed through into the home learning environment (HLE); it improves two-way access to information; and it encourages appropriate ambitions for the child.

Early experiences support a vast array of children's communication skills, including their awareness of verbal and non-verbal communication; their knowledge of sound, pattern, rhythm and repetition; their awareness of symbols such as print and pictures; the opportunities they have to become familiar with and enjoy print in a meaningful way; and the opportunities they have to use mark-making materials. These broad communication skills in turn play a key role in the development of their literacy skills. Furthermore, children's awareness of materials, shape, space, pattern and difference, classifying, matching, comparing and ordering are important for the development of numeracy. The knowledge, skills, attitudes and dispositions developed in these early years impact significantly on their later learning experiences. Research has shown how important the quality of home and early years environments (socially and materially) is to children's dispositions to be actively literate and numerate. Where families are actively involved in literacy and numeracy activities children develop larger vocabularies, faster vocabulary growth and better cognitive abilities than children from homes with less engaged parents.

Literacy and numeracy are key elements of communication. Improving literacy and numeracy standards is an urgent national priority and in 2011 the Department of Education and Skills published *Literacy and Numeracy for Learning and Life: The National Strategy to Improve Literacy and Numeracy among Children and Young People 2011–2020* (DES 2011). The strategy identified six key areas of for action among those working in the education sector, including those in the early years:

1   Enabling parents/communities to support literacy/numeracy development.
2   Improving teacher and early childhood education and care professional practice through in-service and pre-service training.
3   Building the capacity of school leadership.
4   Getting the content of literacy right at primary and secondary level.
5   Targeting resources to special areas of need.
6   Improving the use of assessment processes.

Literacy development usually occurs naturally through hearing, imitating and observing others. Reading and writing (being literate) can be encouraged through experiencing reasons to read and write. Early years practitioners have a critical role in literacy and numeracy development, both directly and indirectly. Practitioners have a direct influence on children in the early years setting through the provision of literacy- and numeracy-promoting environments: offering opportunities for extensive engagement with these materials; making literacy visible through carefully considered pedagogical documentation inclusive of a number of children; using materials to extend vocabulary; encouraging conversation and active listening. Practitioners also have an indirect influence on children through their work with families, such as: sharing pedagogical documentation; offering book lending schemes; sharing particular interests of individual children; and being sensitive to literacy needs of parents – particularly those for whom English is a second language. Early years practitioners contribute to improved general literacy and numeracy by ensuring that their practice in settings is facilitating the development of the underlying skills necessary to later literacy and numeracy competence: by fostering the enjoyment of story and narrative through storytelling, conversation, dialogues, reading stories and listening actively to stories read aloud; by creating awareness of the language of number and its everydayness; by promoting interest and enjoyment of literacy and numeracy activities to encourage an improved attitude to reading, writing and numbers; and by working with parents and other professionals to raise public awareness of the importance of oral language and listening skills to later literacy.

The strategy identifies the early years as an important stage for the implementation of the strategy and recognises the important role that practitioners can play. In referencing both Síolta and Aistear, the strategy points out that 'the introduction of these frameworks in recent years, together with the higher qualifications being demanded within state-supported provision, has resulted in new opportunities to focus on supporting early literacy and numeracy in the full range' (DES 2011:28). In its outcomes for the strategy it sees the early years as having a key role in improving 'the communication and oral-language competence of young children . . . and their readiness to develop early mathematical language and ideas' (DES 2011:17).

The strategy document also recognises that engagement with parents should be a core part of the literacy and numeracy plans of early years settings. They suggest that settings should be welcoming and accessible for parents and should make meaningful provision for the involvement of parents in the setting, and beyond, in activities that support the development of better literacy and numeracy skills. The strategy notes that all parents need to be aware of the relevance of literacy and numeracy for their children's future and the influence that they have over their children's educational development; and that parents with literacy difficulties need particular support.

Facilitating emergent literacy and numeracy can happen in the everyday activities of the setting; there is no need for formal activities such as workbooks or structured table-top exercises. It is far more effective to locate facilitation and promotion of literacy and numeracy skills within the familiar and the meaningful for the young child. Improving early years outcomes for children through improving oral language competence and developing the language of maths in young children in early years settings takes time, careful planning and a keen awareness in the practitioner of appropriate learning goals for individual children. Whitehurst and Lonigan (2001) provide some guidance on how both literacy and numeracy can be facilitated with young children in the day-to-day routines of an early years setting. They list the following strategies for developing the various skills required.

1   Language ability:
    * speak, listen and understand
    * increase vocabulary
    * increase comprehension of narrative through story and conversation.

2   Letter identification:
    * knowing letter sounds
    * recognising letters.

3   Phonological awareness:
    * identification of sounds of spoken language
    * manipulation of such sounds.

4   Understanding print
    * left to right
    * top to bottom
    * across and back the page

5   Literacy promotion
    * visible in the environment
    * not overcrowded or chaotic
    * child/adult literacy material through setting-generated written words
    * daily routine reading and writing associated with everyday activities and planning (by adults).

Our current understanding of literacy and numeracy development recognises that literacy skills (as opposed to skills of reading and writing) develop from birth, that there is a strong link between language development and literacy skills, and that early literacy experiences in the HLE and the early years setting influence children's lifelong attitude or disposition to reading. However, calls for early literacy and numeracy should not diminish attention to and investment in the development of personal capacities such as initiative, self-confidence, self-regulation, persistence, curiosity, love of learning, co-operativeness, conflict management and resolution.

Some examples of literacy activities

1 *Shared reading.* Vocabulary development, listening comprehension, understanding print concepts (such as reading from left to right and top to bottom of the page, importance of spaces in sentences, relationship between length of the written word and the sound of the word as well as the relationship between sound and letters).

2 *Book selection.* Relevant, age-appropriate material: babies love clear, bright pictures and novelty; older children like pictures with lots of detail.

3 *Reading style of the adult.* Pauses, expressions, repetition all contribute to the experience.

4 *Exposure to print.* Pedagogical documentation provides an inclusive context within which to create a literacy-rich (and numeracy-rich) environment. Carefully recording the child's own explanation of a photograph, a plan or a picture brings its meaning alive and shows the power of literacy when, for instance, the child shows it to another without the adult being present or guiding beyond suggestion, 'This is me when we . . .'

5 *Language games.* Naming, sentence completion, potential (and dangers) of computers. (Communicating through computer/text/Skype and so forth.)

6 *Songs and rhymes.* These are key for cadence and rhythm.

Communication is central to the creation of a learning community where both adults and children recognise themselves as learners. But it is not only communication that matters – it is the act of communicating; and this point is captured by the title Aistear gives to this theme, which is *Communicating*.

The table outlines the four Aistear aims for the Communicating theme and expands on them by reference to twenty-four learning goals.

AISTEAR'S AIMS AND LEARNING GOALS: COMMUNICATING

Communicating	
Aims	**Learning goals**
Aim 1 Children will use non-verbal communication skills	In partnership with the adult, children will 1 use a range of body movements, facial expressions, and early vocalisations to show feelings and share information 2 understand and use non-verbal communication rules, such as turn-taking and making eye contact 3 interpret and respond to non-verbal communication by others 4 understand and respect that some people will rely on non-verbal communication as their main way of interacting with others 5 combine non-verbal and verbal communication to get their point across 6 express themselves creatively and imaginatively using non-verbal communication.

...ed	Learning goals *continued*
...n 2 Children will use language	In partnership with the adult, children will 1 interact with other children and adults by listening, discussing and taking turns in conversation 2 explore sound, pattern, rhythm, and repetition in language 3 use an expanding vocabulary of words and phrases, and show a growing understanding of syntax and meaning 4 use language with confidence and competence for giving and receiving information, asking questions, requesting, refusing, negotiating, problem-solving, imagining and recreating roles and situations, and clarifying thinking, ideas and feelings 5 become proficient users of at least one language and have an awareness and appreciation of other languages 6 be positive about their home language, and know that they can use different languages to communicate with different people and in different situations.
Aim 3 Children will broaden their understanding of the world by making sense of experiences through language	In partnership with the adult, children will 1 use language to interpret experiences, to solve problems, and to clarify thinking, ideas and feelings 2 use books and ICT for fun, to gain information and broaden their understanding of the world 3 build awareness of the variety of symbols (pictures, print, numbers) used to communicate, and understand that these can be read by others 4 become familiar with and use a variety of print in an enjoyable and meaningful way 5 have opportunities to use a variety of mark-making materials and implements in an enjoyable and meaningful way 6 develop counting skills, and a growing understanding of the meaning and use of numbers and mathematical language in an enjoyable and meaningful way.
Aim 4 Children will express themselves creatively and imaginatively	In partnership with the adult, children will 1 share their feelings, thoughts and ideas by story-telling, making art, moving to music, role-playing, problem-solving, and responding to these experiences 2 express themselves through the visual arts using skills such as cutting, drawing, gluing, sticking, painting, building, printing, sculpting, and sewing 3 listen to and respond to a variety of types of music, sing songs and make music using instruments 4 use language to imagine and recreate roles and experiences 5 respond to and create literacy experiences through story, poetry, song, and drama 6 show confidence in trying out new things, taking risks, and thinking creatively.

Source: www.ncca.biz/Aistear/pdfs/PrinciplesThemes_ENG/PrinciplesThemes_ENG. pdf.

In the practice illustrations that follow, the theme of Communicating is considered across a variety of settings with a sample of children of different ages. These illustrations are intended as a starting point from which you can begin to take examples of your own day-to-day practice and reflect on them, alone or with colleagues, in the context of both Aistear and Síolta. This can form the basis for regularly reviewing your own practice, questioning the ethos of practice in your setting, and it can also provide a language with which you can consider the practice of others and explain your philosophy of practice as necessary. It should also present you with new questions and challenges, which in turn can enrich your practice, its effectiveness and your own professional satisfaction.

BUILDING PARTNERSHIPS BETWEEN PARENTS AND PRACTITIONERS

Illustration 1

- Aim 3 and Learning Goal 2
- Age Group: Young children
- Setting: Home and infant class (primary school)

Kara (four years) is in junior infants. Her parents left school early. They have difficulties with literacy and know this is a disadvantage. They really want Kara to do well in school and get a good education. But Kara says she doesn't like school. Kara and her family have the support of a home school community liaison co-ordinator, Betty. Betty encourages Kara's parents to talk to her teacher, Ms Nugent, and she suggests some questions they might ask. Ms Nugent encourages them to help Kara in whatever way they can. She suggests that they use a picture book to read a story or to tell her stories themselves about when they were children. They can draw pictures together at home and talk about them. If they have time they can come in some days and help out in the classroom.

Ms Nugent also encourages Kara in school by asking her what kind of books she likes to look at and read. Kara replies, 'Books about babies are good and books about dressing up and going to my friend's house.' Ms Nugent regularly uses books on these topics when reading stories to Kara and her friends. She puts dress-up clothes and props such as tiaras, dolls, buggies, and handbags in the pretend play area. Ms Nugent regularly talks to Kara's mam to see how they can continue to work together to support Kara at home and in school. Betty also regularly liaises with Ms Nugent and Kara's parents to ensure that Kara and her family have positive school experiences.

 Reflection: What can I do to give extra support and encouragement to some parents? (NCCA 2009b:12)

This vignette is presented under the Aistear theme of Communicating and relates specifically to Aim 3: 'Children will broaden their understanding of the world by making sense of experiences through language' and Learning Goal 2: 'In partnership with the adult, children will use books and ICT for fun, to gain information and broaden their understanding of the world' (NCCA 2009a:35). In the description above, the practitioner has seen the value of working closely with parents in developing an interest in stories and books so that Kara will be able to avail of the opportunities in the classroom to extend her language and literacy skills. She points to the value of picture books and of telling stories as an initial lead-in to stories. From stories she points to the value of drawing pictures, representations, and talking about them. In the meantime she is careful to introduce books and related play opportunities and maintains the link with the family.

This example can also be considered by reference to a number of Síolta standards. Standard 3: Parents and Family – 'Valuing and involving parents and families requires a proactive partnership approach evidenced by a range of clearly stated, accessible and implemented processes, policies and procedures' (CECDE 2006:31) points explicitly to the importance of parental involvement as an aspect of quality practice. Component 3.1: 'Staff and parents have both formal and informal opportunities for communication and information sharing about the child' (CECDE 2006:33) notes that there are informal as well as more formal ways in which to involve parents. Signpost for Reflection 3.1.1 asks, 'What kind of arrangements are in place to facilitate regular formal meetings between parents and staff?' while at Signpost for Reflection 3.1.4 we are asked to consider 'What kind of opportunities are in place for informal, regular conversations with parents?' Both signposts have a number of Think Abouts that provide useful ideas for review in light of the illustration above or with respect to your own practice experiences.

Standard 12: Communication – 'Communicating effectively in the best interests of the child requires policies, procedures and actions that promote the proactive sharing of knowledge and information among appropriate stakeholders with respect and confidentiality' (CECDE 2006:87) is also relevant to the illustration above, particularly given the focus of the practitioner's engagement with the parents and the sensitivities around their own literacy skills. Under this standard there are four components, all of which have some points appropriate to the example. Take Component 12.2: 'The setting is proactive in sharing information, as appropriate, in the best interests of the child, with other stakeholders' (in this instance the parents). How the information is shared needs to be carefully considered, and a good selection of suggestions are provided under Signpost for Reflection 12.2.2: 'How is information shared?' (CECDE 2006:89). One of these points relates specifically to information for parents and it redirects the reader to Standard 16: Community Involvement – 'Promoting community involvement requires the establishment of networks and connections evidenced by policies, procedures and actions which extend and support all adults' and children's engagement with the wider community' (CECDE 2006:105). This standard provides a context within which to consider supports and sources of information beyond the immediate setting. At Component 16.1: 'The setting has gathered and made available a comprehensive range of information on resources at local, regional and national levels', we are prompted to ask exactly what resources there are and how we can use them to maximum effect. Signpost for Reflection 6.1.1 – 'What information do you have available on the range of amenities, services and opportunities available at local, regional and national level that can be used to support and complement the goals and objectives of your service?'

– provides a variety of different professionals and community-based services that can be called on to support your work. In the example above, the practitioner avails of support from the home school community liaison co-ordinator in working with the parents. As the year progresses they can both record how Kara is getting on and together ensure that the parents are supported in creating an HLE that supports the work being done in the setting. We know from research that the HLE has a profound impact on how children learn and develop.

LEARNING AND DEVELOPING THROUGH INTERACTIONS

Illustration 2

- Aim 1 and Learning Goal 1
- Age Group: Babies
- Setting: Home

Leah (thirteen months) and her Dad are feeding the ducks at the lake. Leah is pointing towards the ducks animatedly. Her Dad points to the ducks and agrees, 'Yes they are ducks, Leah, and now we are going to feed them.' Leah points to the bread. Her Dad gives her some, smiles and comments, 'You like feeding them, don't you, Leah?' Leah nods. She babbles, 'kak, kak'. Her Dad affirms her contribution, 'The ducks say "quack, quack", don't they, Leah?' He recounts a rhyme about ducks and she claps her hands and points excitedly at the ducks while he does this.

 Reflection: How can I use everyday experiences to help children understand more about the things around them? (NCCA 2009b:32)

In this example we see how a rich learning experience can be made from a regular activity – walking and feeding the ducks. The dad in the example is finely tuned to Leah's behaviour and he builds on her behaviour (pointing to the ducks) and her vocalisations. Further, he extends the experience by reciting a rhyme – which can be returned to even when they are not looking at the ducks, and this will assist Leah in developing her working memory, an important element of our executive function. The example is linked to Aistear Aim 1: 'Children will use non-verbal communication skills' and Learning Goal 1: 'In partnership with the adult, children will use a range of body movements, facial expressions and early vocalisations to show feelings and share information' (NCCA 2009b:35). You can see how the learning goal is being addressed in the responses of the father, who takes every opportunity to encourage and expand Leah's vocalisations by responding in accurate language and – through the rhyme – expanding the words that can be associated with the experience of seeing, hearing and feeding the ducks.

This example can be linked to Síolta Standard 5: Interactions – 'Fostering constructive interactions (child/child; child/adult; adult/adult) requires explicit policies, procedures and practice that emphasise the value of process and are based on mutual respect, equal partnership and sensitivity' (CECDE 2006:39). We can see that the dad is showing respect and fostering the interaction so that it becomes a real learning experience and continues to be an enjoyable and not too taxing experience for the child. Under this standard we can consider Component 5.3: 'The adult uses all aspects of the daily routine (both formal and informal) to interact sensitively and respectfully with the child' (CECDE 2006:43) and, in particular, Signpost for Reflection 5.1.1 – 'What kind of daily interactions do you have with the child during your daily care routines?' Very often with young children there are rich learning and development opportunities in the most basic of routine activities. For the adult the challenge is to recognise and be engaged by these possibilities.

Síolta Standard 6: Play – 'Promoting play requires that each child has ample time to engage in freely available and accessible, developmentally appropriate and well-resourced opportunities for exploration, creativity and "meaning making" in the company of other children, with participating and supportive adults and alone, where appropriate' (CECDE 2006:49) is also useful in relation to this illustration because Leah is engaging in playful wordplay. Take, for instance, Component 6.3: 'The opportunities for play/exploration provided for the child mirror her/his stage of development, give the child the freedom to achieve mastery and success, and challenge the child to make the transition to new learning and development' (CECDE 2006:52). The dad in the example above uses the potential of the walk to feed the ducks to interact with Leah in a way that expands the experience for her in a playful way. Signpost for Reflection 6.3.3 asks, 'How are these opportunities giving the child a sense of control and of being competent?' You can see this where Leah gets excited at the rhyme and points to the ducks, showing that she recognises her role in the whole event. This idea of giving children a sense of competence, whatever their age, reflects the application of Standard 1: Rights of the Child – 'Ensuring that each child's rights are met requires that she/he is enabled to exercise choice and to use initiative as an active participant and partner in her/his own development and learning' (CECDE 2006:13). In particular it is an illustration in action of Component 1.2: 'Each child has opportunities and is enabled to take the lead, initiate activity, be appropriately independent and is supported to solve problems' (CECDE 2006:15). This is particularly useful as it is often difficult to put words to exactly how we can meet the rights of the very young child in practice. While we may feel that what we are doing is respectful and realising their rights, we do not always have the vocabulary to articulate this to parents or other professionals. Examples like the one above, which may at first glance appear very simple, are full of important quality early years practice.

Illustration 3

- Aim 1 and Learning Goal 3
- Age Group: Toddlers
- Setting: Childminding

Zoe (twenty months) can't do up her zip, so Emma, her childminder, asks Conor (nearly three years) to help her to do it. She observes from nearby to make sure that Conor is able to do up the zip and thanks him for his help. She asks Zoe and Conor if they would like to hold hands on the way out to the garden and supports them in playing together outside with the clothes pegs, which they give her as she hangs the clothes on the washing line. Spotting the doormat at the entrance to the utility room, Conor begins to attach pegs, making a decorative edge for the mat. Intrigued by what he is doing, Zoe joins him and together they empty Emma's clothes peg basket. Though Zoe has few words, her big smile and her body language show that she is clearly delighted to be playing with Conor.

 Reflection: Do children have lots of opportunities to spend and enjoy time with each other? (NCCA 2009b:48)

How easy it would have been for Emma to have speeded things up by quickly doing up Zoe's zip for her and directing her out into the garden – but what is the value of that? What would any of them have gained? While hanging out the washing is necessary, it is clear from the example that Emma recognises how important time is to children and allows them the freedom to move around and play with the everyday objects of pegs and the door mat. In this way she is nurturing their development and providing rich learning experience for them both. The illustration comes under Aistear's Aim 1: 'Children will use non-verbal communication skills' and Learning Goal 3: 'In partnership with the adult, children will interpret and respond to non-verbal communication by others' (NCCA 2009a:35). Sensitivity to body language is an important skill to develop as it may be the only way to assess the feelings and needs of very young children. In the example above, Emma judges that Zoe is content by reference to her body language.

This example is a good description of quality practice in a family home environment and it reflects Síolta Standard 7: Curriculum – 'Encouraging each child's holistic development and learning requires the implementation of a verifiable, broad-based, documented and flexible curriculum or programme' (CECDE 2006:55). It allows us to consider the breadth of possibilities that come under the term 'curriculum', a term not often thought appropriate for the day-to-day activities of children and adults in a home or family setting. And yet we see from the illustration the careful consideration given by Emma to assisting peer learning, her use of observation, her provision of guided learning opportunities and her sensitivity to the learning and development that is happening. All of these features reflect a learning environment that is understood and planned carefully by an adult who understands how young children develop. Component 7.3: 'The curriculum/programme is reflected in and implemented through the child's daily routine, spontaneous learning opportunities, structured activities and activities initiated by the child' (CECDE 2006:58) is also realised in this example. The activities described are clearly part of the daily routine and Emma is confident of the value of allowing Conor take the everyday objects of the door mat and pegs to extend his play and of including Zoe so that she can participate in the spontaneous learning opportunities provided by the everyday.

It also reflects Standard 6: Play – 'Promoting play requires that each child has ample time to engage in freely available and accessible, developmentally appropriate and well-resourced opportunities for exploration, creativity and "meaning making" in the company of other children, with participating and supportive adults and alone, where appropriate' (CECDE 2006:49) and, in particular, Component 6.2: 'When the child is engaged in play/exploration, the equipment and materials provided are freely available and easily accessible to her/him' (CECDE 2006:51). Although it is not stated explicitly, one can assume that Emma had enough clothes pegs to hang out all the washing while also allowing the children to play with as many pegs as they needed for their activity. Finally, it also reflects Standard 2: Environments – 'Enriching environments, both indoor and outdoor (including materials and equipment) are well-maintained, safe, available, accessible, adaptable, developmentally appropriate and offer a variety of challenging and stimulating experiences' (CECDE 2006:19) and the associated components.

LEARNING AND DEVELOPING THROUGH PLAY

Illustration 4

- Aim 2 and Learning Goal 6
- Age Group: Babies
- Setting: Full- and part-time daycare (crèche)

Pema's mother Marta is keen that Pema (seventeen months) grows up able to speak both Polish and English. Pema's grandpa Thomas, who is from Poland, has come to stay with Marta and Pema for a month. As always, he brings some new books and toys for Pema. This time he brings a doll with long black hair. They name her Paula. Every afternoon Thomas, Pema and Paula sit together in the kitchen reading the new books. Thomas proudly points to the pictures and names them in Polish. Pema copies him and looks at him with delight as he smiles to affirm her efforts.

Pema attends the local crèche from 9 a.m. to 1 p.m. three days a week while Marta works. This morning Thomas, Marta and Pema are walking together to the crèche. Pema and Paula are in the buggy. They have time to stop and point to interesting things along the way: a dog, an ambulance going by with its siren flashing, flower sellers and the church. Thomas takes time to name the objects and describe them in Polish as Pema points and attempts some of his words. Thomas repeats the words, nods and smiles to encourage Pema.

When they arrive at the crèche Aveen, the practitioner, greets the family with 'Hello' in Polish. Marta proudly shows her father the family wall where there are photographs of all the families in the crèche and a welcome sign in the mother tongue of every child. Marta and Thomas give Pema a kiss and a hug and Aveen takes her to the window so she can wave bye-bye before they play with Paula.

 Reflection: Can I do more to bring the children's home language into the setting? (NCCA 2009b:65)

There are many settings in Ireland, particularly in urban areas, where the children attending have English as their second language. To assist them in settling in and developing a sense of belonging, along with a secure sense of identity, it is important to consider how we can incorporate the home languages of the children into the setting and the daily activities. This example comes under Aistear Aim 2: 'Children will use language' and Learning Goal 6: 'In partnership with the adult, children will be positive about their home language, and know that they can use different languages to communicate with different people and in different situations' (NCCA 2009a:35). In fact, children often have less difficulty with this than the adults whose first language dominates. It is also important to remember that what matters most initially is the communication – we can work with the accuracy of vocabulary and grammar later.

Síolta Standard 14: Identity and Belonging – 'Promoting positive identities and a strong sense of belonging requires clearly defined policies, procedures and practice that empower every child and adult to develop a confident self- and group-identity, and to have a positive understanding and regard for the identity and rights of others' (CECDE 2006:95) is the standard most directly relevant to this illustration. Each setting does need to have explicit policies and procedures in relation to the way it works with children and families from different backgrounds. In the illustration above there is reference to the family wall; this and many other approaches to making settings welcoming for all need to be carefully considered and understood if they are to achieve the aim of supporting all. It is also important to be careful not to put too much pressure on children and their families. Component 14.3: 'The setting promotes positive understanding and regard for the identity and rights of others through the provision of an appropriate environment, experiences and interactions within the setting' (CECDE 2006:99) is important as it has an extensive set of Signposts for Reflection, each with detailed questions worth considering in some depth, for instance 14.3.2, 'How do the ongoing experiences of the child within the setting promote positive understanding and regard for the identity and rights of others?' In an extension of this reflection the question is posed, 'Are there strategies in place to support and maintain the first language of the child while she/he is learning an additional language (e.g. training/staff resource library, signs and labels in the first language, contact with families etc.)?' In addition, are there strategies for 'encouraging and supporting parents to share aspects of their culture or background with all the setting (e.g. food recipes, story-telling, customs and culture etc.)' (CECDE 2006:99)? This last Think About links directly back to Standard 3: Parents and Family – 'Valuing and involving parents and families requires a proactive partnership approach evidenced by a range of clearly stated, accessible and implemented processes, policies and procedures' (CECDE 2006:31).

In addition to these standards, Standard 5: Interactions – 'Fostering constructive interactions (child/child; child/adult; adult/adult) requires explicit policies, procedures and practice that emphasise the value of process and are based on mutual respect, equal partnership and sensitivity' (CECDE 2006:39) is also important. In this particular example we can look at Component 5.3: 'The adult uses all aspects of the daily routine (both formal and informal) to interact sensitively and respectfully with the child' (CECDE 2006:43). We see in the example above how Aveen settles Pema into the setting by bringing her to wave bye-bye and then she stays on to play with Pema and her doll Paula. Later she may refer back to the doll or introduce her to a broader story time or circle time.

Illustration 5

- Aim 4 and Learning Goal 3
- Age Group: Toddlers
- Setting: Full- and part-time daycare (nursery)

Emily (2½ years) is a shy, quiet little girl. She attends the local nursery every day while her ma, a lone parent, works. When she dances in the nursery Emily's whole expression changes and her sense of happiness and delight are clearly communicated. She particularly enjoys the songs 'I'm a Dingle Dangle Scarecrow' and 'Five Fat Sausages'. She also loves singing and doing the actions for 'I'm a Little Teapot' and 'Ring-a Ring-a Rosy', particularly when they are sung in Latvian. She and her two special friends, Victoros and Seán, fall about the place laughing at the end. Victoros loves to hear his home language being used in the setting and starts to talk excitedly in Latvian when he hears it in the nursery rhymes.

Emily also enjoys it when the room leader suggests they take out the musical instruments. She loves marching around the room with her friends making lots of music and noise. She loves it especially when she gets the opportunity to do this outside. Máire, the room leader, often makes video recordings of the children's music making and dancing so that the children can share these experiences with their parents. Expressing herself in a variety of ways is important for Emily. Although her mastery of language is excellent, she is quite reserved when interacting with other children, yet she loves to dance and move to music.

 Reflection: How can I help children express themselves in a variety of ways? (NCCA 2009b:65)

This is an important example. It shows that not all children want to be actively involved in everything, but there may be some particular activities in which they are happy to participate in the group, and these should be provided for. However, it is also important to respect Emily's reserved nature and not to force her too far. This example is presented under Aistear Aim 4: 'Children will express themselves creatively and imaginatively' and Learning Goal 3: 'In partnership with the adult, children will listen to and respond to a variety of types of music, sing songs and make music using instruments' (NCCA 2009a:35). A varied curriculum is essential if we are to address all the learning and development needs of young children. Music and movement has a profound impact on a wide variety of developmental areas, including the obvious skills around balance and physical development and the less obvious aural skills of active listening and listening in a way that assists in the discrimination of different sounds.

Under Síolta there are a number of standards of quality practice that have relevance to this illustration. Perhaps we can begin with a key standard across so many of the examples of practice outlined in the Aistear curriculum framework, Standard 1: Rights of the Child – 'Ensuring that each child's rights are met requires that she/he is enabled to exercise choice and to use initiative as an active participant and partner in her/his own development and learning' (CECDE 2006:13). Sensitive practitioners will not force a shy child to be part of group activities: instead, they will observe and get to know the child so that they can provide those activities in which she/he does participate spontaneously. From that base you can work to integrate children into the setting so that they feel they belong, but this must be done in a way that respects the child's own dispositions. There is a clear distinction between the child who likes her/his own company and the child who is, for one reason or another, neglected or rejected by the group. These latter instances can be picked up by an observant practitioner and require a different approach. Component 1.1: 'Each child has opportunities to make choices, is enabled to make decisions, and has her/his choices and decisions respected' (CECDE 2006:14) should guide your practice, while you should recognise that as an adult you may often have to provide different choices to a child so that they can actually make a choice. You might look back to Illustration 3 in Chapter 5 for an example of how to guide a child away from an inappropriate choice by providing two more appealing choices – while still respecting the right of the child to make a choice.

Standard 5: Interactions – 'Fostering constructive interactions (child/child; child/adult; adult/adult) requires explicit policies, procedures and practice that emphasise the value of process and are based on mutual respect, equal partnership and sensitivity' (CECDE 2006:39) is also worth considering in relation to this example. The key to children's positive development and learning in the early years is the quality of the interactions the child has with other people and with the overall environment. This important point is captured by Component 5.4: 'The adult interactive style is focused on process as opposed to outcomes. It is balanced between talking and listening, offers the child a choice of responses and encourages expanded use of language. It follows the child's lead and interests, and challenges the child appropriately' (CECDE 2006:44). This is further elaborated in the Signposts for Reflection, such as 5.4.10: 'In interacting with an individual child or a group of children, what are the challenges for you in making sure the child does most of the talking?' (CECDE 2006:44).

SUPPORTING LEARNING AND DEVELOPMENT THROUGH ASSESSMENT

Illustration 6

- Aim 1 and Learning Goal 1
- Age Group: Young children
- Setting: Sessional service (naíonra)

Caoimhín (three years) attends a naíonra. He enjoys responding to music. His parents have discussed with Eimear, the stiurthóir (playgroup leader), how he finds it difficult to express his emotions clearly and how this frustrates him. Over recent weeks Eimear has taught Caoimhín and the other children action songs about different emotions. They have also been using instruments while singing the songs and moving to different pieces of music, in order to help them express different feelings. Throughout these experiences, and during play, Eimear has been observing Caoimhín to see how he expresses himself. She makes detailed notes about some of his learning experiences. This documentation shows the progress Caoimhín is making in showing his peers how he feels. Eimear shares this information with his mammy and daddy next time she is talking to one of them.

Examples of Eimear's notes in her practitioner's file:
Monday 18 February, 12.10 p.m. Outside play.
Caoimhín plays by himself in the sandpit. He shovels sand into a play truck. Anraí and Sorcha come over to try to help him. Caoimhín says, 'Ná dean' ('Don't') and offers them a spare bucket beside him.

Wednesday, 27 February, 9.40 a.m. Indoor play.
Caoimhín, Eoin, Niamh and Amy are playing with the tea set. Eoin serves Caoimhín tea. Amy asks Eoin if she can have some tea, Eoin ignores the request and Amy gets upset. Caoimhín offers her his cup of tea.

 Reflection: Do I take time to review my detailed observations of children's learning experiences as a way of seeing the progress they are making? (NCCA 2009b:93)

This is an interesting illustration of the use of observation to guide the practitioner; it refers to music as a location for developing Caoimhín's self- management of his feelings and emotions. It then presents the record of two observations of peer interactions in which Caoimhín exhibits an understanding of the feelings and emotions of others and behaves positively in both cases. The assumption underlying this may be that the music and movement has settled Caoimhín and he is more responsive to the feelings of others; however, this is not made clear. The illustration is responding to the Aistear Aim 1: 'Children will use non-verbal communication skills' and Learning Goal 1: 'In partnership with the adult, children will use a range of body movements, facial expressions and early vocalisations to show feelings and share information' (NCCA 2009a:35).

This example of the use of observation in practice provides an opportunity to consider some of the more administrative standards of quality practice outlined in Síolta (2006). Standard 10: Organisation – 'Organising and managing resources effectively requires an agreed written philosophy, supported by clearly communicated policies and procedures to guide and determine practice' (CECDE 2006:75) – emphasises the importance of an agreed ethos or philosophy of practice. Using observations to evaluate practice and document children's progress requires time and an understanding within settings that this is an important element of quality practice. There are seven components associated with this standard. Component 10.4: 'All adults working in the setting are valued, supported and encouraged in their individual roles and responsibilities' (CECDE 2006:78) points to the value of a cohesive team approach to practice and has six signposts for reflection. Signpost for Reflection 10.4.3, 'How are adults working in the setting valued and supported sensitively, in a manner designed to motivate and encourage?', underlines the importance of leadership and clear role identity. In order to feel free to make observations and discuss these with parents it is critical that practitioners have the necessary skills and recognise that they are supported in the effort. These points are also expanded on in Standard 11: Professional Practice – 'Practising in a professional manner requires that individuals have skills, knowledge, values and attitudes appropriate to their role and responsibility within the setting. In addition, it requires regular reflection upon practice and engagement in supported, ongoing professional development' (CECDE 2006:81). This standard is strengthened under Component 11.3: 'The setting supports and promotes regular opportunity for practitioners to reflect upon and review their practice and contribute positively to the development of quality practice in the setting' (CECDE 2006:84).

This example can also be linked to the Síolta Standard 8: Planning and Evaluation – 'Enriching and informing all aspects of practice within the setting requires cycles of observation, planning, action and evaluation, undertaken on a regular basis' (CECDE 2006:63), which stresses the importance of observation and the use of observation records to inform practice directly within the setting and also to inform engagement with parents on the learning and development of their children attending the setting. Of the four components of this standard I have chosen to consider Component 8.3: 'There is a mechanism in place to ensure that review process leads to change in practice' (CECDE 2006:65). This component is phrased to draw attention to the fact that our practice can always be improved and that reflection and review should be part of daily practice. In Signpost for Reflection 8.3.1 we are asked to consider, 'When change is indicated by the review process, how is that change incorporated into practice?' It is often moving from suggesting a change to actually implementing it in practice that can be most difficult and so extending reflective practice to considering how best to incorporate change, and then doing it, is very important.

Illustration 7

- Aim 2 and Learning Goal 1
- Age Group: Young children
- Setting: Infant class (primary school)

Ms Clarke teaches twenty-nine senior infant boys. As part of the school's assessment policy Ms Clarke uses a literacy screening test with the whole class in late January. When correcting the tests she identifies six boys who score below the test threshold. Through observations and conversations, she has been carefully monitoring these boys as she knows they sometimes find letter sounds challenging, and two require ongoing support in developing listening skills. She considers the possibility that their low scores on the test may be attributable to factors other than difficulties in literacy. She takes account of particular factors, such as the language, the complexity of the instructions, and the anxiety that the testing situations can create for some children. Having talked with the boys' parents, Ms Clarke refers them to the learning support teacher, Mrs Fitzgerald. After establishing a good relationship with the children, this teacher carries out individual diagnostic tests.

Having considered all the available information, Mrs Fitzgerald invites the parents of the six boys to take part in an early intervention programme for six to eight weeks, in order to assist them in supporting specific aspects of their children's learning. Ms Clarke and Mrs Fitzgerald also agree on some additional learning activities that Ms Clarke can use with the boys on both an individual and a group basis.

At the end of the early intervention programme the six children are re-tested. Five now score well. While the sixth child has made some progress, Ms Clarke plans to continue to give one-to-one support to him in class. He will also have further diagnostic assessment and support with Mrs Fitzgerald.

> (?) *Reflection:* Does my school have a screening policy in place to help identify children who may need extra and/or specialised support? (NCCA 2009b:99)

The importance of early identification of difficulties that children may be having cannot be overstated and it is one of the key reasons that early years services require well-trained practitioners. If left unaddressed, a simple difficulty with, for instance, paying attention may lead on to more difficult behaviours which can disrupt a child's learning and development in a more serious and long-term way. The illustration comes under Aim 2: 'Children will use language' and Learning Goal 1: 'In partnership with the adult, children will interact with other children and adults by listening, discussing and taking turns in conversation' (NCCA 2009a:35) and is addressing the issue of assessment. Taking the time to observe children carefully on an ongoing basis can help identify children who may need additional help to overcome the immediate difficulty or who may, in fact, need more specialised help. In this example the setting uses a general screening test, which identifies the six children with difficulties. The response of the practitioner and the learning support practitioner leads to a situation where, after two months, only one child is still having difficulties. The importance of involving parents in the intervention is also highlighted.

Síolta Standard 3: Parents and Family – 'Valuing and involving parents and families requires a proactive partnership approach evidenced by a range of clearly stated, accessible and implemented processes, policies and procedures' (CECDE 2006:31) emphasises the importance of parental involvement in general and it is particularly important with respect to any child who may have additional needs, however transient they may be. While all the components under this standard are important, Component 3.3: 'Staff are responsive and sensitive in the provision of information and support to parents in their key role in the learning and development of the child' (CECDE 2006:34) is perhaps most relevant to the example in question. The Signpost for Reflection 3.3.1, 'How do you provide information for parents?', offers us an opportunity to consider how best to inform parents about issues of concern. In this regard it is not clear in the example above whether or not the parents of the six boys were seen individually in the first instance – but I imagine they were. Once all had been informed it would be easier to work with them as a group, but given the sensitive nature of the issue one would want to meet them separately in the first instance.

It is also worth considering Standard 12: Communication – 'Communicating effectively in the best interests of the child requires policies, procedures and actions that promote the proactive sharing of knowledge and information among appropriate stakeholders with respect and confidentiality' (CECDE 2006:87). If we are collecting assessment data to use for determining children's progress, it is essential that we have a system of record keeping that is secure and confidential. Component 12.1: 'The setting undertakes the collection of relevant and appropriate information on all children and stores it in a safe manner' (CECDE 2006:89) challenges us to consider what information is relevant, how we use it, how we store it and with whom we share it. There is only one Signpost for Reflection under this component: 12.1.1 – 'How does your setting collect information on individual children (both formally and informally)?' It has an extensive list of Think Abouts to consider when reviewing and reflecting on the example above and/or examples drawn from your own experiences of practice.

While the illustrations in this chapter have presented opportunities to link specific samples of daily practice with the standards of Síolta and the learning goals of Aistear, they do not directly present ideas for achieving the aims of Aistear under the theme of Communicating. Attention to actual practice can be found in a series of Sample Learning Opportunities in the Aistear document. The suggestions are set out according to age groups and provide useful ideas on how to really look at your own practice and check it for its potential in expanding and enriching young children's communication skills, so crucial to early learning and development. Below I present the main practice styles suggested for maximising children's learning opportunities under the theme Communicating. The content of the situations derives from the children and the adults and will be unique to each opportunity that presents itself. When considering how to carry through these suggestions you will be greatly assisted by applying your knowledge and understanding of child development, relevant research and the processes that assist learning and development most appropriately for individual children. The ages act as a guide, but they are overlapping in order to capture the reality that children have different developmental trajectories across aspects of development.

- When working with babies – birth to eighteen months – practitioners should:
  - interact non-verbally with babies and use appropriate and supportive techniques to encourage communication
  - provide opportunities for babies to learn language from others
  - create a print-rich environment and foster babies' enjoyment of books
  - support language development using stories, games, songs and rhymes with actions, finger movements and visual props
  - foster listening skills using voice tone, music, movement, songs and rhymes
  - support creative expression.

- When working with toddlers – twelve months to three years – practitioners should:
  - support toddlers in developing their language
  - create a print-rich environment and foster toddlers' love of, excitement in and understanding of books
  - encourage toddlers to communicate creatively through story, song, sculpture, rhyme, play, music, dance and art
  - count and use mathematical language in everyday situations.
- When working with young children – 2½ to six years – practitioners should:
  - encourage young children to develop their non-verbal communication
  - help young children develop their listening skills
  - encourage young children to think and talk about their own and others' feelings
  - support young children in developing their language
  - ensure that young children experience a print-rich environment and foster their love of, excitement in, understanding of and use of books
  - provide opportunities for young children to make sense of their experiences by representing their thoughts and ideas through mark-making and early writing
  - develop young children's understanding of number in the environment
  - help young children to express themselves creatively through art, cookery, drama, language, music, scientific exploration and stories.

(NCCA 2009a:36–41)

SUMMARY

This chapter explored the complex theme of communicating. Initially it considered the elements of communication in the individual, the verbal and non-verbal nature of communication and the multiple ways in which we all communicate. The role of the early years practitioner in communicating with and assisting the communication of children was discussed in some detail. The crucial role of the early years practitioner in communicating with children's families and other professionals was also noted, particularly in relation to developing shared understandings of child development. Suggestions for practice were presented and this was followed by a sample of practice illustrations from Aistear used as examples for linking Aistear and Síolta when reflecting how practice can achieve the potential of the communicating theme.

You will notice that the focus of the learning opportunities and practice examples presented is on the practitioner and child/children relationship, the quality of listening and communicating and the provision of opportunities from within the ordinary and the lived experiences of the children and adults who make up the learning environment. The opportunities require the practitioner to be attuned and sensitive to the learning possibilities that arise in the most ordinary of events. This challenges you to take your time, to give plenty of time and to use time carefully. There are many opportunities presented for capturing the learning moments that arise when individual children are concentrating on a task or when a group of children are playing a game, solving a problem or messing about. Most of all, the examples reflect the democratic nature of excellent early years practice, a practice that respects all children, that celebrates difference, that listens to children and hears them, that engages children in conversations, facilitates conversations between children and that provides a context within which they grow in competence and confidence in their own communicating skills and styles.

CHAPTER 7

Exploring and Thinking

Children have to be educated – but they also have to be left to educate themselves. (Dimnet 1928)

C hildren are actively making sense of their world and their place in it. Through their activities and their relationships they are learning about themselves, what they can do, where they need help, whether they are good or bad. They are also learning how to manage feelings, how to respond to difficult situations, how to respond to others. Through their engagement with the world and the people, objects and materials they find there, they are learning new facts, new words, new ways of doing things; they learn how to wait, how to plan, how to negotiate and how to participate in groups. Exploring and thinking are just two of the important processes that assist children in their meaning-making. Aistear characterises exploring and thinking as 'active learning', which involves children using their senses to 'explore and work with objects and materials around them and they interact enthusiastically with the adults and other children' (NCCA 2009a:10). It is through this dynamic process that 'children develop the dispositions, skills, attitudes and values that will help them to grow as confident and competent learners' (NCCA 2009a:10).

While presented as a theme in itself, exploring and thinking are processes that are also relevant to the three previous themes. For instance, in relation to the theme of communicating we find the observation, '[B]y capturing children's interest and curiosity and challenging them to *explore* and to share their adventures and discoveries with each other, this environment can fuel their *thinking*, imagination and creativity, thereby enriching communication' (NCCA 2009a:34). We see here the importance of early years practitioners creating an environment that invites children to explore and communicate about their experiences, which will enhance the development and refining of their thinking.

In elaborating the underlying focus of this theme, Aistear notes that it is 'about children making sense of the things, places and people in their world by interacting with others, playing, investigating, questioning and forming, testing and refining ideas' (NCCA 2009a:43). The active participation of the child – whether an individual child or a child in a group of children – is central to the vision for this theme. Doing, pointing, asking questions, seeking solutions, setting up theories, making links with previous understandings, interacting with others, with objects, playing with words, laughing, crying, teasing, chortling, exploring and thinking all represent examples of how children learn through their active engagement with their environment in a playful and enriching way. Not only do they increase their knowledge and vocabulary, they also learn new skills, strengthen dispositions and refine their communication and co-operation strategies.

Recognising that children, even very young children, are using their senses to learn more about their world and to make sense of that world and their place in it, this theme argues that children 'refine their ideas through exploring their environment actively and through interacting and communicating with adults and other children' (NCCA 2009a:34).

Creating and sustaining a learning environment to provide opportunities to achieve these ambitions for children takes effort. We know from research that the most effective early learning settings – those where children are engaged and interested and where they show positive indicators for development, learning and well-being – are those where practitioners intentionally plan for learning. They create learning environments that encourage communication, they strike a balance of attention to assisting children in the development of knowledge and understanding of the world and they maintain a language- and literacy-rich environment. In less effective early years settings, on the other hand, practitioners spend considerable time and effort focusing on children's physical and creative development (Siraj-Blatchford *et al.* 2004). Creative development is important, but it is most effective where the early years practitioner moves beyond simply providing the materials and the time so that, through attentive dialogue with the children, their own narrative abilities and conceptual skills can be extended. In short, the broad outcomes for children are enhanced when practitioners themselves take an active role in creating and sustaining the learning environment, engage directly and meaningfully with children and know when it is best to stand back and observe, to listen or to question young children.

Early years setting should be attractive to children so that they can explore and play, be creative and take risks, question their ideas and their understandings and arrive at new problems for solving. In the main children are curious about their surroundings, they enjoy playing and getting to know how – and why – things work as they do. Challenges are good for children but it is important to ensure that those provided take account of the individual child's capabilities and dispositions.

Thinking is defined in the Aistear document as including: questioning, making connections, reasoning, evaluating, problem solving and creative thinking. Thinking is also categorised into higher-order thinking and lower-order thinking. Lower-order thinking refers to learning and remembering factual and procedural knowledge: here the main responsibility of the practitioner is to be clear in transmitting knowledge and procedural routines. Higher-order thinking, on the other hand, refers to the metacognitive skills: manipulating ideas, evaluating and analysing information. It includes the skills of problem solving, predicting, questioning and justifying. In this instance the practitioner's role is to provide activities, objects, materials, space and time in learning environments that present opportunities for children to engage in higher-order thinking.

It is important to understand that both lower- and higher-order thinking develops in parallel in the social context. We do not first acquire lower-order thinking skills and then move on to higher-order thinking. To help children realise their higher-order thinking, practitioners should provide challenge and should expect children – even very young children – to be capable, competent, thoughtful and reflective and assist them in their learning so that both types of thinking develop. Studies have found that where practitioners have high expectations of children they are more successful at developing and refining thinking skills. Where expectations for children are lower, adults are more likely to do things *for* rather than *with* children, for example to organise activities that direct children in their behaviour rather than providing opportunities for them to explore and discover new things for themselves. While such environments may yield short-term performance in children they are unlikely to facilitate children in becoming independent and confident learners. Achieving and sustaining early years practice that balances careful planning with the provision of opportunities for children's self-directed learning is challenging. It requires an understanding of child development, and knowledge of individual children and their experiences so that the fine balance between child-initiated play, guided play and adult-led learning can be achieved. It is, however, worthwhile as the evidence indicates that learner-centred practice, which invites children to explore and think about their world, yields the best outcomes for children.

Aistear provides a useful framework to assist in this task and the theme of exploring and thinking is particularly valuable. A review of early years literature confirms that play is regarded as a critical element of early childhood education and care and considered a central aspect of children's learning and development. The word 'play' is used to mean many things and is considered by some to be somewhat trivial and childish and relatively unimportant to the important task of growing up. The apparently non-productive nature of play poses a problem for those of us who recognise its central role in the process of child development. In an atmosphere where there is growing political attention to measurable academic and skill achievement of even very young children, the value of play to children's learning is often lost. In such a climate there is a real danger that the foundational value of play can be missed in those areas of education where it is most important. In their paper on the right to play, the International Play Association (IPA) notes that 'The irony is that the very "purposelessness" of play, its spontaneous and apparently frivolous nature, is its core value, the element that produces flexibility, creativity and social competency' (Fronczek 2009:26). It is a central process in childhood and it is through play that children explore and develop their thinking. Play also helps children build resilience through acquiring such important aspects of development as self-regulation, emotional health and physical health. It is within the relatively safe context of play that emotions can find expression and management and children learn the complexities of interpersonal relationships (Lester & Russell 2008).

Through play children can follow their curiosity and their interests. An essential feature of play is that it is a free and meaningful activity and carried out for its own sake. It is a safe place where children can overcome any sense of helplessness they have. Play makes sense to the player – it has meaning. The fundamental motive for play is the experience itself – the process. Play has an intrinsic value and facilitates the expression of feelings of risk, anticipation, effort and intensity. Novelty is motivating and can be the space within which practitioners can encourage thoughtful exploration and concentration, and create opportunities for discussion and questioning. Playful exploratory learning requires risk-taking, and this can challenge practitioners who are, rightly, concerned with meeting basic standards of health and safety. However, a totally risk-free environment does not provide sufficiently for children's learning and developmental requirements. In planning learning environments where play is a meaningful activity and children are free to learn through their play, successful practitioners build in safe risk opportunities and, through their engagement, observations and awareness they can avoid situations of dangerous risk and enrich and extend children's learning.

Research has found that settings where children are regularly left to engage in long periods of undirected free play are the least successful learning environments (McLachlan, Fleer & Edwards 2010). In fact the evidence is that play-based learning is most beneficial to children when it is interactive and involves both adults and children in interesting and challenging environments. The key feature seems to be the dynamic interplay between adults and children, which involves practitioners who are engaged, resourceful and attuned and children who are motivated, curious and confident. It also seems that the best outcomes for children come when there is a balance between child-directed play, guided play and adult-led learning (Marbina, Church & Tayler 2011:3–4). Furthermore, research has found that practitioners must intentionally plan for and provide a balance between communication, language and literacy, knowledge and understanding of the world. From this we can see that to really encourage children to explore and to think about their behaviour it is important that practitioners are intentional in their engagement with children and provide a wide range of options to children so that those with different learning styles can find something for them that will extend their learning and fuel their curiosity to learn more. In an effort to capture this integrated approach to early years practice the Victoria Early Years Learning and Development Framework developed the figure below.

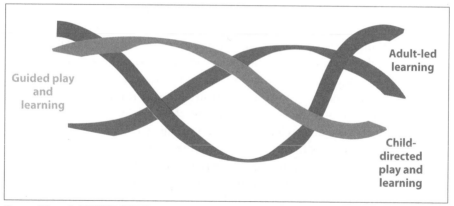

Adult-led learning

Guided play and learning

Child-directed play and learning

Source: Victoria DEECD (2009).

The diagram characterises integrated teaching and learning as a weave between the threads of guided play and learning, child-directed play and learning and adult-led learning. It is within this flow that children will learn best and practitioners will find satisfaction and reward for the work they do. This integrated approach to early years practice challenges practitioners to provide experiences in the context of a curriculum that balances play, varied and rich learning activities and engaged, sensitive and guiding practice. We have seen that early years practitioners often struggle to articulate what it is about play that promotes learning and may have difficulty defending it in the face of those who expect us to be providing school-like educational opportunities for even the youngest children. Both the Aistear and Síolta frameworks provide a common language of early years practice, and strengthening this shared language through reflection and questioning will enhance practitioner skills in explaining and defending quality early years practice.

In reflecting on how practice uses play to meet the learning goals and aims of particular Aistear themes you can explain why there is a balance between what you as an adult do for and with children. More experienced and well-informed practitioners not only understand the importance of this balance but can also describe why it is good early years practice to integrate adult-led with child-initiated activities and why play can, in and of itself, provide an excellent context in which young children develop and learn. Such reflection and questioning of practice can become a routine part of the daily practice in an early years settings and contribute to creating and maintaining an atmosphere of learning that is both professionally satisfying and developmentally rewarding for children.

The science of learning confirms that children are active deciders rather than passive absorbers. The role of the practitioner includes creating environments that invite children to participate, that actively engage both children and adults to provoke their curiosity and exploration. Fostering the development of both the metacognitive and affective dimension to learning in early education can enable children to become ready, le learners (Claxton 1990; Carr 2001). Children are ready when they are se a particular skill or piece of knowledge to achieve something; they are they can recognise when it is relevant to call on those skills or that knowledge; and they are able when they know how to do something. The early years practitioner has an important role to play in motivating, guiding and supporting children to become confident and capable learners who are ready, willing and able in most learning situations. Metacognitive and affective development is particularly important in young children as it facilitates the acquisition, comprehension, retention and application of what is learned; it helps improve their learning efficiency, critical thinking and problem solving; and it gives them control or self-regulation over thinking and learning processes and products. Through the opportunities provided in early years settings, children can, in their exploring and thinking, develop and refine their learning and development.

The table outlines the four Aistear aims for the Exploring and Thinking theme and expands on them by reference to twenty-four learning goals.

AISTEAR'S AIMS AND LEARNING GOALS: EXPLORING AND THINKING

Exploring and Thinking	
Aims	**Learning goals**
Aim 1 Children will learn about and make sense of the world around them	In partnership with the adult, children will 1 engage, explore and experiment in their environment and use new physical skills including skills to manipulate objects and materials 2 demonstrate a growing understanding of themselves and others in their community 3 develop an understanding of change as part of their lives 4 learn about the natural environment and its features, materials, animals, and plants, and their own responsibility as carers 5 develop a sense of time, shape, space, and place 6 come to understand concepts such as matching, comparing, ordering, sorting, size, weight, height, length, capacity, and money in an enjoyable and meaningful way.
Aim 2 Children will develop and use skills and strategies for observing, questioning, investigating, understanding, negotiating, and problem-solving, and come to see themselves as explorers and thinkers	In partnership with the adult, children will 1 recognise patterns and make connections and associations between new learning and what they already know 2 gather and use information from different sources using their increasing cognitive, physical and social skills 3 use their experience and information to explore and develop working theories about how the world works, and think about how and why they learn things 4 demonstrate their ability to reason, negotiate and think logically 5 collaborate with others to share interests and to solve problems confidently 6 use their creativity and imagination to think of new ways to solve problems.

Aims (continued)	Learning goals (continued)
Aim 3 Children will explore ways to represent ideas, feelings, thoughts, objects, and actions through symbols	In partnership with the adult, children will 1 make marks and use drawing, painting and model-making to record objects, events and ideas 2 become familiar with and associate symbols (pictures, numbers, letters, and words) with the things they represent 3 build awareness of the variety of symbols (pictures, print, numbers) used to communicate, and use these in an enjoyable and meaningful way leading to early reading and writing 4 express feelings, thoughts and ideas through improvising, moving, playing, talking, writing, story-telling, music and art 5 use letters, words, sentences, numbers, signs, pictures, colour, and shapes to give and record information, to describe and to make sense of their own and others' experiences 6 use books and ICT (software and the internet) for enjoyment and as a source of information.
Aim 4 Children will have positive attitudes towards learning and develop dispositions like curiosity, playfulness, perseverance, confidence, resourcefulness, and risk-taking	In partnership with the adult, children will 1 demonstrate growing confidence in being able to do things for themselves 2 address challenges and cope with frustrations 3 make decisions and take increasing responsibility for their own learning 4 feel confident that their ideas, thoughts and questions will be listened to and taken seriously 5 develop higher-order thinking skills such as problem-solving, predicting, analysing, questioning, and justifying 6 act on their curiosity, take risks and be open to new ideas and uncertainty.

Source: www.ncca.biz/Aistear/pdfs/PrinciplesThemes_ENG/PrinciplesThemes_ENG.pdf.

In the practice illustrations that follow, the theme of Exploring and Thinking is considered across a variety of settings with a sample of children of different ages. These illustrations are intended as a starting point from where you can begin to take examples of your own day-to-day practice and reflect on them, alone or with colleagues, in the context of both Aistear and Síolta. This can form the basis for regularly reviewing your own practice, questioning the ethos of practice in your setting, and it can also provide a language with which you can consider the practice of others and explain your philosophy of practice as necessary. It should also present you with new questions and challenges, which in turn can enrich your practice, its effectiveness and your own professional satisfaction.

BUILDING PARTNERSHIPS BETWEEN PARENTS AND PRACTITIONERS

Illustration 1

- Aim 1 and Learning Goal 5
- Age Group: Babies and young children
- Setting: Home and childminding

Every evening Luke reads a bedtime story to his son Jack (5½ years) and his baby daughter Kate (sixteen months). As they snuggle up to their Daddy, Kate helps to turn the pages and points to her favourite characters. She loves 'lift the flap' books and Luke told Kate's childminder, Mags, about this when she was starting a few months ago. Mags has a number of these books and Kate loves to sit on her knee on the garden seat looking at them.

Luke also told Mags about Jack's interest in books, especially books about sport. Luke is originally from New Zealand and he and Jack love to read about rugby. Jack has taught the other children at Mags' to play rugby, and a few weeks ago Luke arranged for Mags and the four children she minds to go to a local school rugby match. She also purchased two books about New Zealand as Jack and his family are planning a trip there during the summer to visit his grandparents. The children and Mags are learning a lot about New Zealand. They are finding out about the weather, the sports people play, the food they eat and the types of farm they have. They are also comparing these with the village in Co. Tipperary where they live. The children are really excited about Jack and his family flying on a huge aeroplane. They are even building one just like it in Mags' playroom. It's massive!

 Reflection: How can I build on children's interests to enhance their learning and development, and to strengthen their sense of identity? (NCCA 2009b:11)

This example is a good illustration of how the interests of different children can be brought into the daily routine of the early years settings. It is located under the Exploring and Thinking Aistear theme and under Aim 1: 'Children will learn about and make sense of the world around them' and Learning Goal 5: 'In partnership with the adult, children will develop a sense of time, shape, space and place' (NCCA 2009a:44). This particular illustration addresses this aim and learning goal by reference to a different country far away, which has different weather, food, culture and customs.

A number of Síolta standards of quality practice are also relevant to the example. For instance, the possibilities used in the example reflect Standard 5: Interactions – 'Fostering constructive interactions (child/child; child/adult; adult/adult) requires explicit policies, procedures and practice that emphasise the value of process and are based on mutual respect, equal partnership and sensitivity' (CECDE 2006:39). Clearly Mags has a good partnership relationship with the parents of the children attending her setting. This openness reflects Component 5.5: 'Interactions between the adults within, and associated with the setting, act as a model of respect, support and partnership for the child' (CECDE 2006:46). The first Signpost for Reflection, 5.5.1, is 'How do your interactions with parents model friendly respect and partnership?' It is clear from the illustration that Mags does listen to the parents and incorporates what she learns from them into her daily activities with their children and also the other children in the setting. Mags is also open to availing of the opportunities (such as attending a local school rugby match) presented to her. This is in keeping with Standard 16: Community Involvement – 'Promoting community involvement requires the establishment of networks and connections evidenced by policies, procedures and actions which extend and support all adults' and children's engagement with the wider community' (CECDE 2006:105) and Component 16.4: 'The setting actively promotes children's citizenship in their local, regional and national community' (CECDE 2006:106). It particularly reflects Signpost for Reflection 16.4.2, which asks practitioners, 'How do you enable babies and young children to be present/participate in events and activities within the community?'

From a pedagogical point of view this example also links to Standard 6: Play – 'Promoting play requires that each child has ample time to engage in freely available and accessible, developmentally appropriate and well-resourced opportunities for exploration, creativity and "meaning making" in the company of other children, with participating and supportive adults and alone, where appropriate' (CECDE 2006:49). In the example we see how freely the children can expand on an idea with, for instance, the reference to making a model of the aeroplane. Component 6.4: 'Each learning area and each activity in the setting has plenty of equipment and materials for the child' (CECDE 2006:50) provides practitioners with a challenge, particularly when the setting is a private home (as in this example). Yet we see how responsive Mags is to the learning and development possibilities of the information she receives from the parents and sees its potential beyond a single news item or single story for story time.

LEARNING AND DEVELOPING THROUGH INTERACTIONS

Illustration 2

- Aim 2 and Learning Goal 5
- Age Group: Young children
- Setting: Infant class (Gaelscoil)

Múinteoir Seán is talking to his class of twenty-three junior and senior infants. Ruairí the puppet is worried because he has to go to hospital to have his tonsils removed. Múinteoir Seán asks the children how they would feel if they had to go to hospital. He gets a variety of responses. He then asks the children how they could help Ruairí to feel better about the trip to hospital. Many children empathise with Ruairí's feeling of worry and nervousness, and about being alone and away from family and friends.

Myra (almost six years), who has cystic fibrosis, starts to talk about her long and frequent stays in hospital. She has a captive audience. Her contribution starts a discussion about hospital and why you go there. Many of the children share their own stories and Múinteoir Seán adds his. The discussion leads to a series of conversations over the next few days when the children explore why people get sick, what makes them better and why some people die when they are sick.

Later in the week, and after much collecting of resources from home, Múinteoir Seán and the children assemble a collection of props and dressing-up clothes to make a hospital. There are four very sick people – Ruairí, Teddy, Nora the SNA and Múinteoir Seán. Múinteoir Seán divides the children into four groups and asks each group to work together to attend to the needs of one of the four patients. Within minutes four teams of doctors and nurses appear, as do visitors for Ruairí, Teddy, Nora and Múinteoir Seán. Over the next week, the groups have opportunities to treat each of the patients, as well as new patients, and all the children get opportunities to be doctors, nurses, visitors and patients. This planning enables Múinteoir Seán to spend time with each of the four groups introducing new language in context and developing their understanding of being in hospital.

Múinteoir Seán plans to use some of the quandaries and ponderings raised in the discussions and play scenarios to promote learning in different areas of the curriculum over the following few weeks.

 Reflection: How can I help children explore new situations and experiences through discussion and pretend play? (NCCA 2009b:34)

This example shows how play activities can address a number of different learning goals. These include the standard academic development one might expect in a school setting, such as increased vocabulary, aspects of emotional development around issues of separation, illness and so forth and the development of thinking and exploring skills that assist effective learning. To capture this complexity the illustration provided comes under Aistear Aim 2: 'Children will develop and use skills and strategies for observing, questioning, investigating, understanding, negotiating and problem solving and come to see themselves as explorers and thinkers' and Learning Goal 5: 'In partnership with the adult, children will collaborate with others to share interests and to solve problems confidently' (NCCA 2009a:44).

There are a number of Síolta standards that could be used to review the practices in the example above. For instance, Standard 2: Environments – 'Enriching environments, both indoor and outdoor (including materials and equipment) are well-maintained, safe, available, accessible, adaptable, developmentally appropriate and offer a variety of challenging and stimulating experiences' (CECDE 2006:19) points to the necessity to plan for providing a wide range of materials in the learning environment. This challenge is addressed well in the example above where the practitioner includes the children themselves in gathering the materials over time. Component 2.6: 'The indoor environment provides a range of developmentally appropriate, challenging, diverse, creative and enriching experiences for all children' (CECDE 2006:26) is well addressed in this setting. For instance, the whole project was initiated by reference to a puppet. Puppets are a useful conceit for introducing difficult or emotionally challenging ideas to a group of children. This was well planned and allowed space for Myra to recount her experiences of illness and hospital. Under the Signposts for Reflection associated with this component, 2.6.5 – 'What different areas/spaces within the settings are offered to the child?' – is a useful one to consider, particularly given the attention paid to the important role of pretend play in developing such key skills.

Standard 5: Interactions – 'Fostering constructive interactions (child/child; child/adult; adult/adult) requires explicit policies, procedures and practice that emphasise the value of process and are based on mutual respect, equal partnership and sensitivity' (CECDE 2006:39) is also relevant for consideration. The practitioner in this illustration is very sensitive to how to get the best from a situation. He plans carefully how to move an activity from a simple puppet story, through a real-life example, on to a general discussion, and then the inclusion of the children themselves in preparing for the extensive pretend play hospital project that he allows to run over a series of days. Under this standard a number of components have been addressed. Taking Component 5.4: 'The adult interactive style is focused on process as opposed to outcomes. It is balanced between talking and listening, offers the child a choice of responses and encourages expanded use of language. It follows the child's lead and interests, and challenges the child appropriately' (CECDE 2006:44), which has twenty different Signposts for Reflection, we can see how it offers a useful context for considering how to reflect in some depth on this example. Signpost for Reflection 5.4.4 draws our attention to the child – 'How can your responses support a child towards new learning and meaning?' – while 5.4.17 asks us to consider our pedagogical approach: 'In your interactions, what process characteristics do you emphasise?' This latter signpost offers a selection of techniques, which can be useful in reflecting on your own practice.

We can also consider this illustration by reference to Standard 6: Play – 'Promoting play requires that each child has ample time to engage in freely available and accessible, developmentally appropriate and well-resourced opportunities for exploration, creativity and "meaning making" in the company of other children, with participating and supportive adults and alone, where appropriate' (CECDE 2006:49). Here we are challenged to consider how to offer enriched play experiences in well-equipped learning environments. Component 6.3: 'The opportunities for play/exploration provided for the child mirror her/his stage of development, give the child the freedom to achieve mastery and success, and challenge the child to make the transition to new learning and development' (CECDE 2006:52) provides guidance on how we might evaluate the quality of our practices and the extent to which they are truly offering learning experiences that challenge children each along their own developmental trajectory.

Illustration 3

- Aim 3 and Learning Goal 1
- Age Group: Toddlers and young children
- Setting: Home

Jenna is a single parent and is at home with her two children, Robert (2½ years) and Rebecca (five years). They live in a disadvantaged area in the city centre. At times Jenna finds it hard to cope with the children, especially as the flat has no access to a garden and the nearest park is a bus ride away. Pat, the family support worker, has been helping Jenna to join in with the children in their play. Pat and the family have been to the local electrical shop to get an assortment of empty boxes. Jenna and the children play together to turn these into garages and apartment complexes. Pat provides paints, glitter and glue and the whole family work together happily in the kitchen deciding who is going to do what. At school Rebecca paints pictures, which she takes home to decorate the apartments. Jenna helps Robert to make a ramp for his car to get into the garage. Later that week, Jenna, Robert and Rebecca go for a walk and compare their garages and apartments to the ones in their locality. They have fun walking along and suggesting things to add to their cardboard apartments.

 Reflection: What resources and materials can I get in my community to help improve the learning environment for my children? (NCCA 2009b:43)

The value of this illustration lies in the emphasis on how you can get a great deal of learning opportunities from using fairly readily available materials. (However, experience suggests that it may be necessary to ask local shops to hold cardboard boxes as they generally have them ready for refuse collection quite early in the day: so this does need some planning.) The introduction of the family support worker is also of interest and suggests that Jenna is currently having some difficulty in managing her family. For that reason it is also important to recognise that Pat, the family support worker, is a well-qualified professional who can convince Jenna of the value of a fairly messy but creative and exciting activity. The example comes under Aistear Aim 3:

'Children will explore ways to represent ideas, feelings, thoughts, objects and actions through symbols' and Learning Goal 1: 'In partnership with the adult, children will make marks and use drawing, painting and model-making to record objects, events and ideas' (NCCA 2009a:44) and it describes how you can prepare for an activity, guide the activity and then take the ideas captured in the exercise to relate to the local community.

From the perspective of standards of practice Síolta provides a number of important standards. Standard 16: Community Involvement – 'Promoting community involvement requires the establishment of networks and connections evidenced by policies, procedures and actions which extend and support all adults' and children's engagement with the wider community' (CECDE 2006:105) relates to sourcing materials from the community and then linking the product arising from the activity to aspects of the local community. Component 16.2: 'The setting has established links which have the potential to extend and develop its involvement in the wider community' (CECDE 2006:108) explores the standard and offers Signposts for Reflection such as 16.2.1: 'How do you make use of the(se) amenities and services to enhance the children's/parents' experience, awareness and appreciation of their own local community?' Taking this as a starting point, there are a number of valuable points worth reflecting on, both in relation to the illustration above and also in your own experiences of practice.

Standard 2: Environments – 'Enriching environments, both indoor and outdoor (including materials and equipment), are well-maintained, safe, available, accessible, adaptable, developmentally appropriate and offer a variety of challenging and stimulating experiences' (CECDE 2006:19) is also a valuable source for individual and group reflection. Looking at Component 2.4: 'The environment promotes the safety, both indoors and outdoors, of all children and adults' (CECDE 2006:23) we see the importance of how careful we need to be in what we decide to introduce into a setting. For instance, in the example above it is noteworthy that Jenna accompanies the children in exploring the local community.

Finally, Standard 6: Play – 'Promoting play requires that each child has ample time to engage in freely available and accessible, developmentally appropriate and well-resourced opportunities for exploration, creativity and "meaning making" in the company of other children, with participating and supportive adults and alone, where appropriate' (CECDE 2006:49) points to the importance of allowing time and space for activities, particularly those that could be considered messy. This can be particularly difficult in confined spaces.

Illustration 4

- Aim 4 and Learning Goal 6
- Age Group: Babies
- Setting: Full- and part-time daycare (crèche)

Darragh (fourteen months) and Ian (sixteen months) are playing outside. Susan, their key worker, makes some red jelly and when it is set she gives it to Darragh and Ian to explore. The boys are sitting on a rug beside a sheet of paper, which is stuck to the grass. Susan scoops out a little jelly and offers it to Darragh and Ian. Ian is eager to get his hands on some of the jelly and squeals to make sure that Susan knows he wants it. Darragh doesn't appear to be interested. Ian rubs his jelly into the paper and is delighted to see red marks appearing. Susan makes some marks of her own. 'You are having great fun with the jelly, aren't you, Ian?' she comments. 'What about you, Darragh, would you like to try some?' Darragh watches Susan and Ian and puts his hand out tentatively towards the jelly. Susan encourages him to explore it and to make marks on the paper with it. Darragh watches as Susan makes long red lines on the paper. Susan is observing his reactions closely. She kneels beside him and helps him to make a mark. She describes the jelly and Darragh and Ian's mark-making activities. Darragh puts some of the jelly in his mouth; he likes the taste of it and has another piece. Ian follows. After a few minutes Darragh starts to take pieces of jelly out of the bowl and offers some to Ian. The boys place the jelly on the paper and then pick it up to put it back in the bowl again. Darragh and Ian become engrossed in what they are doing. Not wanting to interrupt their concentration and thinking, Susan sits quietly beside them. Ian and Darragh's body language and the smears of red jelly on their faces show that they are loving the experience!

 Reflection: What new experiences can I provide for children, which will capture their curiosity and encourage them to try new things? (NCCA 2009b:44)

This example is a challenging one. It is likely that some readers will question using food as a source of messy play. In fact, jelly can be used in many different ways – for instance you can 'hide' objects in it before it sets and allow children to explore it. The reference to a key worker is a useful reminder of how valuable this idea can be, particularly in a busy crèche with children as young as those in the example. The illustration refers specifically to Aistear Aim 4: 'Children will have positive attitudes towards learning and develop dispositions like curiosity, playfulness, perseverance, confidence, resourcefulness and risk-taking' and Learning Goal 6: 'In partnership with the adult, children will act on their curiosity, take risks and be open to new ideas and uncertainty' (NCCA 2009a:44). The explicit reference to dispositions under Aim 4 is very helpful because the development of dispositions is a core outcome from our early experiences and the quality of early experiences influences the quality of our dispositions.

Although this setting relates to toddlers in a crèche it is clear from the description that there is a curriculum in place. For this reason Standard 7: Curriculum – 'Encouraging each child's holistic development and learning requires the implementation of a verifiable, broad-based, documented and flexible curriculum or programme' (CECDE 2006:55) is an important one to explore in some detail. Under this standard there are six components. For this example, Component 7.4: 'Curriculum/programme implementation is achieved through a variety of adult strategies, close and supportive relationships in the setting and a wide range of experiences, which are made available to the child' (CECDE 2006:59) seems most appropriate for further consideration. Although the illustration describes just one activity in any detail it is clear from the context – outside on a rug but with a sheet of paper already stuck to the grass beside them – that a great deal of attention is given to the curriculum in this setting. Also of interest is Standard 5: Interactions – 'Fostering constructive interactions (child/child; child/adult; adult/adult) requires explicit policies, procedures and practice that emphasise the value of process and are based on mutual respect, equal partnership and sensitivity' (CECDE 2006:39). Susan, the key worker in the example, is presented as a calm, well-organised adult who is happy to trust children to explore new materials and willing to stand back and observe the behaviour of the two children without being too intrusive. Component 5.4: 'The adult interactive style is focused on process as opposed to outcomes. It is balanced between talking and listening, offers the child a choice of responses and encourages expanded use of language. It follows the child's lead and interests, and challenges the child appropriately' (CECDE 2006:44) emphasises the value of focusing on the process rather than on any explicit product or outcome. Once again this requires trusting children and understanding their development and their learning styles. To be able to plan and gain from this activity it is crucial that the adult knows the children well. We can expect that Susan will make some practitioner notes on her observations once the activity is complete and use this to plan other activities and learning opportunities for both Darragh and Ian.

Standard 6: Play – 'Promoting play requires that each child has ample time to engage in freely available and accessible, developmentally appropriate and well-resourced opportunities for exploration, creativity and "meaning making" in the company of other children, with participating and supportive adults and alone, where appropriate' (CECDE 2006:49) offers us the opportunity to consider the planning for play in the example. Susan has prepared the environment, she has worked out the timing (she has to make the jelly and allow it to set) and she allows the children to set the pace of the activity. In Component 6.6: 'The child has opportunities for play/exploration with other children, with participating and supportive adults and on her/his own, as appropriate' (CECDE 2006:53) we see the importance of a 'participating and supportive adult' and this is explored further in Signpost for Reflection 6.6.1, which asks us to consider, 'How often do you participate in play with the child?'

LEARNING AND DEVELOPING THROUGH PLAY

Illustration 5

- Aim 4 and Learning Goal 5
- Age Group: Young children
- Setting: Infant class (primary school)

The senior infant class of twenty-eight boys are getting ready for story time. They make themselves comfortable on the mats on the floor at the back of the classroom near the library area. The teacher has his storytelling hat on and has a series of props ready to assist him in his telling of Jack and the Beanstalk. He reads the story with the help of some of the boys who have been chosen to take on different roles in the story.

During discussion time Mr O'Donnell asks the boys to describe the different characters in the story. He also asks some questions, such as: 'Was it right for Jack's mother to send him off on his own to sell the cow?'; 'Was it okay for Jack to keep stealing from the giant?' Some very interesting conversations ensue. Later that day the boys play word games with some key words from the story. They love doing this and especially like making up nonsense words.

The following day Mr O'Donnell revisits the story and asks them to think of alternative endings for it. Later, during drama time, the boys re-enact the story of Jack and the Beanstalk. They incorporate the new endings such as Jack and the giant becoming friends, Jack selling the cow for a lot of money, running away and not giving the money to his mother, the guards catching Jack walking along the road with the cow and taking him to the station, the principal of his school ringing his Mam to see why he isn't at school. The teacher builds on their ideas and helps them to develop their stories. Over the next two days, working in pairs, the boys write their own story of Jack. They use words from the whiteboard based on their various discussions and they use their own spelling for other words. The children add illustrations to their stories. When Mr O'Donnell suggests to them that they could staple the pages together to make little story books, some children decide to add their names as authors and illustrators. They add page numbers and some even add ISBN codes! The following week the boys visit the junior infants classroom to read to the children in small groups. Parents get a chance to read the books when they drop the boys off in the morning or when they are collecting them in the afternoon.

 Reflection: How can I use storytelling to promote higher-order thinking skills? (NCCA 2009b:69)

This example is a description of how you can use a very familiar story to extend children's thinking by providing guidance, suggestions, materials and opportunities. In line with this it is presented under Aistear Aim 4: 'Children will have positive attitudes towards learning and develop dispositions like curiosity, playfulness, perseverance, confidence, resourcefulness and risk-taking' and Learning Goal 5: 'In partnership with the adult, children will develop higher-order thinking skills such as problem solving, predicting, analysing, questioning and justifying' (NCCA 2009a:44).

As you might expect, there is a close link to Síolta Standard 7: Curriculum – 'Encouraging each child's holistic development and learning requires the implementation of a verifiable, broad-based, documented and flexible curriculum or programme' (CECDE 2006:55). With that connection in mind I will look at two of the components under this standard, which provide a valuable context within which to reflect on practices, both in the example provided but also in relation to your own experiences. Component 7.2 reads, 'There is a well-referenced curriculum or programme in operation, based on established and verifiable principles of child development' (CECDE 2006:58). This example is set in a school classroom and the practitioner is following the primary school curriculum and using aspects of the Aistear framework to inform his practice. Signpost for Reflection 7.2.1 poses the question, 'How does the curriculum/programme support your setting's aims and objectives for development and learning?' It is helpful to take time to reflect on this in relation to your own setting experiences as well as in the context of the primary curriculum. All practitioners should be able to explain – in broad terms and clear language – the principles that underpin their practice. Another component of importance to this setting example is Component 7.3: 'The curriculum/programme is reflected in and implemented through the child's daily routine, spontaneous learning opportunities, structured activities and activities initiated by the child' (CECDE 2006:5). This component is realised in a number of ways in the illustration above. For instance, the creation of the opportunity for peer tutoring in allowing the senior infants to read their stories to small groups of junior infants is an example of new learning opportunities. In school settings this would take time, co-operation and careful organisation to arrange and it is such a useful learning opportunity. Many of the Signposts for Reflection are relevant here, but one worth thinking about is 7.3.6 – 'What aspects of child learning and development are being addressed in this activity?' We know from the reflection question at the close of the example that the ambition is to develop higher-order skills, but this signpost affords us the opportunity to actually name the different skills that are being developed. If we can't do that, how can we explain to others what it is that is so important about our practices?

Standard 1: Rights of the Child – 'Ensuring that each child's rights are met requires that she/he is enabled to exercise choice and to use initiative as an active participant and partner in her/his own development and learning' (CECDE 2006:13) is being met here. There is a clear sense that the children are respected and the importance of their attention and co-operation is recognised. Component 1.3: 'Each child is enabled to participate actively in the daily routine, in activities, in conversations and in all other appropriate situations, and is considered as a partner by the adult' is actively realised in this example of good practice. Signpost for Reflection 1.3.5 is worth further examination, both in relation to the example above and your own experiences. It poses the question, 'How do you ensure that each child joins in the shared activities in a way that suits her/his own disposition?' This is a particular challenge in a setting with twenty-eight children of five and six years old.

SUPPORTING LEARNING AND DEVELOPMENT THROUGH ASSESSMENT

Illustration 6

- Aim 3 and Learning Goal 2
- Age Group: Babies, toddlers and young children
- Setting: Childminding

Bernie, a childminder, looks after Jack (sixteen months), Sorcha (three years) and Rhiannon (five years) in her home. Bernie plans lots of activities for the week to build on some of what Sorcha has been doing in playgroup and Rhiannon in school.

On Monday they all go for a walk to the shops. On the way they count the red cars parked along the street. Rhiannon and Sorcha look for 1, 2 and 3 on car number plates (Rhiannon does this for 4, 5 and 6 too). Rhiannon spots numbers on houses and shop doors. They identify these and Bernie explains their purpose. They reach the post box. Sorcha and Rhiannon each take a letter for posting and Rhiannon notices a 5 on the stamp. They ask Bernie what the number is and she explains about the cost of the stamp. Bernie makes sure Jack is included by drawing his attention to things. From time to time she kneels beside Jack in his pushchair and points to and describes things around him.

On Wednesday Bernie bakes with the children. Jack sits at the table in his high chair and the girls sit on chairs in their aprons. They are making top hats. Bernie gives Jack a dish of softened fruit and a spoon for him to mix and eat while she and the girls count out bun cases, making sure there is one for each person and their mama and dad and siblings. 'How do we make these buns, Bernie?', enquires Rhiannon. Bernie explains. She adds the melted chocolate and the girls put a marshmallow in each case followed by a small strawberry, which the girls picked in Bernie's garden that morning.

On other days they look for numbers in the kitchen, for example on the washing machine dials, on food packets and in storybooks. 'Two! What that for?', asks Sorcha as she and Rhiannon help Bernie load clothes in the washing machine and set the correct cycle. Bernie describes these experiences to Jack and includes him in the conversations. The children also help Bernie in her day-to day activities in caring for the house and Bernie talks to them about how and what they are learning through these hands-on experiences.

 Reflection: Do I encourage children to ask me questions as part of their conversations with me? (NCCA 2009b:85)

This illustration may appear fairly simple but in fact it hides a great deal of complexity in its simplicity. For instance, Bernie has to handle all the transitions experienced by the children she is caring for, whether from home to her setting or from playgroup or school. There will also be times when they come to her directly from home and this too has to be considered. In addition she has to prepare for their transitions from her setting to their own at the end of the day. While this may all be part of most children's experiences, it can become troublesome if careful attention is not given to clear rules and roles. In addition, the illustration gives us many examples of how children can widen their knowledge of number and develop their numeracy. This example is presented under Aistear's Aim 3: 'Children will explore ways to represent ideas, feelings, thoughts, objects and actions through symbols' and Learning Goal 2: 'In partnership with the adult, children will become familiar with and associate symbols (pictures, numbers, letters and words) with the things they represent' (NCCA 2009a:44).

This example could be linked to a number of Síolta standards, for instance Standard 13: Transitions – 'Ensuring continuity of experiences for children requires policies, procedures and practice that promote sensitive management of transitions, consistency in key relationships, liaison within and between settings, the keeping and transfer of relevant information (with parental consent), and the close involvement of parents and, where appropriate, relevant professionals' (CECDE 2006:91). Although this is not necessarily the standard one might expect to consider in relation to this particular illustration, it does highlight the importance of the careful and sensitive management of transitions. Component 13.2: 'The setting promotes smooth transitions by ensuring there is appropriate liaison within the setting and between settings' (CECDE 2006:93) outlines a key element of successful transitions, and the Signpost for Reflection 13.2.1 poses the question, 'How do you support the child's transition into/within/from your setting?'

Also relevant to the example is Standard 5: Interactions – 'Fostering constructive interactions (child/child; child/adult; adult/adult) requires explicit policies, procedures and practice that emphasise the value of process and are based on mutual respect, equal partnership and sensitivity' (CECDE 2006:39). As Bernie works on her own as a childminder she has sole responsibility for maintaining the relationships between the setting and its activities and the various adults in the life of the children she caters for. Component 5.5: 'Interactions between the adults within, and associated with the setting, act as a model of respect, support and partnership for the child' (CECDE 2006:46) is probably the one most relevant to this example as it captures the importance of respectful relationships, and it can be related to professional practice through Signpost for Reflection 5.5.1, which asks, 'How do your interactions with parents model friendly respect and partnership?' Component 5.3: 'The adult uses all aspects of the daily routine (both formal and informal) to interact sensitively and respectfully with the child' (CECDE 2006:43) is also a useful standard to consider in light of this example. It is particularly relevant when considering Bernie's interactions with Jack and the ways she includes him in the general activities of the setting.

Standard 7: Curriculum – 'Encouraging each child's holistic development and learning requires the implementation of a verifiable, broad-based, documented and flexible curriculum or programme' (CECDE 2006:55) has particular relevance to this illustration. We see how carefully Bernie encourages the children to practise what they are learning in their different settings by reference to the everyday experiences they have with her as she goes about her daily routines. Building on the different curricular experiences of each child, she is expanding their learning and their development. Through her practice she is meeting Component 7.3: 'The curriculum/programme is reflected in and implemented through the child's daily routine, spontaneous learning opportunities, structured activities and activities initiated by the child' (CECDE 2006:58).

Illustration 7

- Aim 2 and Learning Goal 3
- Age Group: Toddlers and young children
- Setting: Sessional service (preschool)

Mary, the preschool leader, creates the following story to document Claire's, Robert's and Kyle's learning through an activity at the water table.

Twins Claire and Robert (four years) and their friend Kyle (nearly three years) are playing at the water tray. They are filling and emptying containers and pouring water into waterwheels and watching them turn.

The children experiment with placing different objects such as balls and cubes in the waterwheels. Claire likes to use the teapot to pour water. Robert joins her in doing this. He uses the small watering can from the vegetable patch to put water over the blocks he has placed in the waterwheel. Kyle watches, quietly choosing not to do any pouring at the waterwheel.

Claire picks up an orange ball and puts it on top of the waterwheel. Robert and Kyle watch as she pours water from the teapot. The ball begins to rotate at the top of the waterwheel. 'Mary, come quick. Look what happens,' Claire shouts excitedly. Mary kneels down to see what is happening. Kyle kneels too. Mary asks Claire to pour more water. They all watch carefully as the ball rotates. 'My

---

goodness, look at that,' responds Mary. Robert pours more water on top of his cubes. 'Mine don't spin. That's not fair,' he concludes. 'Maybe try a ball like Claire did,' Mary suggests. Robert takes out the cubes and inserts the ball he has been holding in his hand. He pours water over it with the watering can and it begins to spin too. 'Yes!' shouts Robert in delight. Kyle smiles. He visits the water tray again by himself later in the day and tries out the spinning balls.

Mary shares the story and the photographs with the children next day. They put the story on display on the pre-school wall. Over the next few days Mary and the children investigate further why the cube wouldn't spin while the balls did.

 Reflection: How can I make time to document some of children's learning and development using the storytelling approach? (NCCA 2009b:90)

This example is intended to illustrate how it is possible to document children's learning as you work with them in the daily routines of the curriculum/programme. Clearly it is important to plan how to do this, but with careful attention it is possible. The illustration is presented under Aistear Aim 2: 'Children will develop and use skills and strategies for observing, questioning, investigating, understanding, negotiating and problem solving and come to see themselves as explorers and thinkers', Learning Goal 5: 'In partnership with the adult, children will collaborate with others to share interests and to solve problems confidently' and Learning Goal 3: 'In partnership with the adult, children will use their experience and information to explore and develop working theories about how the world works, and think about how and why they learn things' (NCCA 2009a:44).

In reviewing the Síolta standards we find a number that are relevant. For instance, Standard 8: Planning and Evaluation – 'Enriching and informing all aspects of practice within the setting requires cycles of observation, planning, action and evaluation, undertaken on a regular basis' (CECDE 2006:63) is particularly relevant, given the attention to documentation in the examples. Component 8.3: 'There is a mechanism in place to ensure that review processes lead to changes in practice' (CECDE 2006:65) is the component that identifies the importance of evaluation and the importance of planning for it so that practice can continue to be critically reviewed. The single Signpost for Reflection (8.3.1) under this component focuses less on using the documentation as a means of planning the curriculum and focuses more directly on practice: 'When change is indicated by the review process, how is the change incorporated into practice?' As mentioned previously, the challenge is to move beyond recognising the need for change and towards actually implementing change in practice.

Standard 12: Communication – 'Communicating effectively in the best interests of the child requires policies, procedures and actions that promote the proactive sharing of knowledge and information among appropriate stakeholders with respect and confidentiality' (CECDE 2006:87) points to the importance of having a clear sense of why what is done in a setting is done. Placing the child at the centre of practice requires that you state clearly what this means for practice. Component 12.2 states: 'The setting is proactive in sharing information, as appropriate, in the best interests of the child, with other stakeholders' (CECDE 2006:89). In the example above the documented story is displayed on the preschool wall so that it can be referred to by the children themselves, thus assisting their working memory and other aptitudes that hone their thinking skills. It can also be referred to with parents and visitors to offer a visible explanation of the importance of the work being undertaken in the setting and guided by a knowledgeable staff. This answers Signpost for Reflection 12.2.2, 'How is information shared?'

Finally, this example can be seen as a realisation of Standard 11: Professional Practice – 'Practising in a professional manner requires that individuals have skills, knowledge, values and attitudes appropriate to their role and responsibility within the setting. In addition, it requires regular reflection upon practice and engagement in supported, ongoing professional development' (CECDE 2006:81). The reflection question at the conclusion of the example is about professional practice in that it asks, 'How can I make time for documentation . . .', showing a reflective attitude and an understanding of the value of pedagogical documentation. Component 11.4 reads: 'Adults within the setting are encouraged and appropriately resourced to engage in a wide variety of regular and ongoing professional development' (CECDE 2006:84). The Signpost for Reflection that offers a context for further consideration of the practice described in the example is 11.4.2 – 'How are practitioners encouraged to engage in professional development?' – and it notes the importance of allocating resources, such as time, funding and materials to assist in professional development.

While the illustrations above presented opportunities to link specific samples of daily practice with the standards of Síolta and the learning goals of Aistear, they do not directly present ideas for achieving the aims of Aistear under the theme of Exploring and Thinking. Attention to actual practice can be found in a series of Sample Learning Opportunities in the Aistear document. The suggestions are set out according to age groups and provide useful ideas on how to really look at your own practice and check it for its potential in expanding and enriching young children's exploration and thinking skills, which are so crucial to early learning and development. Below I present the main practice styles suggested for maximising children's learning opportunities under the theme Exploring and Thinking. The content of the situations derives from the children and the adults and will be unique to each opportunity that presents itself. When considering how to carry through these suggestions you will be greatly assisted by applying your knowledge and understanding of child development, relevant research and the processes that assist learning and development most appropriately for individual children. The ages act as a guide but they are overlapping in order to capture the reality that children have different developmental trajectories across aspects of development.

- When working with babies – birth to eighteen months – practitioners should:
    - promote a warm and trusting relationship with babies through play and exploration
    - provide opportunities for babies to develop physical skills and spatial awareness
    - create opportunities for babies to experience cause and effect
    - provide opportunities for sensory exploration that help babies to develop ideas about how the world works
    - play hiding games to help babies to develop the concept of object permanence (the knowledge that things still exist even when they are out of sight)
    - provide all babies with opportunities to play and explore.
- When working with toddlers – twelve months to three years – practitioners should:
    - encourage physical activity and the development of an understanding of space
    - help toddlers to experience and talk about the world around them
    - support toddlers in making theories about how things work and in understanding cause and effect
    - enable toddlers develop an understanding of concepts like measures – weight (heavy/light), height (bigger/smaller), volume, money and time
    - help toddlers understand the process of change
    - encourage toddlers to follow an interest
    - provide opportunities for toddlers to compare, sort, categorise and order things
    - draw toddlers' attention to the use of pictures, numbers and printed words in the environment and in their play.
- When working with young children – 2½ to six years – practitioners should:
    - enable young children to develop physical skills
    - extend young children's knowledge about their world
    - encourage young children to get involved in projects which enable them to explore a topic that interests them or an experience they really enjoyed
    - encourage young children to think deeply about things by using discussion techniques, listening carefully to them and building on what they know
    - use play and real-life experiences to classify, sequence, sort, match, look for and create patterns and shapes
    - enable young children to develop an understanding of concepts like measures (weight, height, volume, money and time)
    - build on young children's natural curiosity and help them to experiment and investigate change
    - encourage young children to experiment with colour, shape, size and texture to represent ideas

- use symbols to help young children learn from and use their environment
- model the writing process and help young children to record their experiences and thoughts.

(NCCA 2009a:45–52)

SUMMARY

The final theme of Aistear, Exploring and Thinking, was introduced in this chapter. As both these activities are fundamental to overall learning and development it is difficult to consider them in isolation. The important role that play offers as both a site for developing skills and understandings and a process of learning and development was discussed. In the context of providing opportunities to facilitate meaningful exploration and extend thinking, the critical role of the early years practitioner as an intentional and engaged adult was highlighted and linked to the characteristics of high-quality settings. Specifically, the value of an integrated approach to practice, providing for learning through child-directed play, guided play and adult-led learning was examined.

You will notice that the focus of the learning opportunities and practice examples presented is on the practitioner and child/children relationship, the quality of listening and communicating and the provision of opportunities from within the ordinary and the lived experiences of the children and adults that make up the learning environment. The opportunities require the practitioner to be attuned and sensitive to the learning possibilities that arise in the most ordinary of events. Specifically noted was the provision of learning opportunities that invite children to explore, that are challenging and that encourage co-operation and risk-taking while being supported and safe. This theme challenges you to take your time, to give plenty of time and to use time carefully. There are many opportunities presented for capturing the learning moments that arise when individual children are concentrating on a task or when a group of children are playing a game, solving a problem or messing about. Many of the suggestions require practitioners to create space and time for the sustained shared thinking that Siraj-Blatchford and her colleagues found to be so important to practice in quality early years settings and which most benefited young children. Most of all, the examples reflect the democratic nature of excellent early years practice, a practice that respects all children, that celebrates difference, that listens to children and hears them, that engages children in conversations, facilitates conversations between children and that provides learning environments that are rich in possibilities, and where children feel secure and free to explore and to think about the world and their place in it.

CHAPTER 8

Reflecting on Practice

I hear babies cry, I watch them grow
They'll learn much more than I'll ever know. (Thiele & Weiss 1967)

This final chapter presents an opportunity to review the theory and practice sections of the book, to reflect on the key aspects that contribute to quality early years practice and to consider how best to utilise this knowledge to enhance your own early years practice with children from birth to six years of age. The content of this book is based on the premise that the most effective early childhood practice is that which is always open to new knowledge and new ideas and has a sound theoretical basis.

Our own history and experiences of learning influence our practice in a way that may be less than useful. We carry with us into our practice our knowledge and some of the myths from our past. But our understanding of child development and learning is expanding all the time and some of our tacit knowledge is out of date. Unless we are willing to challenge and explore our own assumptions we may never really provide our young children with the rich learning environments they need to experience in order to be able to adapt to the changing world. The 'knowledge' we routinely use and rarely reflect on or question provides us with a familiar structure but one that replicates what has always been done, where there is a danger of repeating mistakes or failed approaches to practice, and that restricts the space within which to challenge ourselves and develop our professionalism. This taken for granted, tacit knowledge is rarely articulated, discussed or made visible – it is just the way things are.

In Chapter 1 I presented six personally influencing beliefs about young children, which were then considered in more detail from the perspective of contemporary research knowledge. These beliefs are still valid and bear repetition:

1 Children are central to quality practice.
2 Children are basically good.
3 Interactions are the key process through which we learn and develop.
4 Children have agency and contribute to their learning.
5 Early years experiences are critical to the journey of learning and development.
6 Adults play a crucial role in providing quality early years experiences.

These beliefs were further elaborated and linked directly to themes for analysing early years practice by Hayes and Kernan (2008) in *Engaging Young Children: A Nurturing Pedagogy*. They are presented below as a framework for practitioners within which to review day-to-day practice.

In the first instance we hold that *young children are active agents in their own learning*. This concept has emerged as a key consideration for early years practitioners as it may present tensions between your structuring or planning for practice and the agency in children's lives. Second, we understand the *dynamic, social and interactive nature of early learning*. While the child is located at the heart of practice, we acknowledge the interdependent nature of the relationship between the child and adult as they engage in joint learning. Research confirms the social nature of development and highlights the critical role of positive interactions and relationships in brain development and the associated executive functions in the early years.

Thus, in the view of early years practice presented here, attention is paid to the *critical role of the adult* in supporting children's learning. The key finding from the research is that it is the quality of the early years practice that impacts most on young children. In support of the critical nature of early years experiences the concept of *early childhood education and care practice* is reconceptualised as a *nurturing pedagogy*. The concept of nurture, proposed by early childhood pioneers such as Margaret McMillan, has a contemporary relevance in that it allows us to view care as an educative process. It is reformulated to emphasise the educative nature of care and to place as central the critical and active role of the adult in effective, engaging and quality early education (Hayes 2007). The fifth theme emphasises the idea *of content-, language- and risk-rich learning environments*. Children's interactions with their social and physical environments are the central location of development and should be challenging and rich in both language and content; the onus is on the practitioner to provide and support such enabling environments. A sixth theme stresses the *importance of play and playfulness as a pathway to learning*. As with other themes of analysis, play is considered from the perspectives of both the child and the adult, recognising the importance of the process of play to children, as well as the role of play as a window for the adult into the world of the sensing, active and playful child. The final theme concerns the *affective dimension of learning*. This dimension of learning is less easy to measure than the more familiar cognitive dimension, but is no less important; it is the dimension that allows consideration of valuable learning dispositions such as motivation, learner identity and confidence. These themes have applicability across the range of early years settings.

> **Themes for analysing early years practice**
> * Young children are active agents in their own learning.
> * The dynamic, social and interactive nature of early learning.
> * The critical role of the adult.
> * The nurturing dimension of early years practice.

- • The role of content-, language- and risk-rich environments
- • The importance of play and playfulness as a pathway to learning.
- • The affective dimension of learning, particularly the sense of security and belonging.

Adapted from Hayes and Kernan (2008:3–4).

A key point for synthesis here is that practice happens in the ordinary reality of the day to day and in the context of a particular group of children and adults. That context is unique and it has its challenges and opportunities. The two practice frameworks available to Irish practitioners, Síolta and Aistear, provide a rich vision for working effectively and in a satisfying way with young children. These frameworks are almost too rich in their possibilities and can be daunting when first approached. However, they are not prescriptive but are designed to act as guides to good practice and they are rich in illustrations and examples from practice against which your own practice can be analysed.

WHAT MAKES A GOOD EARLY YEARS PRACTITIONER?

Early years settings that are of high quality, beneficial to children and their families and professionally satisfying are those where adults are knowledgeable and up to date with contemporary understanding of how young children learn and develop and exhibit engaged and intelligent practice. This requires appropriate initial training and ongoing professional development. Well-trained practitioners provide appropriate sensory input and stable, responsive relationships for the infants and young children they work with and provide a strong foundation of learning, behaviour and health across time. It is clear from research evidence that the interactions between children, adults and environments are key to development and it is here that the adult has a primary role. One cannot overstate the importance of relationships in the early years. We now know that brains are built over time. Research tells us that policies and practices that 'promote supportive relationships and rich learning opportunities for young children create a strong foundation' (NSCDC 2007a:2). The brain architecture is constructed through a process that begins before birth and the process is enhanced by stable, secure and caring early life experiences. Engaged interactions, which are responsive to the child's natural tendency to interact reciprocally and are sensitive to the natural give and take that can be seen in infants as young as days old, have a profoundly positive effect on early development.

A balanced practice that integrates practitioner input with child-initiated activities provides a dynamic context for learning and development. The idea of integrated learning is not new; Dewey stressed the importance of interest as a motivating force for activity and reflection and saw the role of the adult in the process as that of guide or mentor. A respectful and democratic early years environment provides children with the opportunity to develop those skills essential to participation in a democratic society. Even very young children are now recognised as socially competent and active in their engagement with the people, places and things that comprise their learning environments. The evidence suggests that early education that emphasises the affective dimensions of learning and those cognitive skills, the executive functions, associated with the planning and organisation of knowledge positively influences children's later academic cognitive development in relation to content knowledge, literacy and numeracy skills. This approach yields foundational short-term benefits and sustainable long-term benefits across social and educational dimensions. This highlights once again the crucial nature – the centrality – of relationships to learning and development. The child's interactions, whether with an adult, another child, an object, materials or the natural world, are the site of learning. The relational process itself is a key part of the educational experience and, as such, deserves reflection and analysis in and of itself.

Recognising the importance of the social context to development supports the view that development is not an isolated, individualistic pursuit and that children's participation within a social context transforms their experiences. The research also suggests that learning environments that facilitate more involvement with and attention to activities by children themselves result in their learning more skills and concepts, including the kind of knowledge that is tested by achievement measures. In addition, children from such settings show more cognitive advance and variety in verbal and social skills. This may arise because attending longer or more intently to interesting activities gives children practice in attending, a skill highly valued by early years practitioners, or because making decisions and having some responsibility for their own learning and actions may help children internalise control or engender 'the dispositions in children that enable them to achieve greater success' (Schweinhart, Barnes & Weikart 1993). Perhaps the explanation lies in the fact that children may just be happier, and so better motivated, and may, in turn, be responded to more positively by practitioners. Contemporary studies of development move beyond the individual to consider the interactive, integrated nature of learning and development, the role of the individual and the environment as actors that each have the potential to transform the other. Early years practitioners who are knowledgeable, skilled and well trained have an important role to play in creating positive early years environments, facilitating healthy interactions and, where relevant, the early identification of, and response to, difficulties or problems.

WHAT DOES GOOD EARLY YEARS PRACTICE LOOK LIKE?

The evidence suggests that good early years practice is informed by a combination of experience and a contemporary understanding of early child development. A review of research suggests that the following early years practice strategies are pivotal:

- *Listening to children* across the ages to find out about the learning strategies children themselves bring to a problem or an activity, the strengths they have and the opportunities that allow more knowledgeable others (peers or practitioners) to help.

- *Listening to and co-ordinating with parents and family members* to establish children's strengths, interests and dispositions and to find out how the child's development and learning is mediated through the home. Children can also benefit from the influence early years practitioners can have on the home learning environment through sharing with parents aspects of their practice and their understandings of an individual child's development.

- *Establishing common knowledge* through using the opportunities presented by situations where children are together in groups; this provides examples of common experiences and therefore common ground for expanding children's thinking.

- *Encouraging children to recall* experiences associated with a shared task can help children build learning continuity and establish new or enriched concepts and understandings.

- *Using positive modelling* is a powerful way to assist children to extend their meta-cognitive strategies to regulate task achievement. (What is the problem I am working on? What is my plan? How will I proceed? What has worked to solve this problem? How do I know?)

- *Asking children to build theories* that can explain events in which they show interest is thought to keep children interested and active in particular tasks. In such situations it is helpful for practitioners to use open-ended questions to give children a real chance to expand their thinking and strengthen their skills of communication.

- *Finding ways to look beyond the obvious* or the familiar and to reflect in words to babies and young children what they are doing in action. This helps them to clarify processes and ideas and acts as a form of scaffolding.

- *Giving specific instructions* in certain areas. Games may be used to practise and build repetition. Strategies for solving problems can be modelled for children and the thinking process made explicit.

- *Spending time in observation* either through standing aside from or joining in children's tasks with sensitivity to the learning situation. Gathering observation records as a basis for reflection or a source of planning enriches practice.

- *Celebrating diversity* through expanding children's knowledge and understanding of diverse languages, music, stories, images and rituals.

- *Focusing through recall and restatement.* This requires careful questioning, clear responses and explanations linked to events or activities.

- *Ensuring that young children have many situations* in which to speak and listen so that their communication experiences are broadened. (OECD 2007; Marbina, Church & Tayler 2011)

These practice strategies challenge practitioners to be present and engaged and ready to facilitate children in extending their learning through their activities. In a presentation to the UK Association for the Professional Development of Early Years Educators on how practice supports sustained shared thinking, Siraj-Blatchford (2005) drew a useful distinction between sustained shared thinking and sustained shared conversations. It is often through sustained shared conversations that practitioners can use sustained shared thinking. Engaging meaningfully and intelligently with young children in extra talk provides a powerful context for developing their thinking and the metacognitive skills that strengthen their executive function. It can function to equip children, even very young children, with the language and thinking skills that are important to later personal learning style. Much of the talk that is observed in early years settings has been found to be of a fairly low level, largely managerial or organisational in style, for example 'Put on your coat' or 'Pick it up' or 'Do this' or 'Tidy up time.' While such demands can be an important part of the organisation of a setting they are very limited as models of conversation for children and they do nothing to extend children's learning or thinking. Siraj-Blatchford argues that to really enhance children's development practitioners have to work together with children in an intellectual way to solve problems, clarify ideas or extend narrative. She offers the following strategies for engaging in effective sustained shared conversations:

- *Tuning in:* listening carefully to the child, to what is being said, observing body language and what the child is doing
- *Showing genuine interest:* giving your full attention to the child, maintaining eye contact, affirming, nodding and smiling.
- *Respecting children's own decisions* and choices by inviting children to elaborate: saying things like, 'I really want to know more about this' and listening to and engaging with the response.
- *Recapping:* 'So you think . . . ?'
- *Offering your own experience:* 'I like to listen to music when I make supper at home.'
- *Clarifying ideas:* 'Right, Darren, so you think that this stone will melt if I boil it in water?'
- *Suggesting:* 'You might like to try doing it this way.'
- *Reminding:* 'Don't forget that you said that this stone will melt if I boil it.'
- *Using encouragement to further thinking:* 'You have really thought hard about where to put this door in the castle . . . Where will you put the window?'
- *Offering an alternative viewpoint:* 'Maybe Goldilocks wasn't bold when she ate the porridge?'
- *Speculating:* 'Do you think the three bears would have liked Goldilocks to come and live with them as a friend?'
- *Reciprocating:* 'Thank goodness you were wearing wellingtons when you jumped through those puddles, Kwame. Look at my feet – they are soaking wet!'
- *Asking open questions:* 'How did you . . .?'; 'Why does this . . .?'; 'What happens

next?'; 'What do you think?'; I wonder what would happen if . . .?'
- *Modelling thinking:* 'I have to think hard about what to do this evening. I need to take my cat to the vet because he has a sore foot, take my books back to the library and buy some food for dinner tonight. But I just won't have time to do all these things.'

She provides a list of useful *positive phrases and questions* that can be used to extend thinking:
- 'I don't know, what do you think?'
- 'That's an interesting idea.'
- 'I like what you have done there.'
- 'Have you seen what X has done? Why . . .?'
- 'I wonder why you had . . .?'
- 'I've never thought of that before.'
- 'You've really made me think.'
- 'What would happen if we . . .?'

And also a list of what she calls *'making-sense' words*:
- I think
- I agree
- I imagine
- I disagree
- I like
- I don't like
- I wonder.

Finally, she offers some suggestions on *styles of practice:*
- Repeat and use children's own words – restate.
- Be active about introducing new and interesting words to children.
- Limit questioning – sometime it can seem like interrogating.
- Encourage children to describe their efforts, their ideas, their products.
- Use encouragement rather than praise – too much praise can be insidious as it can make children dependent on it.
- When you use praise, be specific – focus on the children's actions and what they are doing rather than on whether it pleases the adult. Rather than saying, 'That's a lovely painting,' try something like, 'I wonder how you made all those layers of colour?'

These strategies for practice illustrate how powerful the practitioner is to the quality of children's early years experiences and they provide a guide that is useful for when you reflect back on your practice, whether alone or with the team.

REFLECTIVE PRACTICE

The term 'reflection' is often used in the current literature to describe a variety of practices, from simply thinking of one's own plans to considering the social, ethical and even political implications this thinking has on actual practice. The word 'reflection' carries with it the idea of looking back, which can lead one to consider that reflection is something that happens after the event. We plan an activity and carry it out; and we review and reflect on it later. However, reflective practice is richer when it is considered in the context of being present in the moment, an inclination towards careful consideration of what exactly is happening in the moment, a reflection in process. This is a deep level of reflection, which requires an awareness and engagement with the moment rather than wondering how this moment will impact on some distant outcome. It suggests an interest in the potential of this moment for you and those children you are working with. Such practice emerges from a well-established understanding of what early years practice is about and it depends on careful planning that allows you to unlock the possibilities of practice in the present.

There are many levels and types of reflection in the growth of reflective practice. Some definitions of reflective practice focus on the connection between practice and identified learning goals and outcomes, through reviewing and analysing one's own actions, decisions or choice of materials. Other definitions characterise reflective practice as a lifelong attempt involving a longer and more lasting commitment to the ongoing learning and continuous improvement of the quality of one's professional practice (York-Barr *et al.* 2006). Still other definitions consider reflective practice as requiring one to move beyond a focus on isolated events to consider the broader context, including the personal, pedagogical and societal as well as the ethical contexts associated with professional work (Larrivee 2005).

There is general agreement that reflection can be considered as functioning on the following three levels:

1   The *surface level* is the level that focuses on the practice skills, actions and roles, generally looking at each teaching episode as an isolated event. The focus is often on the practitioner reflecting on approaches and techniques used to reach particular goals.

2   The *pedagogical level* is a more advanced level, at which the practitioner considers the theory of and rationale for current practice. At this level the practitioner is expected to be working towards understanding the theory behind a particular practice and applying these theories to their practice.

3   The *critical level* represents the higher order, where practitioners examine the social, ethical and political consequences of their educational processes and practices. At this level, they also inspect both their professional and personal convictions and how they impact, directly and indirectly, on children.

Larrivee (2005) recognises that new practitioners and students in training may be at a pre-reflective stage, requiring guidance in developing the skill of reflective practice. She notes that practitioners who are truly self-reflective examine how expectations and assumptions, family influences and cultural conditioning impact on children and their learning. They also recognise that there are tensions between theory, policy and practice, which they need to reconcile. This level of reflection moves practitioners to look not only at their own practices but also at the social implications of these practices.

A reflective practitioner is one who regularly reviews their practice, asking 'Why am I doing this? Of what value is it to the child, the group, my colleagues, parents, community?' Such reflection shows an understanding that part of working professionally in the early years is to be willing to recognise that there is always something more to learn about child development, learning environments, practice in general. As noted in Chapter 2, the word 'why' should be a key word in quality early years practice. It acknowledges the need for constant reflection on the quality of the early years environment and its impact on young children. Furthermore, when answered, it can give practitioners confidence when they are called upon to defend the value of early years practice to professionals and parents.

HOW ASSESSMENT CONTRIBUTES TO QUALITY PRACTICE

We saw in Chapter 3 how assessment can be used in early years practice as either assessment *for* learning or assessment *of* learning and we noted that assessment *for* learning has a powerful contribution to play in informing early years practice and planning. Here we consider assessment in greater detail to illustrate how assessment can be used in the daily routine of an early years setting.

Dynamic assessment is an interactive form of assessment; it is neither an assessment instrument nor a method of assessing. Rather it is a framework for considering practice and assessment as an integrated activity useful in understanding young children's abilities while supporting their development. It draws on Vygotsky's concept of the zone of proximal development, which highlights the developmental importance of providing supports to learners that encourage them to stretch beyond their own independent performance. Effective dynamic assessment represents a unification of theory and practice: the theory offers a basis to guide practice but at the same time practice functions to refine and extend theory.

A key element in dynamic assessment for learning is the expectations that practitioners have of the children they are working with. Research has shown that adult expectations have a profound effect on children's learning. In particular there is evidence to suggest that practitioners working with children from disadvantaged backgrounds may assume that children who come from environments that are limited are themselves limited. This is problematic: most children can be challenged and enthused to learn if presented with an engaged adult who provides do-able activities in a safe and secure environment where the child has a sense of belonging, of being an active member of the group that comprises the adults and children of an early years setting. Where practitioners are engaged and attuned to young children and have high expectations for them they create rich and challenging learning opportunities through which children are more likely to develop positive learning dispositions.

Planning is important for effective practice and is guided by some distant ambition for the future impact of the planned activity or routine. How can we reconcile the tension between the need to plan and ensuring that our practice is meaningful and effective in the moment for the child who is living in the moment? In considering this tension the following example from my own experience may be helpful in understanding how important it is to plan and that careful planning allows for rich, spontaneous practice in the day-to-day practice of early years settings.

> When I am invited to present a lecture or a presentation to a seminar of students or an audience of educators I approach it in the same way. I find a focus and title for the topic, and I draw on my experience and reading to draft an outline for the presentation. Once this is done I can develop, for instance, a PowerPoint presentation and run through the issues and points I want to raise to ensure that they fit in the time I have been allotted.
>
> On the day I use the PowerPoint presentation as a frame within which to present my seminar or lecture. I am well prepared and so I am free to engage in a type of conversation with the audience, add anecdotes that spring to mind in the moment and generally personalise the content to the context and the audience. Thus – when it works – planning creates a framework within which I am free to draw on my experience and knowledge to present key ideas and points to the particular audience in a way that – at its best – is responsive to the moment, natural, flowing and engaging and ultimately satisfying – for both myself and the audience.

Translating from this example to planning for responsive practice in the early years requires a slightly different approach that comprises three elements:

1. The *structure* needs to take account of the characteristics of the learning environment and the profile and age of the children.
2. The *content* can be informed by experience, knowledge, research or guidance from Síolta or Aistear. In practice the exact content emerges from opportunities presented by the children and the learning environment at any given time.
3. The *time* available is guided by the routine, and by the flexibility you have as an adult within the routine. In practice an outline routine is more effective than one that is too tightly defined.

Thus the planning and the content ideas may exist in advance, but the actual practice is guided by the moment, is responsive to the group and engaging for both adult and child.

Planning is greatly enhanced when the practitioner has a sound knowledge base and information about the setting, the children and their families. This can be acquired through the careful collection and management of documentation. There are two types of documentation of use to early years settings: administrative documentation; and pedagogical documentation. The former is essential for meeting the legal and regulatory requirements for providing early years services. For the purposes of this book, however, it is pedagogical documentation that is more important.

For the practitioner, pedagogical documentation is a means of observing learning in action, studying and enriching one's understanding of the whole child. It has a long history going back to the Child Study Movement in early twentieth-century Europe and the USA (Singer 1992; Hayes 2010). Observation is a tool for understanding, for observing how the whole child in context is developing and learning; for hearing what observed behaviour can tell us through reflection and discussion, rather than deciding what the behaviour represents on the basis of our immediate reaction to it. There is a tension between the need to understand how children learn and develop and allowing us to let the child show us their learning and development in action, which can often yield explanations that are both particular to the child or group and also offer a path for practice that is relevant and meaningful.

In early years practice, observation is central to understanding the developing child in the day-to-day midst of life in early years settings. Pedagogical documentation is about getting to know the whole child in context, recognising diversity and acknowledging, valuing and learning from different perspectives and interpretations. It is far more than simply understanding isolated dimensions of development of the child, such as physical or language development. Pedagogical documentation is most valuable when it is carefully gathered, considered and analysed. It is useful to dig deep into the documentation, to go beyond mere recording and reviewing.

In her paper on the use of pedagogical documentation, Alcock (2000) lists a number of elements of documentation that are necessary for it to become an effective element of practice. In the first instance she discusses the tools that can be used. These include cameras, audio recorders, videos, computers, photocopiers, pen, paper and voice. The type of content that can be included in documentation includes: children's work; photographs; plans; drafts of work in progress; audio/video clips of children and adults in action; written transcripts of children's spontaneous articulations; taped language; comments and interviews with children and adults; illustrations, which can be accompanied by child commentary and standard child observations.

A critical dimension in using certain pedagogical documentation is how it is displayed. It requires clear walls with no unnecessary clutter and this, in turn, involves careful team consideration of what exactly constitutes clutter. Careful attention needs to be paid to what to display and why: material can lose its meaning and value if it is dis-embedded from its context when displayed; and it may hold little or no meaning for the children even if it is meaningful to adults. Alcock notes that 'without an analytical explanation or explicit link to learning goals or outcomes these colourful products can create a sense of chaotic clutter rather than inspiring pedagogical reflection' (Alcock 2000:2). Carefully managed documentation can unlock a rich seam of learning opportunities and it can stimulate memories, conversations and reflections on plans met, ideas forgotten, successes, failures and new ideas emerging.

Pedagogical documentation is documentation that documents learning in action. It requires a change in traditional practice, but research suggests that it alters rather than adds to the time in practice. It is not about multiple individual reports for each child or an additional element tacked on to the daily routine; rather it is a change in practice, a revision of routine through a collective dialogue around pedagogical documentation – creating it, displaying it, reflecting on it, making it part and parcel of your daily practice. Simply gathering material and putting it on display is not what we mean when we talk about pedagogical documentation. The name itself suggests that it is recording learning as it happens and reflecting on it. Pedagogical documentation links ideas, events and behaviours, it bridges across time and content, it allows for discussion among children themselves or with an adult – sometimes a parent. It is enriching and informing for the those involved and yields positive change in children, which is visible in their behaviour, their engagement and the overall learning environment. In addition to impacting on adults and children in the early years setting, pedagogical documentation also facilitates the home links and bridges the daily transitions that children make. It also acts as the basis for the larger transition bridge through to the classes in primary school and, in some cases, a personal learning portfolio may be developed for and with the child as part of this.

Documentation, whether for learning, assessment or planning, is most effective when approached collaboratively rather than through isolated individual activity. While individual observations of individual children have a key role to play in aspects of early years practice (such as gathering specific developmental or social information), the more general day-to-day documentation in practice is a social activity and its value rests in that fact. When we talk about collaboration in these contexts it often includes the active participation of the children themselves. Apart from the value of this collaborative engagement in relation to learning and to practice, this also meets the first goal of the National Children's Strategy (DoHC 2000), which is that children's voices will be heard. Realising this in practice with very young children is challenging, but there are many resources that can assist. We have mentioned the work of Carr and her colleagues on the use of visual documentation such as drawings, photos and video clips, which has proved more powerful than traditional written documentation. The visual impact of a photo, for instance, facilitates the inclusion of children who see themselves belonging and who recognise themselves in their past and can reflect on and discuss it in the present. Such practice is democracy in action and facilitates a context where learning becomes more reciprocal, where children learn in an engaged way with adults and other children who respect each other. Such reciprocal practice makes visible for children their place in the setting and enhances their sense of belonging and self-worth.

Contemporary video technology has widened the possibilities of pedagogical documentation. The video introduces a useful temporal or time dimension to pedagogical documentation in a way other materials fail to. However, it needs to be used in a specific way: it is not entertainment, and the content needs to be well understood by the adult to exploit its potential in understanding the children and understanding their stories. To overcome the view that photographing and videoing children is an invasion of their privacy, it is important to respect and include children and their families in your planning. When you understand and recognise the value of this form of pedagogical documentation you will be in a position to share this with parents and engage them in the process as interested and important participants. Over time this becomes a normal part of the setting's practice and routine. In certain situations parents may also wish to share video material from the home learning environment with the early years setting.

Practitioners may also gather less public pedagogical documentation in the form of personal professional learning portfolios. Critical to the effectiveness of such documentation as a pedagogical tool is the way in which it is discussed and reflected on individually, collectively by the team or with a critical friend. This type of self-evaluation is both personally satisfying in giving a language and focus to daily practice and also effective as a form of continuing professional development (CPD) to improve practice and so increase supportive environments for children. It offers a space for connecting theory to practice.

Studies have found that early years practitioners are more likely to be effective when they enjoy and seek out the challenge of practice. The impact of adults who are disengaged or disaffected can be damaging. While everyone has days when they are not all that 'on task', it is crucial that those adults charged with the responsibility of the education and care of young children love what they are doing and recognise both the value and the limitations of their role so that they find satisfaction through their daily practice but do not suffer burnout or boredom. In their report on research into the critical importance of early years experiences of children to their overall development, the USA's National Scientific Council on the Developing Child (NSCDC) argues that 'the essence of quality in early childhood services is embodied in the expertise, skills and relationship-building capacities of their staff' (NSCDC 2007a:13). The report goes on to mention how this might be achieved by: supporting the training of staff, at pre-service and CPD level; identifying effective strategies for retraining qualified staff; career structures that allow for advancement and associated conditions of service; and greater respect for their work as valued professionals in what is a life-changing role for the children they work with.

This book has been designed to contribute to the ongoing professional development of early years practitioners. It is, as outlined in Chapter 1, intended to be the start of a conversation. It presents research evidence to explain why quality early years practice is important and what such practice looks like. Central to the effectiveness of early years practice is the well-informed and knowledgeable early years practitioner; one who knows why certain approaches are best and who is present and engaged in early learning environments that are rich not only in objects and materials but also in opportunities; learning environments that are language-, content- and risk-rich; and where relationships are nurturing and pedagogy maintains and sustains children's learning and development.

In considering practice examples in the context of Síolta and Aistear, this book is contributing to the emergence of a common, shared language of practice with a view to supporting in the development of a cohesive professional identity for practitioners across the range of early years settings. To raise the status of and maintain the support necessary to sustain high-quality early childhood education and care as the norm in Ireland, we need to be confident in the language of early years practice. This can enrich our descriptions of what we do in early years settings and, more important, explain why we do what we do. Through regularly reviewing and reflecting on our practice, individually and collectively, within the language and principles of Síolta and Aistear, we can continue to sustain and enhance the quality and positive impact of our practice. Within this context of reflection, discussion and continued learning we can provide quality early learning environments that are satisfying to practitioners and beneficial to the young children who spend time there, confident that we are getting it right from the start.

References and Web Resources

REFERENCES

Alcock, S. (2000) *Pedagogical Documentation: Beyond Observation. Occasional Report.* Institute for Early Childhood Studies. Wellington, NZ: Victoria University of Wellington.

Alexander, R. (2004) 'Still no pedagogy: principles, pragmatism and compliance in primary education', *Cambridge Journal of Education* 34(1), 7–33.

Berk, L.E. and Winsler, A. (1995) *Scaffolding Children's Learning: Vygotsky and Early Childhood Education.* Washington, DC: NAEYC.

Blair, C. (2002) 'School readiness: integrating cognition and emotion in a neurobiological conceptualization of children's functioning at school entry', *American Psychologist* 57(2), 111–27.

Blakemore, S.J. and Frith, U. (2000) *The Implications of Recent Developments in Neuroscience for Research on Teaching and Learning.* London: Institute of Cognitive Neuroscience.

Bowman, B.T., Donovan, M.S. and Burns, M.S. (eds) (2001) *Eager to Learn: Educating our Preschoolers.* Washington, DC: National Academic Press.

Bredekamp, S. (1987) *Developmentally Appropriate Practice in Early Childhood Programmes Serving Children from Birth through Age 8.* Washington, DC: National Association for the Education of Young Children.

Bredekamp, S. and Copple, C. (eds) (1997) *Developmentally Appropriate Practice in Early Childhood Programmes* (revised edn). Washington, DC: National Association for the Education of Young Children.

Bronfenbrenner, U. and Evans, G.W. (2000) 'Developmental science in the 21st century: emerging questions, theoretical models, research design and empirical findings', *Social Development* 91, 115–25.

Bronfenbrenner, U. and Morris, P. (1998) 'The Ecology of Developmental Processes' in W. Damon and R.M. Lerner (eds), *Handbook of Child Psychology* Volume 1: *Theoretical Models of Human Development* (5th edn). New York: John Wiley and Sons, pp. 993–1028.

Bronson, M.B. (2001) *Self-regulation in Early Childhood: Nature and Nurture.* New York: Guildford Press.

Brooks, D. (2011) *The Social Animal: The Hidden Sources of Love, Character and Achievement.* New York: Random House.

Bruce, T. (2001) *Learning Through Play: Babies, Toddlers and the Foundation Years.* London: Hodder & Stoughton.

Bruner, J. (1996) *The Culture of Education*. Cambridge, MA: Harvard University Press.

Bunreacht na hEireann (1937) Constitution of Ireland. Dublin: Stationery Office.

Carr, M. (1998) 'A Project for Assessing Children's Experiences in Early Childhood Settings', paper presented to the 8th European Early Childhood Education Research Association (EECERA) Conference, Santiago de Compostela, Spain.

— (2001) 'Ready, Willing and Able: Learning Dispositions for Early Childhood?', paper presented at Cultures of Learning: Risk, Uncertainty and Education Conference, University of Bristol, 19–22 April.

— (2012) 'Kei tua o te pae: Tracing Learning Journeys beyond the Horizon', paper presented to the 22nd European Early Childhood Education Research Association (EECERA) Conference, Oporto, Portugal, 29 August–1 September.

Carr, M., Smith, A.B., Duncan, J., Jones, C., Lee, W. and Marshall, K. (2010) *Learning in the Making: Dispositions and Design in Early Education*. Rotterdam: Sense.

Center on the Developing Child (2011) 'Building the brain's "air traffic control" system: how early experiences shape the development of executive function', Working Paper No. 11. Harvard University: Center on the Developing Child.

Centre for Early Childhood Development and Education (CECDE) (2006) *Síolta: The National Quality Framework for Early Childhood Education*. Dublin: CECDE.

— (2007) *Síolta: Research & Digest*. Dublin: CECDE.

Chopra, D. (n.d.) 'The real secret to staying healthy for life', *New Realities*.

Claxton, G. (1990) *Teaching to Learn: A Direction for Education*. London: Cassell.

Connolly, P., Smith, A. and Kelly, B. (2002) *Too Young to Notice*. Belfast: Community Relations Council.

Corsaro, W. (2003) 'Ethnographic Research *With* rather than *On* Preschools in the US and Italy', paper presented at Trinity College Dublin, 26 May.

Costello, L. (1999) *A Literature of Children's Well-Being*. Dublin: Combat Poverty Agency.

Craik, D.M.M. (1859) *A Life for a Life*. London: Hurst & Blackett.

Dalli, C., White, E. J., Rockel, J. and Duhn, I., with Buchanan, E., Davidson, S., Ganly, S., Kus, L., and Wang, B. (2011). *Quality Early Childhood Education for Under-Two Year Olds: What Should it Look Like? A Literature Review*. Report to the Ministry of Education. Wellington, NZ: Jessie Hetherington Centre for Educational Research, Institute for Early Childhood Studies, Victoria University of Wellington.

Daly, M. and Forster, A. (2012) 'Aistear: The Early Childhood Curriculum Framework' in M. Mhic Mhathúna and M. Taylor (eds), *Early Childhood Education and Care: An Introduction for Students in Ireland*. Dublin: Gill & Macmillan, pp. 93–106.

Delors, J. (1996) *Learning: The Treasure Within*. Report to UNESCO of the International Commission of Education for the 21st Century. Geneva: UNESCO.

Department of Children and Youth Affairs (DCYA) (2011) *Children First: National Guidance for the Protection and Welfare of Children*. Dublin: Stationery Office.

Department of Education and Skills (DES) (2010) *A Workforce Development Plan for the Early Childhood Care and Education Sector in Ireland*. Dublin: DES.

— (2011) *Literacy and Numeracy for Learning and Life: The National Strategy to Improve Literacy and Numeracy among Children and Young People 2011–2020*. Dublin: DES.

Department of Health (DoH) (2010) *National Standards for Pre-School Services*. Dublin: Stationery Office.

Department of Health and Children (DoHC) (2000) *Our Children – Their Lives: National Children's Strategy*. Dublin: Stationery Office.

— (2006) *Child Care (Pre-School Services) (No. 2) Regulations 2006 and Child Care (Pre-School Services) (No. 2) (Amendment) Regulations*. Dublin: Stationery Office.

Derman-Sparks, L. and the ABC Task Force (1998) *Anti-Bias Education for Young Children and Ourselves*. Washington: National Association for the Education of Young Children.

Derman-Sparks, L. and Edwards, J.O. (2010) *Anti-Bias Education for Young Children and Ourselves*. Washington: National Association for the Education of Young Children.

Diamond, A. (2013) 'Executive functions', *Annual Review of Psychology* 64:135–68.

Dimnet, E. (1928) *The Art of Thinking*. New York: Simon and Schuster.

Duignan, M. (2012) 'Síolta: The National Quality Framework for Early Childhood Education' in M. Mhic Mhathúna and M. Taylor (eds), *Early Childhood Education and Care: An Introduction for Students in Ireland*. Dublin: Gill & Macmillan, pp. 83–93.

Dunn, J. (1987) 'Understanding Feelings: The Early Stages' in J. Bruner and H. Haste (eds), *Making Sense: The Child's Construction of the World*. London: Methuen.

Dweck, C.S. (1999) *Self-Theories: Their Role in Motivation, Personality and Development*. Philadelphia, PA: Taylor & Francis.

Edwards, C., Gandini, L. and Forman G. (eds) (1995) *The Hundred Languages of Children: The Reggio Emilia Approach to Early Childhood Education*. Norwood, NJ: Ablex.

European Commission (2010) *Europe 2020: A Strategy for Smart, Sustainable and Inclusive Growth*. Brussels: European Commission.

Fleer, M. (2003) 'Early childhood education as an evolving "community of practice" or as lived "social reproduction": researching the "taken-for-granted"', *Contemporary Issues in Early Childhood* 4(1), 64–79.

French, G. (2003) *Supporting Quality Guidelines for Best Practice in Early Childhood Services* (2nd edn). Dublin: Barnardos.

Fronczek, V. (2009) 'Article 31: a "forgotten article of the UNCRC"' in 'Realising the rights of young children: progress and challenges', *Early Childhood Matters* 113, 24–8.

Gaffney, M. (2011) *Flourishing*. Dublin: Penguin Ireland.

Galinsky, E. (2010) *Mind in the Making: The Seven Essential Life Skills Every Child Needs*. New York: Harper Collins.

Gardner, H. (1995) 'Foreword: Complementary Perspectives on Reggio Emilia' in C. Edwards, L. Gandini and G. Forman (eds), *The Hundred Languages of Children: The Reggio Emilia Approach to Early Childhood Education*. Norwood, NJ: Ablex, pp. ix–xv.

Goffin, S.C. (2000) 'The role of curriculum models in early childhood education' (ERIC Document-PS-00-8). Champaign, IL: Clearinghouse on Elementary and Early Childhood Education.

Goleman, D. (1996) *Emotional Intelligence: Why it can Matter More than IQ*. London: Bloomsbury.

Hayes, N. (2007) *Perspectives on the Relationship between Education and Care in Early Childhood*. Background paper prepared for the National Council for Curriculum and Assessment. Dublin: NCCA.

— (2008) 'Teaching matters in early educational practice: the case for a nurturing pedagogy', *Early Education and Development* 19(3), 430–40.

— (2010) *Early Childhood: An Introductory Text* (4th edn). Dublin: Gill & Macmillan.

— (2012) 'Children at the Centre of Practice' in M. Mhic Mhathúna and M. Taylor, *Early Childhood Education and Care: An Introduction for Students in Ireland*. Dublin: Gill & Macmillan.

Hayes, N. and Kernan, M. (2008) *Engaging Young Children: A Nurturing Pedagogy*. Dublin: Gill & Macmillan.

Hedges, H. and Cullen, J. (2005) 'Subject knowledge in early childhood curriculum and pedagogy: beliefs and practices', *Contemporary Issues in Early Childhood* 6(1), 66–79 <http://dx.doi.org/10.2304/ciec.2005.6.1.10>.

Hohman, M. and Weikart, D. (2002) *Educating Young Children: Active Learning Practices for Preschool and Childcare Programs* (2nd edn). Ypsilanti, MI: HighScope Press.

Huizinga, J. (1938) *Homo Ludens [Playing Man]*. Boston MA: Beacon Press.

Johnson, J.E. (1988) 'Psychological Theory and Early Education' in A.D. Pellegrini (ed.), *Psychological Bases for Early Education*. New York: John Wiley and Sons, pp. 1–22.

Katz, L. (1993) 'Dispositions: definitions and implications for early childhood practices', *Perspectives from ERIC/ECCE: A Monograph Series* No. 4.

— (1995a) 'The Distinction between Self-esteem and Narcissism: Implications for Practice' in L. Katz (ed.), *Talks with Teachers of Young Children: A Collection*. Norwood, NJ: Ablex.

— (1995b) 'What can we learn from Reggio Emilia?' in C. Edwards, L. Gandini and G. Forman (eds), *The Hundred Languages of Children: The Reggio Emilia Approach to Early Childhood Education*. Norwood, NJ: Ablex, pp. 19–37.

Katz, L. and Chard, S.C. (1994) *Engaging Children's Minds: The Project Approach* (2nd edn). Norwood, NJ: Ablex.

Kernan, M. and Singer, E. (2010) *Peer Relationships in Early Childhood Education and Care*. London: Routedge.

Kickbusch, L. (2012) *Learning for Well-being: A Policy Priority for Children and Youth in Europe. A Process for Change*. Brussels: Universal Education Foundation.

Laevers, F. (ed.) (2002) *Research on Experiential Education: A Selection of Articles.* Leuwen: Centre for Experiential Education.

Larrivee, B. (2005) *Authentic Classroom Management: Creating a Learning Community and Building Reflective Practice.* Boston, MA: Allyn and Bacon.

— (2008) 'Development of a tool to assess teachers' level of reflective practice', *Reflective Practice* 9(3), 341–60.

Lester, S. and Russell, W. (2008) *Play for a Change: Play, Policy and Practice – a Review of Contemporary Perspectives.* London: National Children's Bureau.

— (2010) 'Children's right to play: an examination of the importance of play in the lives of children worldwide', *Working Paper* 57. The Hague: Bernard van Leer Foundation.

Lockhart, S. (n.d.) 'Play: An important tool in cognitive development', *Extensions,* HighScope Curriculum Newsletter 24(3).

MacNaughton, G. and Williams, G. (2009). *Techniques for Teaching Young Children: Choices in Theory and Practice* (3rd edn). Frenchs Forest, NSW: Longman.

Marbina, L., Church, A. and Tayler, C. (2011) *Practice Principle 6: Integrated Teaching and Learning Approaches.* Victoria Early Years Learning and Development Framework Evidence Paper. Melbourne: University of Melbourne Graduate School of Education.

Marcon, R.A. (1999) 'Differential impact of preschool models on development and early learning of inner-city children: a three-cohort study' *Developmental Psychology* 35(2), 358–75.

Maslow, A.H. (1987) *Motivation and Personality* (2nd edn). New York: Harper and Row.

McLachlan, C., Fleer, M. and Edwards, S. (2010) *Early Childhood Curriculum: Planning, Assessment, and Implementation* Melbourne: Cambridge University Press.

Melhuish, E., Phan, M., Syla, K., Sammons, P. and Siraj-Blatchford, I. (2008) 'Effects of the home learning environment and preschool center experience upon literacy and numeracy development in early primary school', *Journal of Social Issues* 64(1), 95–114.

Mhic Mhathúna, M. and Taylor, M. (2012) *Early Childhood Education and Care: An Introduction for Students in Ireland.* Dublin: Gill & Macmillan.

Ministry of Children and Family Affairs (Norway) (1996) *Norwegian Framework Plan for the Content and Tasks of Kindergartens.* Oslo.

Ministry of Education (New Zealand) (1996) *Te Whariki: Early Childhood Curriculum.* Wellington, NZ: Learning Media Ltd.

Mitchell, L. and Cubey, P. (2003) 'Characteristics of effective professional development linked to enhanced pedagogy and children's learning in early childhood settings: a best evidence synthesis'. Wellington, NZ: Ministry of Education <www.educationcounts.govt.nz/publications/ece/36086/36087>.

Moffitt, T.E., Arseneault, L., Belsky, D., Dikson, N., Hancox, R.J., Harrington, H., Houts, R., Poulton, R., Roberts, B.W., Ross, S., Sears, M.R., Thomas, W.M. and Caspi, A. (2011) 'A gradient of childhood self-control predicts health, wealth and public safety', *Proceedings of the National Academy of Science* 108(7), 2693–8.

Moss, P. (2007) 'Meeting across the paradigmatic divide', *Educational Philosophy and Theory* 39(3), 229–40.

Moyles, J., Adams, S. and Musgrove, A. (2002) *SPEEL Study of Pedagogical Effectiveness in Early Learning*, DfES Research Report 363. London: Department for Education and Skills.

Murray, C. and O'Doherty, A (2001) *'Éist': Respecting Diversity in Early Childhood Care, Education and Training*. Dublin: Pavee Point.

Murray, C. and Urban, M. (2012) *Diversity and Equality in Early Childhood: An Irish Perspective*. Dublin: Gill & Macmillan.

National Council for Curriculum and Assessment (NCCA) (1999) *Primary School Curriculum*. Dublin: NCCA.

— (2004) *Towards a Framework for Early Learning: A Consultative Document*. Dublin: NCCA.

— (2007) *Listening for Children's Stories: Children as Partners in the Framework for Early Learning*. Dublin: NCCA.

— (2009a) *Aistear: The Early Childhood Curriculum Framework*. Dublin: NCCA.

— (2009b) *Aistear: The Early Childhood Curriculum Framework: Guidelines for Good Practice*. Dublin: NCCA <www.ncca.biz/Aistear/pdfs/Guidelines_ENG/Guidelines_ENG.pdf>.

— (2009c) *Aistear: The Early Childhood Curriculum Framework and Síolta: the National Quality Framework for Early Childhood Education: Audit of Similarities and Differences*. Dublin: NCCA <www.ncca.ie/en/Curriculum_and_Assessment/Early_Childhood_and_Primary_Education/Early_Childhood_Education/Aistear_Toolkit/Aistear_Siolta_Similarities_Differences.pdf>.

National Economic and Social Council (NESC) (2009) *Well-being Matters: A Social Report for Ireland*, Vols. I and II. Dublin: NESC.

National Scientific Council on the Developing Child (NSCDC) (USA) (2007a) *The Science of Early Childhood Development: Closing the Gap Between What We Know and What We Do*. Harvard University: Center on the Developing Child.

— (2007b) *A Science-Based Framework for Early Childhood Policy: Using Evidence to Improve Outcomes in Learning, Behavior, and Health for Vulnerable Children*. Harvard University: Center on the Developing Child.

— (website) *Core Concepts in the Science of Early Childhood Development: Healthy Development Builds a Strong Foundation – For Kids and For Society*. Harvard University: Center on the Developing Child <http://developingchild.harvard.edu/index.php/resources/multimedia/interactive_features/coreconcepts/>

Nic Gabhainn, S. and Sixsmith, J. (2005) *Children's Understandings of Well-Being*. Dublin: National Children's Office.

Nsamenang, B. (2008) 'Enhancing a sense of belonging in the early years', *Early Childhood Matters* No. 111, 13–18.

Nussbaum, M. (2011) *Creating Capabilities: The Human Development Approach.* Cambridge, MA: Belknap Press, Harvard University.

Office of the Minister for Children (OMC) (2006) *Diversity and Equality Guidelines for Childcare Providers.* Dublin: OMC.

Organisation for Economic Co-operation and Development (OECD) (2001) *Starting Strong: Early Childhood Education and Care.* Paris: OECD.

— (2002) 'Strengthening Early Childhood Programmes: A Policy Framework', *Education Policy Analysis.* Paris: OECD, pp. 9–33.

— (2006) *Starting Strong II: Early Childhood Education and Care.* Paris: OECD.

— (2007) *Understanding the Brain: The Birth of a Learning Science.* Paris: OECD.

— (2012*) Starting Strong III: A Quality Toolbox for Early Childhood Education and Care.* Paris: OECD <www.oecd.org/edu/preschoolandschool/startingstrongiiiaquality toolboxforearlychildhoodeducationandcare.htm>.

Penn, H. (2009) *Early Childhood Education and Care: Key Lessons from Research for Policy Makers.* An independent report submitted to the European Commission by the Network of Experts in Social Science of Education and training (NESSE). Brussels, European Commission.

Perkins, D.N., Jay, E. and Tishman, S (1993) 'Beyond abilities: a dispositional theory of thinking', *Merrill-Palmer Quarterly* 39(1), 1–21.

Rinaldi, C. (1995) 'The Emergent Curriculum and Social Constructivism', an interview with Lella Gandini in C. Edwards, L. Gandini, and G. Forman (eds), *The Hundred Languages of Children: The Reggio Emilia Approach to Early Childhood Education.* Norwood, NJ: Ablex, pp. 101–11.

— (2006) *In Dialogue with Reggio Emilia: Listening, Researching and Learning.* London: Routledge.

Rosenow, N. (2012) *Heart-Centred Teaching Inspired by Nature.* Lincoln, NE: Dimensions Educational Research Foundation.

Schaffer, H.R. (1992) 'Joint Involvement Episodes as Contexts for Cognitive Development' in H. McGurk (ed.), *Contemporary Issues in Childhood Social Development,* reprinted in H. Daniels (ed.) (1996) *An Introduction to Vygotsky.* London: Routledge.

Schweinhart, L.J. (2002) 'Making Validated Educational Models Central to Preschool Standards', paper presented at the NAEYC Annual Conference, New York.

— (2006) 'The HighScope Approach: Evidence that Participatory Learning in Early Childhood Contributes to Human Development' in N.F. Watt *et al.* (eds), *The Crisis in Youth Mental Health: Critical Issues and Effective Programs* Vol. 4: *Early Intervention Programs and Policies.* Westport, CT: Praeger, pp. 207–27.

Schweinhart, L., Barnes, H. and Weikart, D. (1993) *Significant Benefits: The High/Scope Perry Preschool Study through Age 27.* Ypsilanti, MI: HighScope Press.

Sheridan, S. (2011) 'Characteristics of preschools as learning environments and conditions for children's learning' in Ministry of Education and Research (Norway), *Nordic Early Childhood Education and Care – Effects and Challenges: Research, Practice and Policy Making.* Oslo: Ministry of Education and Research, pp. 19–23.

Singer, E. (1992) *Childcare and the Psychology of Development.* London: Routledge.

Singer, E. and de Haan, D. (2007) *The Social Lives of Young Children.* Amsterdam: SWP.

Siraj-Blatchford, I. (2003) Keynote Address to the Annual Meeting of the Irish Preschool Playgroups Association, Maynooth, September.

— (2005) 'Birth to Eight Matters! Seeking Seamlessness – Continuity? Integration? Creativity?' Presentation to the Association for the Professional Development of Early Years Educators, Cardiff, 5 November.

Siraj-Blatchford, I., Sylva, K., Taggart, B., Melhuish, E., Sammons, P. and Elliot, K. (2004) 'Technical Paper 10: Intensive Case Studies of Practice across the Foundation Stage', paper given at the 5th Annual Conference of the Teaching and Learning Research Programme, Cardiff, 22–24 November.

Siraj-Blatchford, I. and Manni, L. (2008) 'Would you like to tidy up now? An analysis of adult questioning in the English Foundation Stage', *Early Years: An International Journal of Research and Development* 28(1), 5–22.

Siraj-Blatchford, I., Sylva, K., Taggart, B., Sammons, P. and Melhuish, E. (2008) 'Towards the transformation of early childhood practice', *Cambridge Journal of Education* 38(1), 23–36.

Smiley, P.A. and Dweck, C.S. (1994) 'Individual differences in achievement goals among young children', *Child Development* 65, 1723–43.

Start Strong (2011) *If I had a Magic Wand: Young Children's Visions and Ideas for Early Care and Education Services.* Dublin: Start Strong <www.startstrong.ie/contents/213>.

Stephen, C. (2010) 'Pedagogy: the silent partner in early years learning', *Early Years* 30(3): 15–28.

Super, C.M. and Harkness, S. (1986) 'The developmental niche: a conceptualisation at the interface of child and culture', *International Journal of Behavioural Development,* 9, 545–69.

Sylva, K., Melhuish, E., Sammons, P., Siraj-Blatchford, I. and Taggart, B. (2011) 'Preschool quality and educational outcomes at age 11: low quality has little benefit', *Journal of Early Childhood Research* 9(2), 109–24.

Taylor, M., (2012) 'Social Policy and Early Childhood Education and Care' in M. Mhic Mhathúna and M. Taylor (eds) *Early Childhood Education and Care: An Introduction for Students in Ireland.* Dublin: Gill & Macmillan, pp. 63–82.

Thiele, G. and Weiss, R. (1967) 'What a Wonderful World'.

Trevarthen, C. (1992) 'An infant's motives for thinking and speaking' in A.H.Wold (ed.), *Dialogical Alternatives.* Oxford: Oxford University Press.

United Nations (UN) (1989) United Nations Convention on the Rights of the Child, adopted by the UN General Assembly 20 November 1989.

— (2001) Committee on the Rights of the Child, General Comment 1: 'Aims of Education'. Geneva: UN.

— (2005) Committee on the Rights of the Child, General Comment No. 7: 'Implementing Child Rights in Early Childhood'. Geneva: UN <www2.ohchr. org/english/bodies/crc/docs/AdvanceVersions/GeneralComment7Rev1.pdf>.

United Nations Children's Fund (UNICEF) (2007) 'An overview of child well-being in rich countries: a comprehensive assessment of the lives and well-being of children and adolescents in the economically advantaged nations'. Florence: UNICEF Innocenti Research Centre.

Victoria Department of Education and Early Childhood Development (DEECD) (2009) *Victorian Early Years Learning and Development Framework for all Children from Birth to Eight Years*. Melbourne: Early Childhood Strategy Division, DEECD and Victorian Curriculum and Assessment Authority.

Vygotsky, L. (1978) *Mind in Society: The Development of Higher Psychological Processes*. Cambridge: Cambridge University Press.

Wagner, P. (2008) 'Categorisations and young children's social constructions of belonging' in 'Enhancing a sense of belonging in the early years', *Early Childhood Matters* No. 111, 20–4.

Whitehurst, G.J. and Lonigan, C.J. (2001) 'Emergent Literacy: Development from Prereaders to Readers', in S.B. Neuman and D.K. Dickinson (eds), *Handbook of Early Literacy Research*. New York: Guilford Press, pp. 11–29.

Wolfe, C. D. and Bell, M. A. (2007) 'Sources of variability in working memory in early childhood: a consideration of age, temperament, language, and brain electrical activity'. *Cognitive Development*, 22(4): 431–55.

Woodhead, M. and Brooker, L. (2008) 'A sense of belonging' in 'Enhancing a sense of belonging in the early years', *Early Childhood Matters* No. 111, 3–7.

York-Barr, J., Sommers, W.A., Ghere, G.S., and Montie, J.K. (2006) *Reflective Practice to Improve Schools: An Action Guide for Educators* (2nd edn). Thousand Oaks, CA: Corwin.

WEB RESOURCES
Irish websites
Aistear Toolkit: www.ncca.ie/aisteartoolkit

Barnardos: www.barnardos.ie

Comhair Naíonraí na Gaeltachta Teoranta: www.cnng.ie

Department of Children and Youth Affairs: www.dcya.gov.ie

Early Childhood Ireland: www.earlychildhoodireland.ie

Equality and Diversity Early Childhood National Network (EdeNn): www.decet.org/en/partners/pavee-point/edenn.html

Lifestart Foundation: www.lifestartfoundation.org

National Council for Curriculum and Assessment: www.ncca.ie/earlylearning

Síolta: www.siolta.ie

Start Strong: www.startstrong.ie

World Organisation for Early Childhood Learning (OMEP) Ireland: www.omepireland.ie

The developing child

Child Development Institute: http://childdevelopmentinfo.com

Effective Provision of Pre-School Education Project (UK): http://eppe.ioe.ac.uk

National Association for the Education of Young Children (USA): www.naeyc.org

National Institute for Early Education Research (USA): www.nieer.org

National Scientific Council on the Developing Child (USA) – for a comprehensive list of publications and resources see:

- http://developingchild.harvard.edu/activities/council/publications/
- http://developingchild.harvard.edu/activities/forum/

Society for Research in Child Development: www.srcd.org

Talking Point (information on children's communication): www.talkingpoint.org.uk

Models of practice

HighScope: www.highscope.org

Irish Steiner Kindergarten Association: www.steinerireland.org

Montessori:

- St Nicholas Montessori Society of Ireland: www.montessoriireland.ie
- Montessori College Dublin: www.montessoriami.ie

Naíonraí – Forbairt Naíonraí Teoranta: www.naionrai.ie

NCCA – Curriculum Online: www.curriculumonline.ie

OECD Quality Toolbox for Early Childhood Education and Care: www.oecd.org/edu/preschoolandschool/startingstrongiiiaqualitytoolboxforearlychildhoodeducationandcare.htm

Reggio Emilia: www.reggiochildren.it

Te Whariki: www.educate.ece.govt.nz/learning/curriculumAndLearning/TeWhariki.aspx

For valuable literature reviews on issues of practice see the Victoria Early Years Learning and Development Framework and associated papers: www.vcaa.vic.edu.au/pages/earlyyears/index.aspx

Play

International Play Association: www.ipaworld.org

Play England: www.playengland.org.uk

Rights-based approaches to children's policy

Children's Rights Alliance: http://childrensrights.ie

Child Rights International Network: www.crin.org

Diversity in Early Childhood Education and Training: www.decet.org

Eurochild: www.eurochild.org/

OECD: www.oecd.org

Office of the UN Commissioner for Human Rights: www2.ohchr.org/english/law/crc.htm

UN General Comment 7 on implementing the rights of the child: www2.ohchr.org/english/bodies/crc/docs/AdvanceVersions/GeneralComment7Rev1.pdf

UNICEF: www.unicef.org

Index